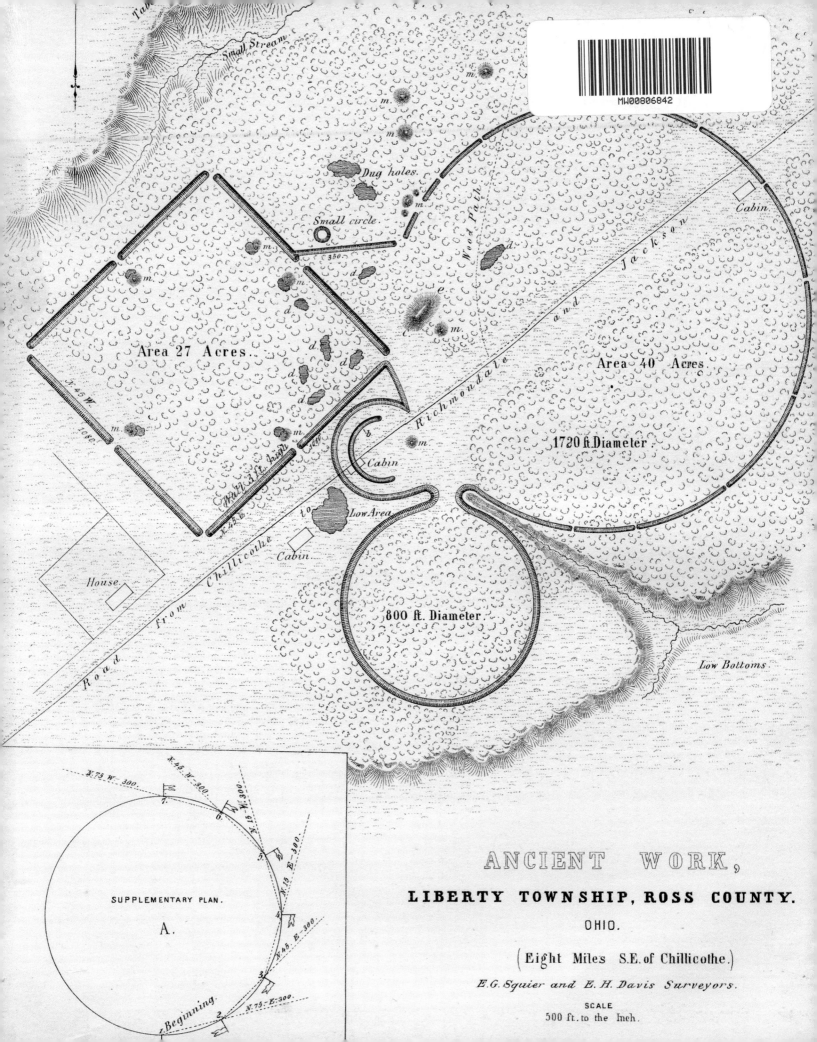

Small Stream

Dug holes.

Small circle.

Wood Path

Cabin

Area 27 Acres.

Area 40 Acres.

1720 ft. Diameter.

Richmondale and Jackson

Wall 3 ft. high

Cabin

800 ft. Diameter.

Low Area

Cabin

House.

Road from Chillicothe

Low Bottoms.

SUPPLEMENTARY PLAN.

A.

N.75.W. 300.
N.45.W. 300.
N.15.W. 300.
N.15.E. 300.
N.45.E. 300.
N.75.E. 300.
Beginning.

ANCIENT WORK,

LIBERTY TOWNSHIP, ROSS COUNTY.

OHIO.

(Eight Miles S.E. of Chillicothe.)

E.G. Squier and E.H. Davis Surveyors.

SCALE
500 ft. to the Inch.

Ohio ARCHAEOLOGY

An Illustrated Chronicle of Ohio's Ancient American Indian Cultures

2007

For Judy,

Happy Birthday!

Steve

ARCHAEOLOGY

An Illustrated Chronicle of Ohio's Ancient American Indian Cultures

Written by
Bradley T. Lepper

✕✕✕

With feature articles contributed by over 20 archaeologists and scholars

ORANGE FRAZER *PRESS*
Wilmington, Ohio

VOYAGEUR
media group, inc.

ISBN 1-882203-39-9

Book design by Orange Frazer Press

Cover: Serpent Mound State Memorial aerial by Richard A. Cook III, Changing Image.

End sheets: Serpent Mound and Liberty Works survey maps by E.G. Squier and E.H. Davis,
Ancient Monuments of the Mississippi Valley, Smithsonian Institution, 1848.

Library of Congress Cataloging-in-Publication Data

Lepper, Bradley Thomas, 1955-
    Ohio archaeology : a visual chronicle of Ohio's ancient American
Indian cultures / written [and edited] by Bradley T. Lepper ; with
feature articles contributed by over 20 archaeologists and scholars.
        p. cm.
    Includes bibliographical references and index.
    ISBN 1-882203-39-9
  1.   Paleo-Indians--Ohio. 2. Indians of North
America--Ohio--Antiquities. 3. Excavations
(Archaeology)--Ohio--History. 4. Ohio--Antiquities. I. Title.
    E78.O3L46 2004
    945'.05--dc22
                                            2004059500

The Ohio Archaeology book was made possible with the generous contributions of:

Bart and Jamae van Eck

MeadWestvaco

MeadWestvaco Papers Group

The Ohio Archaeology Project was made possible with support from:

The George Gund Foundation

The Ohio Humanities Council

The Wohlgemuth Herchede Foundation

The Ohio Archaeological Council

Ancient Ohio
Timeline of Archaeological Periods

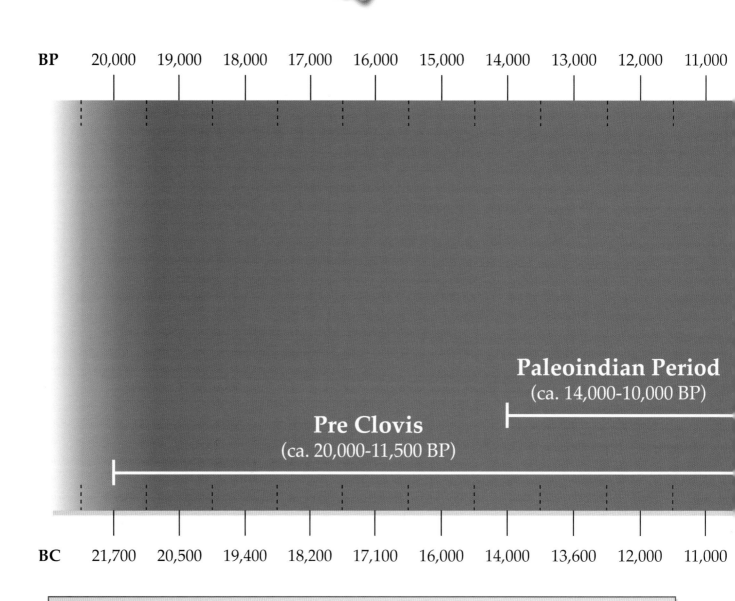

BP   20,000   19,000   18,000   17,000   16,000   15,000   14,000   13,000   12,000   11,000

Paleoindian Period
(ca. 14,000-10,000 BP)

Pre Clovis
(ca. 20,000-11,500 BP)

BC   21,700   20,500   19,400   18,200   17,100   16,000   14,000   13,600   12,000   11,000

Criteria and Key
This timeline is based on published radiocarbon dates or artifact typology. The dates are listed as ca. (about)
BP = Radiocarbon Years Before Present and BC/AD. The "present" is defined by convention as AD 1950, the year
standards were set for reporting radiocarbon dates. The timeline includes the best information available at the time
of publication.

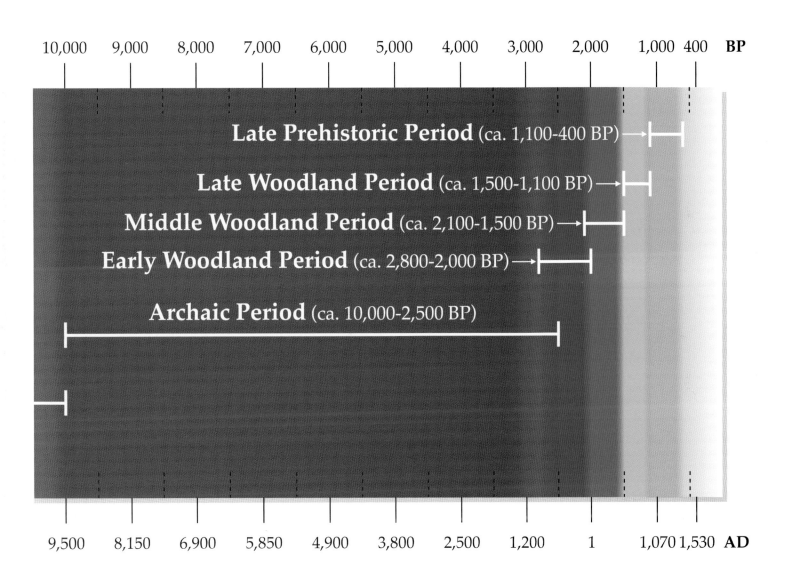

TABLE OF CONTENTS

PREFACE

David Hurst Thomas, Curator, Department of Anthropology, American Museum of Natural History;
Founding Trustee, National Museum of The American Indian, Smithsonian Institution

Brad Lepper has written a dynamite book describing some of America's most spectacular archaeology. Mesa Verde? Chaco Canyon? Cahokia or maybe Moundville? No. Lepper's book is a personal odyssey through the ancient human past that played out within the State of Ohio.

Why Ohio? Why not?

For some curious reason, Americans tend to overlook the extraordinary archaeological real estate of the heartland. The pages that follow will demonstrate to the uninitiated, beyond a doubt, the rich archaeological treasures contained within the Buckeye State. Dr. Lepper presents this long-term history in a straightforward, easy-to-understand narrative, emphasizing the lengthy tradition of scientific archaeology that has been practiced here, but he also highlights the puzzles that remain, the questions still to be answered.

Nobody knows when the first human footprint appeared on Ohio soil. We do not know for sure what the first Ohioan wore, spoke, or thought. We do not know exactly from where these Paleoindians came, what conditions they experienced along the way, or how they ended up in Ohio.

But whenever and however, come they did. The First Ohioans brought with them an Ice Age patrimony. They could make fire, knap stone into tools, hunt game, make shelter, and clothe themselves. Ohio's Native American ancestors explored and settled into their new homeland. Moving along the endless river roadways, they eventually exploited nearly all of Ohio's varied habitats. Spreading out the risk and buffering themselves against the failure of any particular plant or animal species, the Archaic people of Ohio developed increasingly intensive strategies of harvesting native plant crops, presaging the horticultural economies that would follow. As their population increased, native Ohioans exchanged resources over long distances and learned to store food for the future.

Inevitably, some harvested and stored more food than their neighbors, some excelled at trade and barter. In response to growing competition over scarce resources, ancient Ohio society became increasingly rigid and controlling. Two thousand years ago, these ancient Ohioans began erecting earthen mounds and earthworks, some defining sacred geometric spaces that continue to amaze. They captured their wisdom of the heavens in powerful monuments and daily architecture. They buried their dead with exquisite works of art, crafted of exotic materials exchanged across vast distance—volcanic glass from Yellowstone, copper from the Great Lakes, mica from the Carolinas and sharks' teeth from the gulf. For a thousand generations, Ohio's native people wove a story of ingenuity, enterprise, and above, all, survival.

The earliest Europeans who explored Ohio knew nothing of this dramatic history. As the newcomers filtered across the landscape, they became increasingly curious about the earliest Ohioans. Who were they? Where did they come from? And what became of them? The mystery deepened with each new discovery of the ancient monuments found throughout the state. That curiosity remains alive today.

Nineteenth-century scholars framed colorful theories to account for American Indian origins. Maybe the Indians were a long-lost Tribe from Israel. Perhaps they descended from a Welsh colony that arrived in America in A.D. 1170. Could it be that the fabled Island of Atlantis was the ancestral homeland of Native Americans? Many believed that American Indians were relative newcomers who displaced a glorious race of Moundbuilders—the mythical non-Indian people responsible for constructing the thousands of mounds and earthworks that dotted the Ohio landscape.

In 1848, E. G. Squier and E. H. Davis published a classic study entitled *Ancient Monuments of the Mississippi Valley*, triggering an onslaught of meticulous inquiries into Ohio's rich archaeological record. Today, a staggering quantity of archaeological evidence has accumulated from sites throughout the state of Ohio. But the technical sophistication of modern archaeological method and theory renders these raw data almost unintelligible to the lay public.

Fortunately for us all, *Ohio Archaeology* presents a fresh, understandable synthesis of the ancient Native American past. A dirt archaeologist in the best sense of the term, Lepper pulls together the archaeological evidence documenting the Paleoindian pioneer period, the moundbuilding Adena and Hopewell peoples, culminating with the Late Prehistoric people who encountered the earliest Euroamerican explorers and settlers. In the process, Lepper demonstrates the techniques through which modern archaeologists piece together the data of stones-and-bones to reveal the rich panorama of long-term human history.

INTRODUCTION

Bradley T. Lepper, Curator of Archaeology, The Ohio Historical Society

AMERICANS CELEBRATE THEIR HERITAGE IN MANY WAYS. NATIONAL HOLIDAYS commemorate our shared history and historical societies and museums are in nearly every state and county. The Daughters of the American Revolution honor their ancestral ties to our nation's founders and the Mayflower Society looks to even deeper roots. Scandinavian Americans vie with Italian Americans over who should get the credit for discovering America—Leif Eriksson or Christopher Columbus. But often lost in all of the displays of national pomp, patrician pride, or ethnic heritage is the fact that the story of America does not open in AD 1000, 1492, or 1776; and Ohio's history does not begin in 1803. Native American people shared this land with mastodons more than 10,000 years before George Washington was born. They were the first to explore our hills and valleys and the first to till our fields. Their achievements are as much a part of humanity's odyssey as are the voyages of Leif Eriksson, Christopher Columbus, and Neil Armstrong. If this were true, however, why should ignorance about them be so widespread?

There are, of course, fundamental issues related to racism and national guilt over the way European Americans treated the indigenous peoples of this continent. If we honor the heritage of Native America, it might make the usurpation of their lands seem even more heinous. But I believe that some of the blame for modern Americans neglect of Native America's ancient heritage lies with archaeologists.

The Native American saga was not recorded in any chronicle. It is written in the soil with letters of shivered flint, broken pottery, charred seeds, and mounds of earth. It takes an archaeologist to read that obscure alphabet and translate the story for modern readers. Too often, archaeologists have devoted themselves almost entirely to reading and enjoying that story for themselves and have not translated it for the benefit of non-archaeologists. This is unfortunate because the general public is keenly interested in archaeology and has a right to know what archaeologists are learning about America's past. After all, taxpayers are funding much of the archaeology being done in this country. More effective public education efforts may lead to a greater appreciation of the wonders archaeology can reveal and a greater sense of our common heritage. Hopefully, this will engender a deeper understanding of why it is important to invest public dollars in both the preservation and study of archaeological sites.

The main part of this book is my attempt to summarize what archaeologists have learned about the ancient people who made Ohio their home. Archaeology, like other sciences, depends on the work of many people. No individual archaeologist is expert on all aspects of Ohio's past. I have turned to the works of dozens of other archaeologists in preparing this summary. Scientists often disagree with one another, however, and I frequently have had to make choices between conflicting interpretations. As a result, not all archaeologists will agree with every part of my synthesis, but it is doubtful that any broad synthesis of Ohio prehistory would satisfy every archaeologist. I have tried to present an accurate picture of what we think we know about Ohio's past while telling a good story.

The main text is supplemented with numerous sidebars written by other scholars each offering their own expertise and insights on various aspects of Ohio archaeology. It is hoped that these will provide some balance and at least hint at the diversity of perspectives in modern archaeology.

How do we know what we think we know about things that happened so long ago?

Archaeology is the scientific study of the human past. Since we can't travel to the past and see what people were doing, we have to look at the things they left behind and use these as clues to what they were doing. This would seem to rather severely limit the knowledge we can glean about the past but, fortunately, people use a lot of stuff in their daily lives and information about those various activities is encoded in that stuff and how it is distributed in space. The science of archaeology is about learning to decode the information about once-living cultures from the stuff they left behind.

There are four basic categories of evidence that archaeologists can study to learn about ancient people: artifacts, human remains, features, and ecofacts. Artifacts are objects made or used by people. Human remains are the surviving remnants of human bodies. Usually, if any traces of human remains are found at archaeological sites in Ohio, it is only the bones that are preserved. Features are sets of artifacts or non-portable traces of human activity such as pits, hearths, burials, postmolds, or other structures. Ecofacts are unmodified traces of the environmental setting of the human occupation. These include animal bones and plant remains, such as nutshells, seeds, or pollen. All of these lines of evidence, when combined with details about their context, contribute to our understanding of the ways of life of ancient people.

Human remains, features, and ecofacts are, however, relatively rare. Most of what we know about Ohio's ancient cultures is limited to what we have learned from artifacts. Fortunately, you can learn a lot about people from their artifacts. Obviously, we can learn about how ancient people hunted and fished by finding their stone spear points and bone fishhooks, but artifacts also can provide clues to the more intangible aspects of ancient ways of life, such as their religious practices or the structure of their societies.

People use artifacts for a variety of purposes. Some artifacts, like spear points, fishhooks, or pickup trucks help people make a living. There are also artifacts that are used to convey social information such as a diamond engagement ring, a chief's headdress, or a stretch limousine. Finally, there are artifacts that symbolize important religious beliefs or social values such as a crucifix, an American flag, or a totem pole. Every artifact has a story it can tell and by combining the stories of many artifacts with evidence from human remains, features, and ecofacts, archaeologists can get a remarkably complete picture of the people who made and used those artifacts.

Before archaeologists can interpret the artifacts, however, they must first find them. Archaeologists find artifacts in a number of ways. The two most basic are surface surveys and excavations. In surface surveys, archaeologists scan the surface of the ground and look for artifacts. The main limitation of surface surveys is that you only find artifacts that happen to be lying on the surface. Deeply buried artifacts, or artifacts covered by grass or leaves will not be discovered.

Excavation is another way archaeologists find artifacts. Excavation involves digging into the earth to discover artifacts and other remains. Archaeologists excavate with a variety of tools depending on the situation. Sometimes they use trowels and whisk brooms and at other times they use shovels. Occasionally, they even use back hoes!

A frequently asked question is, "How do archaeologists know where to dig?" Usually, archaeologists choose to excavate a site only after it was discovered during a surface survey or accidentally uncovered by someone digging a ditch or a house foundation. Sometimes archaeologists will undertake test excavations to see if any archaeological sites are in an area. Often, archaeologists dig and don't find any artifacts. This tells them at least where prehistoric people didn't live.

Other ways archaeologists find sites are encompassed under the term "remote sensing." Remote sensing includes a variety of techniques for "seeing" beneath the surface of the ground without digging a hole. Aerial photography, ground penetrating radar, metal detectors, magnetometry, soil conductivity and resistivity all are ways of using modern technology to examine the ground for different kinds of traces of human activity.

Whether artifacts are discovered through surface survey, excavation, or remote sensing, archaeologists record detailed information on exactly where the object was found. They make maps, take photographs, and take lots of notes. This information about the context of the discovery is vital to interpreting the significance of the site. Each artifact is like a letter on a page of text. If all the letters on this page were carelessly removed and put in a box, you would be left with a blank page and a jumble of letters conveying no information. You could admire the individual letters, but you could no longer read the message. But if you had carefully recorded the location of each letter before removing it, you could, at any time, reconstruct the text. This is the goal of scientific archaeology: to recover the artifacts, but preserve the contextual information that will allow us to reconstruct the "text" and "read" the history written on the landscape.

Once the artifacts, notes, and photographs are brought back into the laboratory the hard work of analysis begins. Archaeologists clean the artifacts and give each one a unique number. This allows researchers to keep track of individual artifacts throughout the process of analysis and later storage. Then the artifacts are weighed, measured, examined under a microscope, or subjected to various chemical analyses. The results of such studies are summarized in a report and the artifacts are curated (stored in such a way that they can be studied by future scientists who may have different questions to ask) or displayed in a museum exhibit.

The science of archaeology is a highly technical discipline and most archaeologists have advanced college degrees. Many amateur archaeologists, however, have made important contributions to our knowledge about the past. Responsible amateurs look for artifacts in plowed fields, or other places where the ground has been disturbed, and share what they find with professionals. They keep track of where they find artifacts and often label each artifact and keep written records about the sites they discover.

People who collect artifacts as a hobby, but do not take the time to record exactly where they find items, or who dig up artifacts without using the methods of archaeological science, are destroying information about the past. These people sometimes are called "pot hunters" because they are only interested in the pot or the arrowhead, not in what those beautiful objects can tell us about the people who made them.

If you like to hunt for arrowheads or are interested in participating in an archaeological dig, then I urge you to do so responsibly. Many professional archaeologists welcome volunteer assistants in the field and in the lab. If you don't live near a university or a museum with archaeologists on the staff, then you can read books about how to collect artifacts the right way. The Boy Scouts' Archaeology guide is a good place to start.

Archaeology can be an exciting and a fulfilling hobby. You could make discoveries that will contribute to our knowledge of Ohio's ancient people. On the other hand, if you remove artifacts from a site without properly recording the information, you are ripping pages out of Ohio's unwritten history, pages that are irreplaceable.

A word about dates...

Most of the dates I have presented in this book are based on radiocarbon dates. Radiocarbon dating is a marvelous method for determining the age of almost any organic substance, that is, anything that once was alive, such as wood or bone. Archaeologists have obtained hundreds of radiocarbon dates for hundreds of sites in Ohio allowing us to gain a fairly complete and consistent picture of what was happening across the state for the last 10,000 or more years.

The way I have presented dates in this book may be confusing to some readers who are more used to seeing ages given in years BC and AD. Most archaeologists use "years BP" to indicate the ages of the artifacts and sites they study and, usually, it refers to dates determined by radiocarbon dating. "BP" stands for "Before Present" and, technically, it refers to years before AD 1950. Using BP makes it easier to follow a timeline since you're not counting alternately forward and backward.

You also should be aware that radiocarbon years before the present are not quite the same as calendar years before the present. Radiocarbon dating machines determine the proportion of two different kinds of carbon atoms in a sample of organic material. When living things die, those proportions change as the unstable form decays. The rate of decay is known and is more or less constant, like the ticking of a clock or the trickle of sand grains in an hour glass. Unfortunately, the proportion of stable to unstable carbon atoms in living things has not remained constant from decade to decade. So, the "radiocarbon hour glass," in samples of charred wood or bone that are 10,000 years old, started out with less "sand" (or unstable carbon atoms) than one in similar samples that are 1,000 years old. If there is less sand to start with, then it will take less time for the sand to trickle from one glass chamber to the other.

Fortunately, scientists are coming up with increasingly accurate correction factors that allow us to convert radiocarbon years before present into calendar years before present. The dates used in this book have not been corrected. If they had, the Paleoindian period would be said to extend from 17,000 to 12,000 (calendar) years BP instead of from 15,000 to 10,000 (radiocarbon) years BP. This would be more accurate, but it might be confusing to readers who come across conflicting dates in other books or articles on Ohio's prehistory. Fortunately, the difference between radiocarbon years and calendar years generally is greater with increasing age and, by two or three thousand years ago, the ages are nearly equivalent. So the radiocarbon dates for the Middle Woodland period, for example, correspond relatively closely to their true calendar age.

PURPOSE STATEMENT

To the reader:

OVER THE PAST FEW YEARS, VOYAGEUR MEDIA GROUP, INC. HAS BEEN COLLABORATING with scholars representing Ohio's major archaeological and educational institutions on the development of a comprehensive media project about the state's ancient American Indian cultures. The *Ohio Archaeology* book is joined by three other project components; a public television documentary series, the "Ancient Ohio" art series and a companion website for the delivery of educational materials.

Ohio Archaeology is neither a scientific journal, nor a discourse on American Indian studies. The book is designed to introduce readers to what is scientifically known about a series of ancient American Indian cultures that flourished in the state for well over ten thousand years. Dr. Bradley T. Lepper, Curator of Archaeology, Ohio Historical Society, has taken on the challenge of translating complex scientific research into a narrative that is clear, concise and accessible to readers, educators and students. The first six chapters are presented in a chronology based on major archaeological periods. Each chapter includes feature essays contributed by over 20 scholars on specific archaeological sites and investigations.

Ohio Archaeology also includes an historical retrospective, "Early Accounts of Ohio's Mounds," by Dr. Terry Barnhart, Professor of History, Eastern Illinois University. Dr. Barnhart describes an era when the mounds and earthworks of the Ohio Valley drew national attention as American archaeology emerged from the pursuit of "antiquarians" into a true scientific discipline. We close the book with an Epilogue, "Legacies," that summarizes some of the scientific, cultural and social issues that confront modern archaeology in Ohio.

Ohio Archaeology is being published during a time of monumental change. Voyageur's editorial board has made difficult decisions in an attempt to balance the presentation of scientific research with the cultural concerns of American Indians. After discussions with project advisors and tribal leaders, Voyageur has decided not to show images of human skeletal remains, which some American Indians find offensive. Voyageur does present images of artifacts, including funerary objects from public or academic archives. Some American Indians object to the public display of funerary objects. Others do not (see Epilogue).

Our goal is to present Ohio archaeology in a manner that is accurate, engaging and honorable, knowing the inherent conflict among these three core values. Our hope is to generate a greater appreciation for Ohio's ancient American Indian cultures, understanding the fragile nature of this magnificent heritage.

Thomas M. Law
Project Director
The Ohio Archaeology Project
Voyageur Media Group, Inc.

ACKNOWLEDGEMENTS

Voyageur Media Group, Inc.

The production of *Ohio Archaeology* was an enormous task that demanded the collaborative effort of dozens of scholars, archivists, photographers, graphic designers, researchers and publishing professionals. *Ohio Archaeology* was made possible thanks to the contributions of advice, time and resources from individuals, institutions and several Ohio companies that support educational projects. Voyageur would like to thank some of the participants who provided services well above and beyond their professional duties.

We thank the 26 scholars who contributed feature articles about specific archaeological sites and investigations. We thank the archaeologists, archivists and curators who provided some of the over 340 photographs, survey maps and graphics used to illustrate this coffee-table-style book.

We also thank a host of skilled professionals: Wanda Parrott, Proof Perfect, for proofing the manuscript; Steve Orf, All Systems Colour; Audra Jergens, AudDesign, Inc.; J. Miles Wolf, Wolf Photographic Arts; Bill Pickard for lending his personal copies of historic archaeological publications; Dave Barker, staff photographer, Ohio Historical Society, for his large format photography; freelance photographer Jules Angel, who documented fieldwork and artifacts at several Ohio institutions and sites; and John Hancock and Jose Kozan who generously provided 2-D images from the outstanding "Earthworks" project, The Center for the Electronic Reconstruction of Historical and Archaeological Sites, University of Cincinnati. We thank several volunteers and demonstrators, including Tom Grooms, Don Miller, Billy Wagner, The Ohio Atlatl Association, The Flint Ridge Lithographic Society, Nobles Pond FORCE; anthropology students from Northern Kentucky University and Mark Jacobs, Split Rock Conservation Park.

Voyageur greatly appreciates the assistance of graphic designer Jim Giles, Command Z Studio, who provided considerable talent and patience during the creation of numerous illustrations and graphics and all of the original maps and timelines presented in this book. The cartography staff of the Division of Geological Survey, Ohio Department of Natural Resources, generously supplied the new topographic graphics for many of these maps.

We thank archaeologist Martha Potter Otto, Curator of Archaeology, Ohio Historical Society, who supervised the development of the "Ancient Ohio" art series, and provided earnest support during difficult times. We applaud the skills of artist Susan Walton, who created the six extraordinary artworks in the "Ancient Ohio" art series, giving us a vital visual glimpse of the ancient lifeways of American Indians in Ohio. Our gratitude to archaeologist Frank Cowan, F. Cowan & Associates, who found time between investigations to help us sort out the most difficult challenge of this endeavor—the presentation of time. We thank Brent Eberhard, Ohio Historic Preservation Office, for helping us locate archaeological sites on the period maps.

I would also like to personally thank Voyageur's Board of Trustees for their wisdom, including Steve Gillen for his generous legal counsel, and Rebecca Hawkins for her sage advice on so many complex scientific and cultural issues. I thank Brad Lepper for his commitment and passion, and Marcy Hawley, Publisher, Orange Frazer Press, whose encouragement, talent and boundless patience made this project possible. Finally, I thank my wife, Kate, and daughters Emily and Audrey, for their personal sacrifices during this journey.

ACKNOWLEDGEMENTS

Author

THE FOLLOWING FRIENDS AND COLLEAGUES READ ALL OR PART OF THE MANUSCRIPT and offered their comments and suggestions.

Elliot Abrams (Ohio University), James Adovasio (Mercyhurst College), Jonathan Bowen (Ohio Historical Society), David Brose (Schiele Museum of Natural History), Jarrod Burks (Hopewell Culture National Historical Park), Martin Byers (McGill University), Robert Connolly, Robert Genheimer (Cincinnati Museum Center), N'omi Greber (Cleveland Museum of Natural History), Rebecca Hawkins (Voyageur Media Group, Inc.), Gwynn Henderson (Kentucky Archaeological Survey), Kathryn Jakes (The Ohio State University), Benjamin Lepper, Linda McKean Logan, Jerry McDonald, Julie Olds (Miami Tribe of Oklahoma), Martha Potter Otto (Ohio Historical Society), Brian Redmond (Cleveland Museum of Natural History), Katharine Ruhl (Cleveland Museum of Natural History), David Snyder (Ohio Historic Preservation Office), Kent Vickery, Dee Anne Wymer (Bloomsburg University), Sandy Yee (International Archaeological Research Institute).

Their gracious help is acknowledged, but any errors in the book are entirely my responsibility. I did not always heed the advice that was offered.

I thank my family for their many sacrifices without which this book never could have been written. I wish my father could have hung around long enough to see it.

I especially thank my wife, Karen, for carrying my share of the load when I spent all those Saturdays reading and writing in my office.

Finally, I thank Tom Law for his dedication to this project and for his faith in our ability to pull it off. It never could have happened without him.

I dedicate this book to my sons, Benjamin and Peter.

An Illustrated Chronicle of Ohio's Ancient American Indian Cultures

This mural by R. G. Larson in the Illinois State Museum depicts the landscape most common in the Midwestern United States about 16,000 years ago. American Indian family groups would have encoutered a cool, moist climate with ecosystems dominated by spruce, poplar and various wetlands.

THE
THE PALEOINDIAN
PERIOD

Circa 14,000 - 10,000 BP

No one knows when people first set foot upon the land that one day would become known as Ohio. The original discoverers of America were few in number and they lived in small groups who seldom stayed in one place for long. Such people leave few traces for archaeologists to find more than ten thousand years later. So, in order to piece together the puzzle of this earliest period of Ohio's prehistory, we must look beyond the borders of Ohio. Indeed, a global perspective is necessary in order to tell the story of the first Ohioans.

We KNOW THAT MODERN HUMANS EMERGED IN AFRICA AROUND 100,000 years ago and, over the subsequent millennia, our ancestors ranged out from this homeland to discover and settle the "new" worlds of Asia, Europe, Australia, and, eventually, America. The Americas were the last of these continents to be peopled because they were isolated behind formidable barriers of water and ice. To get here from Africa or Europe you needed a sea-worthy boat and the skills of sailors and fisherfolk. To get here from Asia you needed warm clothing and the tools to survive in an arctic wilderness. Crossing either a vast ocean or a frozen wasteland required technologies the earliest humans did not possess. So we find no Australopithecines or Neanderthals in America. But people excel at overcoming barriers and, by 40,000 years ago, they had built boats to cross the ocean separating Asia from Australia and had found ways to survive and thrive on the arctic doorstep of the Americas.

The emergence and dispersal of modern humans occurred during the Pleistocene Epoch, a geological period that is sometimes referred to as the "Ice Age," although it would be more accurate to characterize it as a series of ice ages. Throughout this era, the climate shifted, sometimes quite rapidly, from episodes of glacial cold, to warm intervals with temperatures like those to which we are accustomed. During the cold episodes, glaciers spread across much of northern North America. At their maximum extent, about 22,000 years ago, these ice sheets covered much of northern and western Ohio.

With so much of the world's water frozen in gigantic glaciers, sea level dropped, exposing large areas of continental shelf. At such times, the lowering waters revealed a broad land bridge connecting Siberia with Alaska, and humans along with other animals would have walked between Asia and America. But during the peak of the Ice Age, the glaciers covering northern North America would have formed a wall of ice blocking entrance to the rest of the hemisphere. Rising temperatures eventually caused these ice sheets to melt, opening a corridor to the southern lands, but as the melting ice released its water to the oceans the land bridge was submerged beneath the rising tides.

This complicated dance of ice, land, and water would seem to have set severe limits on when people could have come to America, but by the time humans reached Siberia they likely would have known how to make and use small boats. So they could have crossed the Bering Strait without a land bridge or followed the coastline southward avoiding the glaciers covering the land.

A distance of about 100 miles separates mainland Asia and North America at the Bering Strait. At their closest, Little Diomede Island (Alaska) and Big Diomede Island (Russia) are only 2.5 miles apart as seen in this photograph taken from Siberia. The Bering Strait often freezes in midwinter, making it possible to walk between these two modern continental outposts.

Ancient Ohio
North American Migration

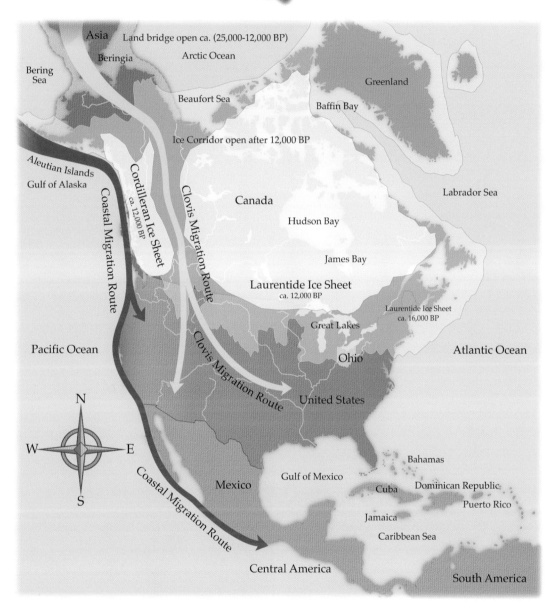

The dates and routes are a matter of considerable debate, but archaeological evidence indicates American Indians discovered the North American continent sometime between 14,000 and 33,000 years ago. The earliest peoples probably followed the coastline along southern Beringia and on southward to North and South America. Later groups, following the herds of big game animals, moved through the interior and down the ice-free corridor between the receding ice sheets centered on the Rocky Mountains and Hudson's Bay. Over many centuries, nomadic family groups worked their way south and east. Rather than a steady eastern expansion, some archaeologists think American Indian family groups may have "leapfrogged" their way across the continent. Once a family group became established in a region, their descendents jumped over known boundaries to explore unknown territories and begin to adapt to the new challenges and opportunities afforded by the newlands. Archaeological evidence suggests that the first American Indians to enter Ohio came up the Ohio River Valley. Some stayed and made this their home. Others pushed on to the north and east.

OHIO GEOLOGY

By Dale Gnidovec, Curator, Orton Geological Museum, The Ohio State University

Archaeologists must be students of Ohio geology in order to understand the state's relatively recent human history. The history of Ohio extends back long before the first settlers, long before the first people and even before the dinosaurs. Such ancient history is geologic history. Deep in the ground are granite, schist and gneiss that formed over a billion years ago. Ohio's oldest rocks exposed at the surface are the limestones and shales of the Cincinnati area, which were deposited in a warm shallow ocean much like that surrounding the Bahamas today. At that time, 450 million years ago, Ohio was in the tropics, around 20 degrees south of the equator, about where Australia is today.

Geologists call that time the Ordovician Period. Ohio's Ordovician fossils are world famous, and include such ocean-dwelling animals as corals, trilobites (ancient crab-like creatures), crinoids (stalked relatives of starfish), brachiopods (with two-part shells like clams but different inside) and cephalopods (ancient relatives of the living chambered nautilus).

Ohio was at or below sea level during most of the succeeding period, the Silurian. Most of Ohio's Silurian rocks are precipitates–limestone, dolomite, gypsum, and salt—showing that highlands were distant. Such conditions persisted for millions of years, until late in the Devonian Period when the east coast of North America collided with Europe as the supercontinent Pangea was forming. That collision formed mountains that shed sediment westward. The resulting dark black shales of Ohio contain fossils of giant carnivorous fish.

By the Carboniferous Period (often divided into the Mississippian and Pennsylvanian Periods) Ohio was at the equator. In vast swamps of scaly-barked trees plant debris accumulated, forming thick deposits of peat that eventually would be compressed into the coal that fueled the industrial revolution. Farther offshore limestone formed, some of which contains lenses of flint that, 300 million years later, would be used by humans for tools and weapons. Early in the Permian Period the sea withdrew. Never again would Ohio be below sea level. That is why there is no rock record of the next 250 million years—we're missing the entire Mesozoic (the time of the dinosaurs) and most of the Cenozoic.

About five million years ago Earth's climate began getting cooler. In Canada snow accumulated to thousands of feet. The weight of the upper layers of snow compressed the lower layers into ice, which began flowing outward. Such a moving sheet of ice is called a glacier. As the ice moved over the land, boulders, rocks and sand frozen in the base of the glacier acted like the teeth of a giant file, grinding the rock beneath them. High areas were shaved and valleys filled with debris.

Glacial Grooves State Memorial preserves a footprint from Ohio's last Ice Age. About 18,000 years ago, rocks frozen into the base of mile thick ice glaciers and melt water carved grooves into the softer limestones bedrock of modern Kelley's Island. The 400 foot long section exposed today is a portion of even larger glacial grooves that were destroyed during quarry operations in the 1830s.

GLACIAL MAP OF OHIO

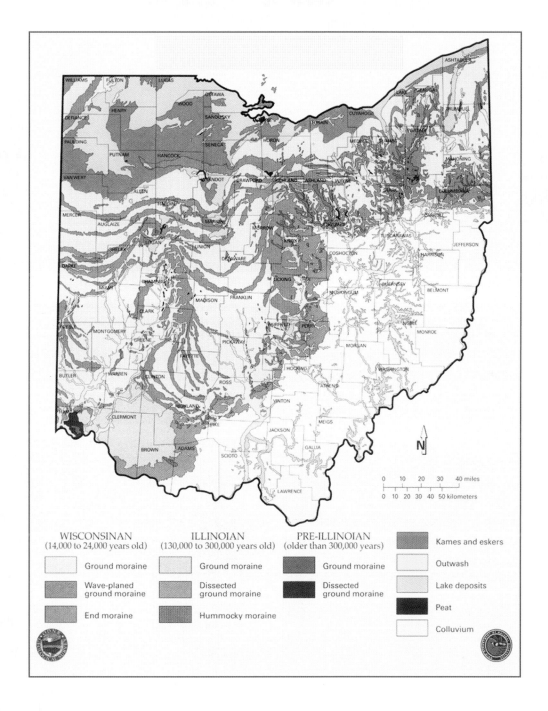

WISCONSINAN
(14,000 to 24,000 years old)

Ground moraine

Wave-planed
ground moraine

End moraine

ILLINOIAN
(130,000 to 300,000 years old)

Ground moraine

Dissected
ground moraine

Hummocky moraine

PRE-ILLINOIAN
(older than 300,000 years)

Ground moraine

Dissected
ground moraine

Kames and eskers

Outwash

Lake deposits

Peat

Colluvium

Archaeologists study Ohio's glacial geology to better understand the relationship between ancient American Indian cultures and their environment. This glacial map by The Ohio Department of Natural Resources shows how the state is divided into the glaciated plains and hills of the northwest and the unglaciated Appalachian Plateau of the southest. The glacial moraines, kames, eskers and outwash deposits between this geological rift provide diverse ecosystems for a rich variety of plant and animal life.

OHIO GEOLOGY

In eastern Ohio the glaciers covered the northern half but were stopped by the foothills of the Allegheny Mountains. Further west, less resistant bedrock and lower elevations allowed the ice to flow all the way to Cincinnati. That is why western Ohio is so flat. The glaciers enlarged some old river valleys, forming the Great Lakes. Sometimes glaciers blocked rivers, forcing them to find alternate routes. That is why many rivers in Ohio flow in one direction for a distance then suddenly change course.

At times the ice front would melt back at the same rate as new ice was arriving. Like a giant conveyor belt, the ice deposited large ridges of boulders, sand and gravel. Averaging about 50 feet high, two miles wide and over 50 miles long, the ridges are called moraines. Sometimes the glacier would leave behind huge chunks of ice. Their melting would leave large pits called kettles that, when filled with water, are called kettle lakes. The glaciers also left rocks carried from distant sources. Such rocks are called erratics. Some erratics are igneous and metamorphic rocks like granite, schist and gneiss, which are far harder than Ohio's native stones and would be put to use by prehistoric people as hammerstones and other tools.

The ice came and melted back numerous times, with warm interglacial periods averaging 100,000 years alternating with cooler times of similar lengths. Each time the ice advanced, plant and animal communities would be pushed south, then reclaim their former territory as the ice retreated. Mastodons, which preferred forested areas, and mammoths, which preferred open grasslands, would follow their preferred habitats. Their human hunters would move with them or switch to other prey. Humans didn't enter Ohio until the very end of the Ice Age or Pleistocene. The ancient seas, Carboniferous swamps, and Pleistocene glaciers laid Ohio's foundations and provided the abundance of natural resources that have made this land so attractive for human habitation. With the entry of people, we end the geologic story and begin the human story.

The power of glaciation is seen on the campus of The Ohio State University in the form of the Orton erratic. Dale Gnidovec leans against this 16-ton granite boulder, which was carried a distance of over 500 miles by glaciers into Ohio from an outcrop near Quebec, Canada.

Photographer Peter Bostrom spent several months gathering this assemblage of 175 early Paleoindian artifacts from institutions and collections throughout America. His stunning image includes fluted spearpoints, scrapers, knives, gravers, several bone rods that may have served as the foreshafts for spears, and a bone shaft wrench probably used for straightening spear shafts. About seventeen of the artifacts pictured here come from Ohio.

THE EARLIEST RELIABLE EVIDENCE WE HAVE OF PEOPLE IN AMERICA IS FROM THE MONTE Verde site in southern South America. Here archaeologists have found the remains of several houses that had been framed with wood and covered with mastodon hides. The few stone tools found among these houses are remarkably simple—long, narrow spear points, spherical, grooved bolo stones, and roughly broken stones with naturally sharp edges. Charcoal from Monte Verde's campfires have given us radiocarbon dates ranging from 12,500 to 33,000 years ago. The earliest dates are from a deep layer that has not been thoroughly studied, but they suggest people discovered America before 33,000 years ago. And if people were at the southern end of South America by then, they must have been in North America considerably earlier.

✕✕✕✕

WE HAVE VERY LITTLE EVIDENCE FOR PEOPLE IN OHIO AT SUCH AN EARLY TIME. BUT IN Pennsylvania, fewer than 20 miles from the Ohio border, there is a small cave, or rockshelter, that disclosed traces of the first Americans in its deepest layers. Meadowcroft Rockshelter is located along a creek that flows into the Ohio River. The creek valley would have been a sheltered environment during the Ice Age and the kinds of plants and animals found in the deepest layers of the rockshelter are similar to those living in the area today. The oldest layers of the site that contain stone tools have been radiocarbon dated to between 13,000 and 16,000 years ago. By this time the glaciers had begun to melt back towards their source near Hudson Bay. There would be more shifts to bitterly cold temperatures and the ice would creep southward again, but never again as far south as Ohio.

The stone tools found in the oldest levels of Meadowcroft Rockshelter include a small, resharp-ened spear point, a triangular flint knife, small, narrow flint blades, somewhat like the replaceable blades in a modern razor, and a few other whole and broken tools. This was the basic stone tool kit used by the hunting and gathering peoples of Europe and Asia during the Upper Paleolithic era, the most recent phase of the Stone Age that began around 35,000 years ago. It represents only a small part of the highly flexible technology of these resourceful people who colonized the entire world by 15,000 years ago (except for Antarctica and the islands of the Pacific Ocean). They also had tools of wood and bone, such as digging sticks, needles, and awls as well as nets, snares, and containers made of cordage, basketry and leather. Unfortunately, most of these things have rotted in the soil and left few traces for archaeologists to find thousands of years later. Such materials generally are preserved only at sites that are very wet, very dry, or very cold.

Many of the flint tools found in the deepest layers of Meadowcroft Rockshelter were shaped from stone quarried in Ohio, from Flint Ridge in Licking County and from the outcrops of Upper Mercer flint in Coshocton County. This supports the idea that the people who made these tools and lived for a time in this small rockshelter were part of the vanguard of the original colonizers of America. Their ancestors had traveled southward from Alaska, along the coast or through the interior, and then moved eastward, generally following the major river valleys. They likely moved up the Ohio River and its tributaries, searching for exposures of flint and pleasant places to live. Some of the people who camped at Meadowcroft Rockshelter had come from Ohio, where they had quarried flint and shaped it into the tools they required for their Paleolithic way of life. They had traveled eastward, perhaps in search of game or marriage partners; or, perhaps they were restless pioneers with their eyes on the horizon, wondering what might be over that next hill.

Meadowcroft Rockshelter, located about 8 miles east of the Ohio River in southwestern Pennsylvania, has some of the earliest evidence of Paleoindian cultures in North America. Dr. James Adovasio conducted extensive excavations here from 1973 to 1978. The upper section shows sediment layers from the Archaic to the historic periods. The lower section, coined the "Deep Hole," holds evidence of early Paleoindian campsites radiocarbon dated to about 16,000 years ago. Archaeologists have recovered over 2 million artifacts from the Meadowcraft Rockshelter, including Paleoindian tools made of flint from sources as far away as New York, West Virginia and Ohio.

This assemblage of Pre-Clovis tools, dating from 11,300 to 12,800 BP, was collected from the deepest occupational layers at Meadowcroft Rockshelter. From left to right: Miller spearpoint, two small blade fragments, two flakes chipped from a biface, and a retouched knife.

A wooden staircase leads visitors up to the Meadowcroft Rockshelter, which is located about 50 feet above Cross Creek. Billed as the oldest and longest continually used human site in North America, the rockshelter is open for seasonal public tours as part of the Meadowcroft Museum of Rural Life.

ICE AGE GIANTS

of the Ohio Valley and Lower Great Lakes Region

By Kenneth B. Tankersley, Ph.D., Anthropologist,
Department of Sociology, Anthropology, and Philosophy, Northern Kentucky University;
Department of Archaeology, Cleveland Museum of Natural History.

Our knowledge about the plants and animals that lived in Ohio during the Ice Age is based on their fossil remains, serendipitously discovered or deliberately excavated from sand and gravel pits, peat bogs and ponds, and deeply buried cave passages. By directly radiocarbon dating the plant and animal fossils and plotting where they were found on maps, we can glean important clues about the Ice Age environment—rates of climate change, adaptation, survival and extinction.

If we had a time machine that could take us back to the end of the last Ice Age, the view would be unlike anywhere found in the world today. We would experience warmer winters and cooler summers, but they would be extremely erratic from one year to the next. We would see a mosaic of plant and animal communities, parklands of spruce and pine, open patches of grassland interrupted by an occasional cedar, and shallow streams and wetlands bounded by willows and poplars.

The waters would be filled with the same variety of fish and turtles, frogs and salamanders, and snakes that we see today. We would see beavers and muskrats swimming toward their lodges, and raccoons washing their paws along the shore. In the sky, we would find the same ducks and geese, hawks and owls, and vultures and eagles, and even bats flying at night. The woodlands would be filled with chipmunks and squirrels, porcupines and woodchucks, mice and voles, white-tailed deer and elk, and an occasional black bear.

Among this modern menagerie of animals, we would also see strange, giant creatures known as megamammals (animals that weighed more than 100 pounds, 45 kilograms) walking, swimming, and flying across the landscape. We would see two very different herds of hairy elephants (the Wooly and Jefferson mammoths) grazing on grasses and riverside willows. They would tower over the hairy elephant-like mastodon, giant deer-like stag-moose, and tapirs browsing in and around the bogs and fens. In the deeper water, we would see bear-sized, beaver-like creatures swimming with cattails and rushes in their mouths. In the nearby parklands, we would find two kinds of giant ground sloth's (the Jefferson and Harlan's) standing on their hind legs, as tall as the trees they bow with their giant claws, browsing on tender green leaves. At salt springs, we would see herds of colossal-sized complex-toothed horses, giant bison, and huge, hairy woodland muskoxen grazing on prairie grasses. In the distance, we would see herds of two kinds of giant hairy pig-like creatures (the long-nosed and flat-headed peccaries). Packs of dire wolves and a short-faced bear would be keeping a watchful eye on the young and weak, as California condors circle overhead waiting for their next meal.

Among these megamammals we would also see unusual smaller animals such as caribou, pine martins and fishers, mink and ermines, and even tiny animals, called micromammals, such as northern bog lemmings, and the mountain-heather, boreal redback, and yellow-cheeked voles.

The climate at the end of the last Ice Age was like a flickering candle flame—unstable and rapidly changing. Not every plant or animal had the same tolerance to this profound climatic change. Some plants and animals were unaffected, remaining in Ohio. Others moved north, south, east, or west. Some became smaller in size, but more than thirty genera could neither adapt nor move—they became extinct.

CARNIVORES

DIRE WOLF (*Canis dirus*)

Est. Max. Height: 3 feet (at shoulders)
Est. Max. Length: 5 feet
Est. Max. Weight: 110 lbs.
Est. Max. Speed: 30 mph
Fossil Range: North America

Description: The dire wolf was larger than the modern grey wolf in both size and weight, but had shorter, more muscular limbs. Its broad head and large, massive teeth and jaws made it a powerful predator and effective scavenger. Heavy wear on the surface of it teeth suggests it broke the bones of large animals. The brain of the dire wolf is smaller than the grey wolf, which may have made it less competitive. It became extinct about 11,000 years ago.

Regional evidence: Specimens have been found at the Sheriden Cave site in Ohio, and in Indiana.

SABER-TOOTHED CAT (*Smilodon fatalis*)

Est. Max. Height: 3 feet (at shoulders)
Est. Max. Length: 9 feet
Est. Max. Weight: 550 lbs.
Est. Max. Speed: 35 mph
Fossil Range: Midwestern North America

Description: The saber-toothed cat was nearly twice as heavy as the modern American mountain lion, and it had a bobtail. Their weight and short tail suggest that it did not chase down prey, but probably ambushed animals using stealth and teamwork. Their canine teeth, up to seven inches long, may have been more important for sexual selection (show) than for hunting. The saber-tooth cat was most likely a social predator, living in prides like African lions. Numerous bone injuries suggest saber-tooth cats took care of wounded pride members. It became extinct about 13,000 years ago.

Regional evidence: Specimens have been found as close as Indiana. As yet, none have been discovered in Ohio.

Illustrations not to scale.

SHORT-FACED BEAR (*Arctodus simus*)

Est. Max. Height: 5 feet (at shoulders)
Est. Max. Length: 11 feet (standing)
Est. Max. Weight: >1,800 lbs.
Est. Max. Speed: bursts of up to 70 mph
Fossil Range: North America (except southeast)

Description: The short-faced bear was the single most deadly predator of the Ice Age. It was bigger, faster and more carnivorous than the polar and grizzly bears. This fierce carnivore had a broad, powerful muzzle filled with sharp canine teeth and jagged molars that could tear through the toughest hides and crush thick bones, including the mastodon and mammoth. Humans would have avoided this awesome predator at all costs. The short-faced bear went extinct about 1,000 years later than the other megamammals. Although it survived the end of the Ice Age, it could not compete with the invasion of both the brown and grizzly bears into the modern habitat.

Regional evidence: Specimens have been found at Sheriden Cave, Wyandot County, Ohio, and a few sites in Pennsylvania and Indiana.

AMERICAN MASTODON (Mammut americanum)

Est. Max. Height:	9 feet
Est. Max. Length:	15 feet
Est. Max. Weight:	6 tons
Est. Max. Speed:	25 mph
Fossil Range:	North America, especially abundant in the Midwest

Description: The American mastodon was smaller than the mammoth, but more robust in build. Adult males and females had long tusks up to 18 feet long, and from eight to twelve molars with deep cusps used to cut and chew wetland plants, abrasive grasses and leafy vegetation. Scientists continue to debate whether the extinction of this animal was caused by human hunting, climactic changes or a combination of both.

Regional evidence: More than 100 individuals have been found throughout Ohio and its contiguous states.

GIANT BEAVER (Castoroides ohioensis)

Est. Max. Height:	4 feet (at shoulders)
Est. Max. Length:	9 feet (head to tail)
Est. Max. Weight:	500 lbs.
Est. Max. Speed:	7 mph
Fossil Range:	North America

Description: The giant beaver was one of the largest rodents ever known, reaching the size of a modern black bear. The common name is somewhat misleading since it lived more like a muskrat than a modern beaver. The giant beaver was well adapted for swimming with powerful, short hind legs and webbed feet. It had a narrow, scaly tail. The cutting edge of their enormous incisors was convex in shape to feed on coarse wetland vegetation. There's no evidence that the giant beaver chewed on trees or built lodges or dams from felled trees. Unable to create its own habitat like the modern beaver, the giant beaver likely became extinct with the rapid and profound warming and drying at the end of the Ice Age.

Regional evidence: Specimens have been found in thirteen Ohio counties, and in Indiana.

ICE AGE GIANTS
HERBIVORES

JEFFERSON'S GROUND SLOTH (Megalonyx jeffersonii)

Est. Max. Height:	>6 feet (at shoulders)
Est. Max. Length:	>9 feet (standing, hind legs)
Est. Max. Weight:	>2,000 lbs.
Est. Max. Speed:	5 mph
Fossil Range:	North America– west coast to Alaska, inland to Idaho, most of the Midwest.

Description: Jefferson's ground sloth had large claws on its front and back paws. This gentle herbivore probably stood upright to browse on the leafy green vegetation of woodland tress and shrubs based on the shape of its pelvis and upper leg bones, and small, dull, rounded teeth. The Jefferson's ground sloth was larger in size and weight than its western cousin, the Shasta ground sloth. It became extinct about 11,000 years ago as the result of climactic change, human hunting or both.

Regional evidence: A specimen was found in Darke County, Ohio. Others have been reported from Fairfield, Holmes and Huron counties in Ohio, and at Big Bone Lick, Kentucky.

STAG MOOSE *(Cervalces scotti)*

Est. Max. Height: 8 feet
Est. Max. Length: 9 feet (standing)
Est. Max. Weight: 1,500 lbs.
Est. Max. Speed: 30-40 mph
Fossil Range: North America midwest

Description: The Stag-moose (aka Scott's moose) was a giant deer about the size of a modern moose. It had long limbs to walk through all types of environments, from open meadows, woodlands to bogs. The stag-moose had massive spreading antlers up to 10 feet in width, which were used to keep lethal predators at bay. It became extinct about 12,500 years ago, most likely from climate change.

Regional evidence: Specimens have been found in five Ohio counties, and Big Bone Lick, Kentucky.

JEFFERSON'S MAMMOTH
(Mammuthus jeffersonii)

Est. Max. Height: >12 feet (at shoulders)
Est. Max. Length: >24 feet
Est. Max. Weight: >6 tons
Est. Max. Speed: 25 mph
Fossil Range: North America midwest

Description: Jefferson's mammoth, like its western cousin the Columbian mammoth, was larger than the wooly mammoth. Jefferson's mammoth had course hair, long incurved tusks up to 16 feet long, an extended broad head, a shallow down-turned chin for feeding on grassy vegetation, and a stiff tail for swatting insects. Its small ears, stout trunk and fat-filled hump helped the Jefferson mammoth survive in cold weather. They were hunted by humans, but it's unknown whether this predation contributed to their extinction about 11,000 years ago.

Regional evidence: Specimens have been found in twenty-eight Ohio counties, Big Bone Lick, Kentucky and contiguous states.

FLAT-HEADED PECCARY *(Platygonus compressus)*

Est. Max. Height: 3 feet
Est. Max. Length: 5 feet
Est. Max. Weight: 200 lbs.
Est. Max. Speed: 30 mph
Fossil Range: North America

Description: The flat-headed peccary, a herd animal, was the most common mammal in North America during the Ice Age. It was about the size of a white-tailed deer and as fast as a modern European boar. Razor-sharp tusks protruding from a slender snout discouraged predators such as the short-faced bear and dire wolf. Its long legs and molars suggest a life in open meadows and the forest edge. The flat-headed peccary died out at the end of the Ice Age from human hunting, habitat loss or increased competition from modern animals such as the American black bear.

Regional evidence: Hundreds of specimens have been found throughout Ohio, and its contiguous states.

Some of the earliest evidence of the first "Ohioans" comes from the Paleo Crossing site, an encampment near a kettle lake in Medina County. Jim Remington (foreground with camera) discovered this rare site, which was investigated by archaeologists from 1990 to 1993.

The artifacts from Paleo Crossing reveal a fascinating tale. A large percentage of the artifacts from this Ohio site, such as the stone fluted points, are made of Wyandot chert from a quarry about 350 miles away in southern Indiana. Dr. Brian Redmond, Curator of Archaeology, Cleveland Museum of Natural History, contends the abundance of this "exotic" stone could mean that the nomadic family groups at Paleo Crossing may have come from the lower Ohio River Valley. "The people who camped at Paleo Crossing may have first used up their Wyandot chert before learning about the local flint quarries in northern Ohio," says Redmond.

THE EVIDENCE FROM MEADOWCROFT, MEAGER AS IT IS, SHOWS US THAT THE EARLIEST PEOPLE IN this region were opportunistic hunters and gatherers. They hunted deer and other game animals, fished in the streams, and gathered a rich variety of nuts, fruits, and other plant foods. There are no mastodon or other giant mammal bones at Meadowcroft. Such mega-mammals would have lived in the region at that time, but if the small groups of pioneers were just passing through, it would have made little sense for them to risk their necks trying to hunt them. Even if they succeeded in killing one of the great beasts without getting killed, the small band couldn't carry enough of the meat to make it worth the effort. And if they stayed by the kill, the smell of the carcass would have attracted unwelcome guests, such as the saber-toothed cat and the giant short-faced bear.

Some Paleoindian groups found a solution to this dilemma. If they managed to kill a mastodon in late autumn and stashed the butchered carcass in the cold waters of a lake or pond, then the meat wouldn't spoil. The band could come back to this Ice Age meat freezer all through the winter. This is just what may have happened at the Burning Tree mastodon site in Licking County. Archaeologists found the bones of a large male mastodon in three separate piles beneath layers of peat. This bog, or fen, had been a shallow pond when the mastodon was alive. Some of the bones had cutmarks on them, indicating that Paleoindians butchered the beast. But whether they killed the mastodon or found it dead and scavenged the meat is a question we cannot, as yet, answer. Daniel Fisher, a paleontologist at the University of Michigan, studied the growth rings in the tusks and concluded the mastodon died in late autumn. Fisher has found other sites in Michigan, and elsewhere in the Great Lakes region, that repeat this pattern suggesting that Paleoindians regularly hunted mastodons in the autumn.

Winter in Ohio was a difficult time for hunters and gatherers. There were no nuts or berries available, and some game animals migrated to other regions or hibernated during the coldest months. A cache of mastodon meat in a frozen pond might have meant the difference between starvation and survival for many Paleoindian bands.

I F PALEOINDIANS WERE LIKE MOST OF THE HUNTERS AND GATHERERS STUDIED BY ANTHROPOLOGISTS around the world, they probably divided up the work between men and women. In such societies, men usually hunted for game, while women gathered plant foods and cared for the children. Of course this does not mean that women never hunted or that men never cared for the children. Meat was highly prized and shared among the members of the band, but the fruits and vegetables collected by the women provided the bulk of the diet. Older children helped their parents and learned the skills they would need to become successful hunters and gatherers.

Paleoindian religion was probably based on shamanism. Men or women might call upon animal spirits to help them find food, heal an illness, succeed in romance, or find consolation at the death of a loved one. We know little of Paleoindian burials for none have been found in Ohio. Archaeologists working at the Crowfield site in neighboring Ontario, Canada, found a pit with many burned and broken artifacts. They interpret the pit as a Paleoindian cremation. If Paleoindians cremated their dead, this would help to explain why archaeologists have found so few burials from this period.

Paleoindians also began to learn the medicinal qualities of the plants in their environment. At Monte Verde, for example, there was a special house separated from the others. Bits of plants found within this structure are from species known to have medicinal properties. Perhaps this was the shaman's dwelling—a combination of church and pharmacy.

The Paleoindian Period Tool Kit,
Circa 14,000 – 10,000 BP

Ice Age Ohio must have been a paradise for hunters and gatherers based on the numbers of Paleoindian artifacts that have been found here.

The spectacular point in the center of this image is a Clovis point. The points spread out above it are in approximate chronological order. Beginning on the left, the points are a Debert point, Ross County point, Cumberland point, Crowfield point, and Plano lanceolate point. Debert points are more common in northeastern North America. Ross County points are named for Ross County, Ohio, but are found throughout the Ohio Valley. Cumberland points are most common in the southern United States. Crowfield points are found predominantly in Ontario. Plano points were used in the Late Paleoindian period. They are more common than earlier fluted point varieties and occur mostly in the Great Lakes andnortheast regions of Eastern North America. Similar points were made and used by many of Ohio's ancient cultures, so it is not always easy to identify Plano points.

The tools along the bottom of the image are endscrapers and a sidescraper. These could have been used to scrape animal hide or to work wood or bone. After more than 10 millennia, most Paleoindian tools of bone, wood, or fiber have decayed.

CHAPTER 1: THE PALEOINDIAN PERIOD

The "Ancient Ohio" Art Series
The Paleoindian Period
(ca. 14,000-10,000 BP)

A group of Paleoindian hunters successfully ambushed a herd of caribou migrating through the till plains of western Ohio. Now one family has butchered an animal, hanging strips of meat on a rack to dry both to preserve it and make it easier to pack and carry to their next camp. The animal also provides hides, which, after stretching, scraping, and tanning, can be made into clothing or thrown over a wood frame for a temporary shelter. All the tools required for these tasks are chipped from flint, sometimes even using heavy caribou bones as the chipping tool.

Archaeological basis: A combination of information from such Paleoindian sites as Paleo Crossing, Nobles Pond, and Sheriden Cave in Ohio, and the Vail site in Maine.

This highly successful way of life, based on mobility and flexibility, changed gradually as people became settlers rather than explorers. By 11,500 years ago, the population of Paleoindians had grown to a point where traces of their activities became more common on the landscape. By this time, their stone tool kit included a distinctive spear point typified by a long groove, or flute, running up from the base. This groove formed a channel that permitted the point to be more securely attached to a shaft. This kind of point is called a Clovis point. It is named for the small town of Clovis, New Mexico, where it was first recognized as a weapon used by Ice Age hunters of mammoth.

Because similar points have been found across North America all dating to about the same period, between 11,500 and 11,000 years ago, archaeologists used to think that all these points were made by the same people who had spread rapidly across the continent. Some archaeologists argued that, in order for people to move so rapidly, they must have been moving across an unoccupied land and that they therefore must have been the very first Americans.

There have always been problems with this idea. For one thing, there are no Clovis points in Asia, so it must not have been a part of the tool kit of the first people to discover America—it is a purely American invention. Also, Clovis points actually are not all the same. Although they look somewhat similar, there are differences in their shapes and in the ways they are made from one region to another. A better way to explain the rapid appearance of the Clovis point over such a broad area is that people already were living in America, and that somebody came up with the idea of adding a flute to the base of their spear point. It was a good idea and it caught on. The idea of making a Clovis point could spread from one group to another very rapidly and each group would end up adapting a flute to their existing stone spear points.

More than 1,000 Clovis points have been found in Ohio. Only Alabama has more Clovis points per square mile than Ohio, so eastern North America, in general, and Ohio, in particular, must have been a Paleoindian paradise. It was rich country during the closing phases of the Ice Age. The environment was a mosaic of different kinds of forest and prairie, with a smorgasbord of resources from upland groves of nut trees to wetlands filled with waterfowl. In addition to deer and beaver, there also were herds of caribou and musk oxen, mastodons, mammoths, and giant ground sloths, as well as predators such as the saber-tooth cat, the short-faced bear, wolves and mountain lions.

Fluted spearpoints made of Wyandot chert from the Paleo Crossing site in Medina County.

Ancient Ohio
Paleoindian Period Site Map

(ca. 14,000-10,000 BP)

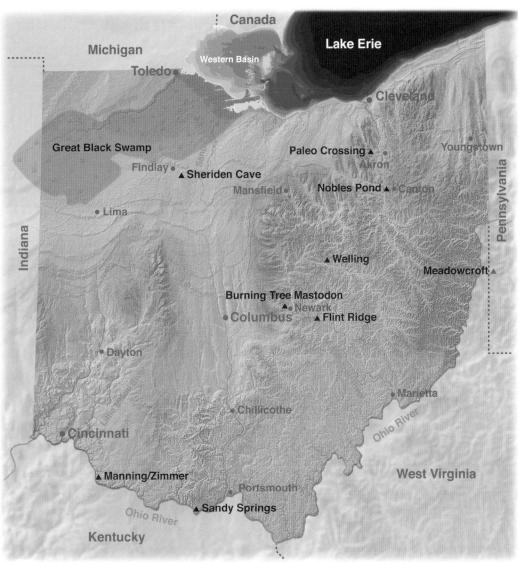

* Sites referenced in text and timelines

▲ – Ohio Archaeological Sites
▲ – Kentucky Archaeological Sites
▲ – Pennsylvania Archaeological Sites
▲ – West Virginia Archaeological Sites
● – Modern Cities

Elevation base map courtesy
Cartography & Editing Group,
Ohio Department of Natural Resources

© 2004 Voyageur Media Group, Inc.

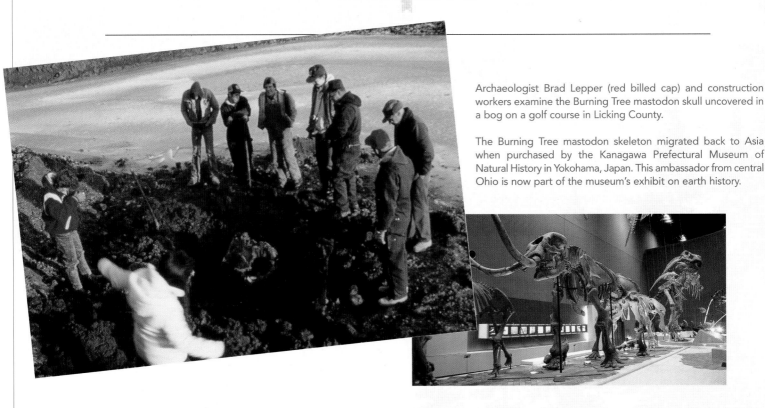

Archaeologist Brad Lepper (red billed cap) and construction workers examine the Burning Tree mastodon skull uncovered in a bog on a golf course in Licking County.

The Burning Tree mastodon skeleton migrated back to Asia when purchased by the Kanagawa Prefectural Museum of Natural History in Yokohama, Japan. This ambassador from central Ohio is now part of the museum's exhibit on earth history.

THE BURNING TREE MASTODON
Licking County

By Dr. Bradley T. Lepper, Curator of Archaeology, The Ohio Historical Society

On a bitterly cold day in December 1989, dragline operator Phil Flowers was excavating peat from a bog at the Burning Tree Golf Course south of Newark, Ohio. While scooping out masses of the soft, decaying vegetable matter, the dragline bucket banged into something unexpectedly hard and massive — something that didn't belong in the peat. It was the giant skull of a mastodon, a distant relative of modern elephants. Without intending it, Mr. Flowers had opened a window onto a lost world. And our understanding of that world has been forever changed because he chose to stop digging thereby giving archaeologists, geologists, and other scientists a chance to excavate the skeleton.

The Burning Tree mastodon was a remarkable discovery. The wonderfully preserved bones lay in three separate stacks: the skull, pelvis, and one back leg in one place, the ribs and backbone in another, and the front legs together with the neck vertebrae in yet another pile. When examined under the microscope many of the bones showed cuts or gashes made by stone tools and a few were marked by scratches or drag marks on the ends. The scientists who studied the bones concluded that Paleoindians killed and butchered this animal somewhere nearby, and then dragged the sections of the carcass to this cold, shallow pond where they could be submerged and stored in a sort of Ice Age meat freezer. For some reason, the ancient hunters never came back to feast upon their frozen McMastodon nuggets, leaving them for Mr. Flowers to uncover. Their failure to return, however, was our good fortune, because this site has been a treasure trove of information about this giant animal and his world.

At Sheridan Cave in Wyandot County, archaeologists and geologists have found a fluted point and other tools associated with a wide range of Ice Age animals. Some of the bones may be the remains of Paleoindian meals, but others might have been brought to the cave by non-human carnivores. Regardless, the abundance of animal bones found here gives us a glimpse of the amazing biodiversity during the Ice Age. By 10,000 years ago, that biodiversity would crash. Part of the explanation for this environmental catastrophe relates to climate change. During the Ice Age, animals such as caribou, musk oxen, northern bog lemmings, and pine martens all lived in Ohio. Today, these animals are confined to the far north. They cannot live in Ohio's modern temperate climate. However, the drastic change in climate at the end of the Ice Age didn't just displace animals. A number of species, dominated by extra large mammals such as mastodons and giant ground sloths, became extinct at the end of the Ice Age. Either they were unable to find a suitable modern environment in which to thrive, or else humans hunted them into extinction. Scientists who favor climate change as an explanation for the extinctions point to the fact that Paleolithic humans were not single-minded carnivores and did not have the technology to kill so many animals in so short a time. Scientists who think overhunting by people was the cause of the extinctions say the animals were especially vulnerable because they had never been hunted by humans before. They also point out that earlier episodes of climate change did not result in the extinction of any big game animal species. Scientists do not agree on whether climate change or human hunting was the main factor behind the extinction of the megafauna, but most accept that both played a role in this ecological disaster.

✂

Flint was another natural resource important to Paleoindians. In some ways it was the key resource, because flint tools were needed in order to hunt game animals and to turn their hides into clothing and moccasins. Paleoindians especially prized the black flint of Coshocton County. Most of the fluted points found in Ohio are made of this high quality flint, and more fluted points have been found in Coshocton County than in any other Ohio county.

Because Paleoindians lived in small, family groups that were always on the move, they needed a way to get several groups together, at least occasionally, so young men and women could find suitable marriage partners. The flint quarries provided a place known to all. Each autumn, when nuts were falling from the trees and the deer were fat, groups from across Ohio might have rendezvoused at Coshocton to dig for flint to replenish their tool kits. They would gather at favorite places, such as the Welling site near Warsaw, and feast, play games, share stories around the campfire, renew old acquaintances, and mourn the passing of friends and family who had died in the past year. Young couples might slip away from the campfires to hold hands in the moonlight and dream about the future. A few days or weeks later, with their bags full of flint, the groups would disperse for the coming winter. Some groups would have a new member, if their son or daughter had successfully wooed a mate. Other groups would be missing a familiar face and the farewells would be bittersweet. But they would meet again at the quarries next year and perhaps there would be grandchildren to welcome into the clan.

Scrapers from the Paleo Crossing site in Medina County.

The location of the Nobles Pond site, seen here in a 1988 aerial photograph, is no accident. This Paleoindian site is situated high and dry on a glacial outwash terrace between two wetlands, a kettle lake (Nobles Pond) and a fen (Jackson Bog State Nature Preserve). Archaeological evidence suggests several mobile family groups may have gathered here (no more than about 75 people) for a winter encampment near this "bottleneck" of established game trails and water sources.

THE NOBLES POND SITE

Stark County

By Dr. Mark F. Seeman, Professor of Anthropology, Kent State University

Nobles Pond, excavated by Kent State University and an extremely dedicated crew of volunteers, is one of the most extensive Paleoindian sites in eastern North America. The site, located in Stark County, Ohio, just west of the city of Canton, covers about 20 acres and is composed of a minimum of 10 distinct artifact concentrations that are situated on a series of slight ridges on a glacial outwash terrace. The terrace is located just east of Jackson Bog (fen), a low swampy area, and immediately adjacent to a glacial kettle lake (Nobles Pond) of approximately 11 acres. It was discovered in 1972 by two amateur archaeologists, Philip Cossentino and Garry Summers, and it has been continuously surface collected ever since. In 1988 the site was faced with imminent destruction due to urban development. The landowners, Kent State University, and a corps of highly motivated volunteers developed a plan to salvage as much information as possible prior to construction. What was initially envisioned as a short-term field project involving machine stripping and hand excavation has evolved into a project that now spans 14 years and has resulted in numerous professional papers, articles, and public presentations. Nobles Pond has already shed considerable light on life in Ohio nearly 11,500 years ago at a time when the climate and vegetation were considerably different than they are today.

Raw lithic material analyses, refit data, and stylistic information at Nobles Pond indicate that between four and six of the circular artifact concentrations or "hotspots" at the site probably were occupied contemporaneously as individual family bands came together for purposes of social interaction, communal hunting, hide processing, and related activities. The available evidence indicates that this was probably a cold season or winter activity and that caribou were among the quarry sought.

To date, Nobles Pond has yielded 43 finished diagnostic early Paleoindian fluted points of the "Gainey style," two miniature fluted points, two later "Crowfield" fluted points, 1,707 trianguloid end scrapers, and a variety of other tools pertaining to the Paleoindian occupations, notably side scrapers, gravers, perforators, and spokeshaves, altogether totaling over 6,835 tools. Waste flakes from the manufacture of tools is comparatively rare. The majority of the tools at Nobles Pond were made of high quality lithic sources obtained 45-70 miles to the south. Their condition and on-site patterning are consistent with a lifestyle requiring high residential mobility within large band territories or home ranges. Early Paleoindian societies were among the most mobile ever to exist. Many tools at Nobles Pond show unusually high rates of salvage and recycling, patterns that are consistent with tool kits that are depleted and in need of replacement, but that must be conserved to finish the tasks at hand. Many tools arrived at the site in heavily worn condition. Nobles Pond is one of perhaps eight to ten early Paleoindian base camps in the lower Great Lakes region. These sites appear to be earlier to the south and somewhat later to the northeast, which presumably reflects changing opportunities for aggregation as environmental conditions changed at the end of the Ice Age. More than that, it represents the story of over 2,000 adult volunteers and 3,500 students saving a significant part of Ohio's ancient past.

Over 4,600 volunteers and school children participated in salvage excavations at Nobles Pond from 1988 to 1996, making it one of the most extensive investigations of a Paleoindian site in eastern North America. Elaine Dowd, Field Director, calls the collaboration among the landowner, Kent State University and a crew of thousands of volunteers "a truly noble effort."

Over 55,000 Paleoindian artifacts have been collected from campsites at Nobles Pond, including this sample of fluted points made of Upper Mercer, Flint Ridge (Vanport) and Attica cherts. Dr. Mark Seeman reports that many artifacts from the site are worn out and burnt. This suggests American Indian hunters may have been recycling their precious flint and chert tools during the winter at Nobles Pond until they could travel to quarries for new supplies.

The work at Nobles Pond didn't end with field excavations. A core of about 12 volunteers, under the banner First Ohioan Research Consortium Excavation or FORCE, gathers every Thursday evening to identify, catalogue and refit artifacts from the site at the Analysis Laboratory on the Stark Campus of Kent State University. Pictured here are (front to back) Mark Seeman, Larry Morris, Elaine Dowd, and Garry Summers.

SHERIDEN CAVE

Wyandot County
Opening a time capsule

By Dr. Brian Redmond, Curator of Archaeology,
The Cleveland Museum of Natural History.

In 1990, the late Richard "Dick" Hendricks, hired a crane operator to dig out a sinkhole behind Indian Trail Caverns, his commercial operation in Wyandot County. About 25 feet below the surface, the crane exposed the entrance to a small cave. Hendricks had uncovered one of the most important archaeological sites in Ohio.

Most Paleoindian sites in Ohio are scatters of artifacts found on the surface. But, Sheriden Cave, filled to the ceiling with earth, was a perfectly preserved time capsule. Investigations by paleontologist Dr. Gregory McDonald revealed that the cave held the bones of over 60 different Ice Age animals, including extinct species such as the short-faced bear, giant beaver, stag-moose and flat-headed peccary. In 1997, archaeologists from The Cleveland Museum of Natural History and Kent State University became involved after volunteers discovered 11,000-year-old stone and bone tools. This research was supported by The Cleveland Museum of Natural History and The National Science Foundation.

Archaeologist Dr. Ken Tankersley learned that other, less obvious Paleoindian stone tools made from flint flakes had been found at the site for years. In addition, a few bones appeared to have charred surfaces, perhaps from cooking. Others showed possible cut marks from stone tools.

The best was yet to come. Archaeologists found the richest concentration of animal remains and artifacts in sediments at the back wall. This area contained the remains of a possible fire pit or hearth feature consisting of a thick layer of wood charcoal. A bone spear point, scraper and complete "fluted" spear point were all found near the hearth. Radiocarbon dating of charcoal from surrounding sediments revealed that these artifacts and features are between 10,500 and 11,000 years old.

Animal bones are buried beneath and within layers of soil with human artifacts. This tells us that animals used the cave before and after humans did. There are several theories about how Paleoindians used Sheriden Cave.

Dr. Gregory McDonald proposed that the open sinkhole pit was a natural trap. Animals occasionally fell into the hole and perished from thirst and hunger. Some peccary bones shows signs of being bitten and chewed by predators. This suggests large carnivores may have used Sheriden Cave like a fast-food drive-through, where an easy meal of fresh peccary could be had with little effort. The cave may have been a convenient den for a short-faced bear.

Based on the fact that we find finished artifacts here, I think Sheriden Cave was a short-term camp for Paleoindian hunters. A small group may have stored their weapons here, but for an unknown reason, never came back to retrieve them. This intermittent use of Sheriden Cave appears to have ended abruptly about 9,000 years ago. At the end of the Ice Age, rainfall and flooding increased. The cave and sinkhole filled with sediments, converting Sheriden Cave into a unique time capsule.

Archaeologists are still analyzing the incredible materials and data from Sheriden Cave. A group of dedicated volunteers continue to process bone-laden sediments from the cave, which is gaining national attention and has been designed by the Ohio Bicentennial Commission as an historical site. Their meticulous fieldwork is helping us better understand the first people to ever occupy Ohio.

Sheriden Cave yielded a wealth of animal bones and artifacts from the Paleoindian period, including this photographic assemblage featuring: the skull of a flat-headed peccary (top); an incised bone spear point (both sides, left and right); a stone fluted point (center); and a scraper (right) made from southern Indian chert.

Archaeologists built a scaffold (right) above sediments near the back of Sheriden Cave so as not to disturb layers of silt from a flood that filled the cavern.

A staircase leads archaeologists down a sinkhole to the entrance of Sheriden Cave in Wyandot County. The sinkhole was filled with earth when excavated in 1989 by Dick Hendricks, owner of the nearby Indian Trail Caverns.

A videographer documents Dr. Brian Redmond and Dr. Ken Tankersley as they watch one of the volunteers who continue to excavate animal bones from Sheriden Cave.

Paleoindian Period Timeline
Archaeological Sites and Natural Events
(ca. 14,000-10,000 BP)

RC Years Ago (BC/AD)	Ohio	North America	World
10,000 BP (9,500 BC)	Manning/Zimmer (✻ ca. 10,000-9,400 BP) Niagara outlet lowers Lake Erie (ca. 10,000 BP)	Climate begins to stabilize (ca. 10,000 BP) Agate Basin, WY (ca. 10,000 BP)	Early grain storage, Mesopotamia (10,000 BP) Jericho, Israel (ca. 10,000 BP) Star Carr, England (ca. 10,000 BP)
11,000 BP (11,000 BC)	Sandy Springs (✚ ca. 10,900-9,000 BP) Sheriden Cave (✻ ca. 11,000-10,500 BP) Nobles Pond (✚ ca. 11,000-10,800 BP) Paleo Crossing (✻ ca. 11,100-10,800 BP) Welling (✚ ca. 11,500-10,900 BP)	Dust Cave, AL (ca. 10,500-10,000 BP) Big Bone Lick, KY (ca. 10,850-10,350 BP) Folsom, N.M. (ca. 10,900 - 10,200 BP) Clovis, N.M. (ca. 11,500 BP) Cactus Hill, VA (ca. 11,500-9,700 BP)	Saharan rock art, Africa (ca. 10,500 BP) Early cultivation, Syria (ca. 11,000 BP) Spirit Cave, Thailand (ca. 11,000 BP) Earliest known pottery, Japan (ca. 11,000 BP)
12,000 BP (12,000 BC)	Burning Tree Mastodon (✻ ca. 11,600-11,300 BP) Flint Ridge State Memorial (Quarries) (✚ ca. 12,000-10,000 BP)	Schaefer Mammoth, WI (ca. 12,440-12,290 BP)	Monte Verde, Chile (ca. 12,500 BP)
13,000 BP (13,600 BC)			Fului Cave, Japan (ca. 13,000 BP)
		Little Salt Spring, FL (ca. 13,450-12,030 BP)	
14,000 BP (14,000 BC)	Wisconsinan glacier retreats from Ohio (ca. 14,000 BP)	Meadowcroft Rockshelter, PA (ca. 14,000-10,000 BP)	Domesticated dogs, Russia (ca. 14,000 BP)
15,000 BP (16,000 BC)			
16,000 BP (17,100 BC)			
17,000 BP (18,200 BC)			Lascaux Cave paintings, France (ca. 17,000 BP)
18,000 BP (19,400 BC)			
19,000 BP (20,500 BC)			Allen's Cave, Australia (ca. 19,000 BP)
20,000 BP (21,700 BC)	Wisconsinan glacier covers most of Ohio (ca. 20,000 BP)	Bering Strait migration (ca. 20,000 BP)	Ishango, Zaire (ca. 20,000 BP) Mal'ta, Siberia (ca. 21,000 BP)

Left-margin period labels:
- Late Paleo (ca. 10,500-9,000 BP)
- Middle Paleo (ca. 10,900-10,500 BP)
- Early Paleo (ca. 14,000-10,900 BP)
- Pre Clovis (ca. 20,000-11,500 BP)

Criteria and Key

This timeline is based on published radiocarbon dates or artifact typology. The dates are listed as ca. (about) BP = Radiocarbon Years Before Present and BC/AD. The "present" is defined by convention as AD 1950, the year standards were set for reporting radiocarbon dates. The timeline includes the best information available at the time of publication. Ohio sites limited to those referenced in text or on maps.

✻ = based on radiocarbon (C^{14}) and other laboratory dates
✚ = based on typology of artifacts and site features

THE PALEOINDIAN PERIOD BEGAN MORE THAN 14,000 YEARS AGO IN OHIO. THE FIRST Ohioans were hunters and gatherers in a bountiful landscape of lakes and streams, forests and prairies. A unique diversity of plants and animals lived here, including tundra plants and oak trees, mastodons and white-tailed deer. But the climate was wildly unstable during this period. It could shift from episodes of glacial cold to warm periods similar to those we presently enjoy within the span of a dozen or so years. The hunting and gathering groups who lived through this period had to be flexible and adaptable. Many of the Ice Age animals with whom these people shared the environment were not able to adapt to the changing climate. Some left Ohio to find a more suitable habitat, but many became extinct. Others may have been hunted to extinction by Paleoindians. The Paleoindians themselves might have become extinct if they had not been able to adapt to the new challenges and opportunities afforded by the changes in the environment; but the hallmark of humans is their adaptability. Archaeologists can see the changes Paleoindians made in their ways of life by observing the changes over time both in their tool kits and in the changing patterns of their distribution across the landscape.

In the waning centuries of the Paleoindian period, the practice of chipping the long groove, or flute, into the bases of their spear points was given up. The spear points of the Late Paleoindian period look like fluted points in outline, but they were no longer fluted. In other ways, however, the way of life of these people appears unchanged.

The subsequent Archaic period is marked by more substantial changes in tool kits. Early Archaic spear points are more diverse in form and they are found in much larger numbers, indicating a substantial growth in population. But the successes of the Archaic peoples were built upon the flexibility of the hunting and gathering way of life established by their Paleoindian forebears.

At the end of the Paleoindian period, Ohio's climate was transforming into the warmer and wetter weather we known today. Large portions of northern Ohio would become wetlands such as the historic Great Black Swamp that once covered an area the size of Connecticut along the Maumee River. This immense wetland was a fertile reservoir for fish, mammals and birds that were important to the food economy of ancient American Indian cultures. About two percent of the Great Black Swamp, survives in preserves such as the Ottawa National Wildlife Refuge pictured here in Ottawa County.

American Indians developed new technologies and methods during the Archaic period for obtaining an increasing variety of plant and animal resources. Moving with the seasons, the Late Archaic peoples had a relatively healthy, balanced diet from hunting, fishing and the collection of turtles, freshwater mussels, roots, tubers and wild berries. But, from the Paleoindian period through the historic era, the white-tail deer (shown here in silhouette) was the most important game animal for American Indians in eastern North America. Deer was important not only for its meat, but also for the hides that provided material for clothing, moccasins, bags and tents.

∋2∈

THE
THE ARCHAIC
PERIOD

Circa 10,000 - 2,500 BP

The archaic period has a name distin-guishing it from the preceding Paleoindian period, but this does not mean that new and different cultures moved into Ohio replacing the earlier groups. Some Ohio Paleoindians may indeed have moved away to search for new hunting grounds, perhaps to find the herds of mastodon or caribou that could no longer be found in this region. Also, some people from other parts of eastern North Americ may have traveled to Ohio and found it to their liking. For the most part, however, the people of the Archaic period in Ohio were the descendants of the Paleoindians who had lived here before them. "Paleoindian" and "Archaic" are not the names of different tribes. The names refer to sets of artifacts and ways of life that archaeologists have recon-structed from material remains. To ask "what happened to the Paleoindians?" is like asking, "what happened to the 'covered wagon people' or the 'model T- Ford people'? they didn't mysteriously vanish; they became something else. In the case of the Model T-ford people— they became us.

ARCHAEOLOGISTS STUDY A CONTINUUM, OR A GENERALLY UNBROKEN SEQUENCE, OF cultural change. It is easier to understand what is happening along that continuum when you can break it up into more manageable segments. In making those divisions, however, we should never lose sight of the fact that we are defining the breaks based primarily on changes in durable technology—artifacts made from materials resistant to decay. A single individual who lived in Ohio 10,000 years ago could have been both a Paleoindian and an Archaic Indian if he or she used fluted spear points as a youth and spear points with notches in later years.

The Archaic period is distinguished from the Paleoindian period by a changed environment, a few technological innovations, a rapidly growing population, and a variety of social changes probably caused, at least in part, by the growth in population. The Archaic has, by far, the longest duration of any of the periods in Ohio prehistory. Fundamentally, this shows how successful the hunting and gathering way of life was in this region.

It does not mean that there were more than 7,000 years of cultural stagnation. On the contrary, this period witnessed the transition from small groups, living much like their wide-ranging Paleoindian predecessors, to much larger groups living in settled communities, making pottery, and planting gardens.

The 7,000-year-long Archaic continuum presents a problem for archaeologists who like to divide the prehistoric record into manageable units of time, like the comfortable spacing of rungs on a ladder. Throughout the Archaic period, there are no abrupt transitions in which one distinctive technology replaces another. All of the momentous cultural change encompassed by the Archaic period took place gradually, at least partly in response to the establishment of a remarkably stable climate following the rollicking unpredictability of the Ice Ages. Nevertheless, archaeologists have found it useful to chop the Archaic period into three parts, named, with characteristic blandness, the Early, Middle, and Late Archaic.

EARLY ARCHAIC PERIOD: 10,000 - 8,000 BP

The dawn of the Archaic period is marked by the end of the Ice Age, the extinction of a large number of big game animals, an increasing diversity in the shapes of stone spear points, and the appearance of a new technology: the pecking and grinding of particularly hard stones to make tools such as axes, adzes, and pestles. Like their Paleoindian predecessors, the hunters and gatherers of the Early Archaic period lived in small groups scattered throughout

The Archaic period marks a time when the climate of Ohio became much warmer and drier, similar to the seasonal weather patterns we experience today. This climate change prompted the rise of meadows, pocket prairies and oak-hickory forests that dominated the landscape. The ancient forests would have held mature hardwoods, such as these rare 500-year-old oak trees (left) preserved in Sugar Creek Metropark, Greene County.

Ancient Ohio
Archaic Period Site Map

(ca. 10,000-2,500 BP)

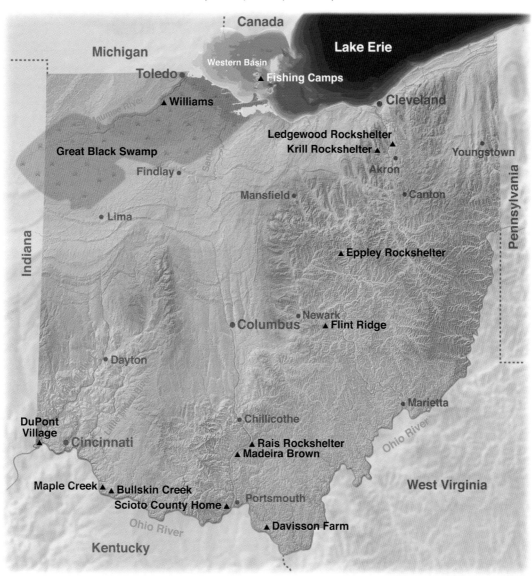

Canada

Michigan

Lake Erie

Western Basin

Toledo

▲ Fishing Camps

Cleveland

▲ Williams

Ledgewood Rockshelter
Krill Rockshelter ▲ ▲

Youngstown

Great Black Swamp

Akron

Findlay

Mansfield

Canton

Pennsylvania

Lima

Indiana

▲ Eppley Rockshelter

Newark

Columbus ▲ Flint Ridge

Dayton

Marietta

DuPont
Village

Chillicothe

Ohio River

Cincinnati

▲ Rais Rockshelter
▲ Madeira Brown

West Virginia

Maple Creek ▲ ▲ Bullskin Creek

Portsmouth

Scioto County Home ▲

Ohio River

▲ Davisson Farm

Kentucky

* Sites referenced in text and timelines

▲ – Ohio Archaeological Sites
▲ – Kentucky Archaeological Sites
▲ – Pennsylvania Archaeological Sites
▲ – West Virginia Archaeological Sites
● – Modern Cities

Elevation base map courtesy
Cartography & Editing Group,
Ohio Department of Natural Resources

VOYAGEUR

© 2004 Voyageur Media Group, Inc.

Ohio. They moved with the seasons and in response to the changing availability of a wide variety of wild foods—hickory nuts, acorns, fruits, berries, fish, deer, bear, rabbits, turkeys, passenger pigeons, and waterfowl. In order to take advantage of all of these resources, the Early Archaic hunters and gatherers had to be able to pick up and move their camps many times a year. Their houses would have been small shelters built with wooden frames and covered with hides, tree bark, or mats woven from reeds or grasses.

Ground stone tools are made by pecking, grinding, and polishing hard stones like granite. These tools take much longer to make, and are heavier and more cumbersome to carry, but they hold up to hard, prolonged use better than similar tools chipped from flint. Their appearance in the archaeological record reflects an increased need for heavy duty woodworking tools such as those needed to make dugout canoes.

Stone nut crackers and seed grinders are sometimes found at Paleoindian sites, but they became much more common in the Archaic period. Their increasing use suggests people were becoming more settled within familiar regions. Because they would not have needed to carry these tools around with them, they likely left them at the groves of nut trees where they would be needed in subsequent seasons. So, although the Early Archaic folk were still highly mobile, their movements across the landscape were becoming more regular and more confined to a particular region. And each region offered a distinctive range of resources, from the sandy margins of Lake Erie to the broad valleys of the Ohio River and its tributaries, and from the Great Black Swamp of the northwest to the hills and hollows of the southeast. This is probably why we see an increasing regional diversity in the styles of spear points through time. Each band had its own territory and, as interaction between bands in different regions declined, the opportunities to share ideas about changing styles

of tools became fewer. As a result, different and increasingly distinctive styles began to diverge. Moreover, the separate bands may have chosen to emphasize these differences to show group identity and solidarity. This increasing emphasis on "us" versus "them" would be storing up trouble for future generations.

Early Archaic spear points and knives are much more abundant than Paleoindian points. This shows us that there were more and more people around during the Archaic period. Upper Mercer flint from Coshocton County and Flint Ridge flint from Licking County continued to be the favorite raw materials for Archaic flintknappers. As they became more familiar with their homelands, however, they found local sources for flint and increasingly relied on these for their chipped stone tools.

American Indians were Ohio's first forest managers. Archaeological evidence suggests American Indians used controlled burns as early as 8,000 years ago in the eastern woodlands to diminish the threat of catastrophic wildfires and to propagate fire-resistant trees that bore edible nuts. Vital to their food supply, American Indians harvested the "fruits of the forest" like this sample plate collected on the grounds of Fort Ancient State Memorial. Several species of nuts are found at Archaic sites after about 6500 BP, including hazelnuts (lower center), acorns (center), hickory (left in steatite bowl), black walnuts (upper center in basket) and chestnuts (top in gourd).

The Archaic Tool Kit
Circa 10,000 – 2,500 BP

The Archaic period is the longest in duration of any of Ohio's archaeological periods. It lasted over 7,000 years, from the end of the Ice Age to the origins of agriculture. This period encompassed an enormous amount of cultural change as groups adapted to changing environments. This is reflected in the diversity of spearpoint styles and in the appearance of ground stone technology.

This selection of spearpoints and knives in the top row is arranged in approximate chronological order, from left to right: Big Sandy; Kirk Serrated; MacCorkle Stemmed; LeCroy; St. Charles; St. Charles; McWhinney Heavy Stemmed; Lamoka; Merom Expanding Stemmed; Brewerton; Susquehanna Broad point; Turkey-tail.
Other tools include the following: Second row: Thebes point/knife (Early Archaic); Hafted scraper (Late Archaic). Third row: Bone atlatl hook and bone handle for an atlatl. Bottom row: Grooved axe (3/4 grooved); Pestle; Grooved axe (full grooved).

FLINT RIDGE STATE MEMORIAL
Licking County

By Dr. Richard W. Yerkes, Associate Professor of Anthropology, The Ohio State University.

The ancient inhabitants of the Ohio Valley were blessed with an abundance of animal, vegetable, and mineral resources, including more than a dozen types of high-quality chert. The best-known type is "Flint Ridge Flint" (Ohio's official gemstone) obtained from large prehistoric quarries in Licking and Muskingum counties. Flint Ridge Flint is part of the Vanport Formation (Allegheny Group) of sedimentary rocks that formed under a shallow sea during the Pennsylvanian Geologic period. The flint beds consist of five colorful, translucent varieties, and outcrop in discontinuous layers with an average thickness of 4 feet. Prehistoric quarries are found along most of the 7 mile length of Flint Ridge, but the greatest concentration is within the 525 acre Flint Ridge State Memorial.

The Flint Ridge quarries were described by pioneer archaeologists like Caleb Atwater (1820), O.T. Mason (1879), and the Salisbury brothers (1862), and were investigated by Gerard Fowke of the Smithsonian (1884) and W. C. Mills of the Ohio Archaeological and Historical Society (1902). They were interpreted as "neutral grounds" where any Indian could come and quarry flint, or as "emporia" where local groups produced stone objects for trade and export. Recent investigations provide more support for the neutral ground legend than the emporia hypothesis.

Flint Ridge has been quarried for over 12,000 years. Paleoindian artifacts were made of Flint Ridge Flint, but its use increased during the Archaic period (10,000 – 3,000 BP). Recent research by Ohio

Flint Ridge State Memorial preserves 525-acres of quarry pits and trails along a more extensive outcrop of Vanport or Flint Ridge Flint in Licking and Muskingham counties. A large nugget of rose-colored Flint Ridge flint (left) sits in front of the site museum.

Hundreds of ancient quarry pits, (right) filled with spring rainwater, sparkle in the morning sunlight at Flint Ridge State Memorial. American Indians have quarried flint here for over 12,000 years.

State University (1987, 1988) and Ohio Historical Society (1997, 2003) archaeologists suggests that Archaic Indians came to Flint Ridge to replace their worn-out and broken points and artifacts, not to produce large quantities of stone tools for trade. During our recent excavations, we found that over half of the projectile points discarded at Flint Ridge were made of other types of chert, not Flint Ridge Flint. No substantial Archaic settlements have been found on Flint Ridge, and it does not look like Archaic groups lived on the Ridge and kept other tribes from using the flint. Small groups of Archaic Indians probably visited the quarries during hunting and gathering trips and replaced their worn out tools. Flint Ridge may have indeed been "neutral ground," where anyone could come for flint.

Extensive quarrying on Flint Ridge probably did not begin until Adena/Hopewell times (2500-1500 BP). During the Late Woodland and Late Prehistoric periods (1500-500 BP) there seems to have been a decline in the use of Flint Ridge Flint. Adena/ Hopewell groups may have visited Flint Ridge to obtain the colorful flint artifacts they presented in ceremonies at their earthworks. These ceremonies strengthened the ties between the mobile, dispersed Adena/Hopewell people. Professor Robert Hall, Department of Anthropology, University of Illinois, reminds us that Adena/Hopewell leaders were not merchant princes that controlled the production and distribution of Flint Ridge Flint (and other elaborate objects made of mica, copper, shell, etc.). Like other North American Indians, they gained prestige not from possessing but from giving to others, often to the point of impoverishing themselves. The bright and varied colors of Flint Ridge flint distinguished it from other cherts found in the Ohio Valley and may explain why it was so important to the Adena/Hopewell.

Flint Ridge Flint is highly localized. The quality and color can change dramatically within a hundred feet," according to archaeologist Bill Pickard, Ohio Historical Society. This photographs shows some of the more common varieties. Top Row (left to right): highly fossiliferous "burr stone" material used to make grind stones in more recent historic times; opaque gray white flint; translucent blue white chalcedony. Bottom Row (left to right): Nethers flint is dark gray to lavender in color with white banding; a high quality blackish translucent variety; a variety that is high and iron content that looks similar (and often fools archaeologists) to Knife River Flint.

Archaeologist Don Miller demonstrates a replica of a traditional atlatl and spear at Split Rock Conservation Park.

The ancient art of flintknapping is carried on by Roy Miller, President, Flint Ridge Lithics Society, (right) which sponsors the annual Knap In at Flint Ridge State Memorial. Hundreds of flintknappers gather each summer for this event to exchange materials and demonstrate their skill in crafting replicas of American Indian points and tools.

Archaic spearpoints were made in a variety of styles from several different sources of chert or flint as seen in this assemblage (above) from Lake County. (Left to right): Thebes, Kirk, MacCorkle, Kirk stemmed, Brewerton and Gennessee.

Early Archaic spear points tended to be long and broad, with notches chipped in the sides of the point near the base. The edges of these so-called "points" were serrated or saw-toothed, like modern steak knives. Perhaps these were hafted onto short handles and used as knives rather than as tips for spears. Another change in the weaponry of the Archaic period was the introduction of the ground stone weight for the spear thrower, or atlatl. Paleoindians probably brought the atlatl with them from Asia, but we have little direct evidence of it from Paleoindian sites in Ohio.

Atlatl is the Aztec name for the spearthrower. It was a rod of flexible wood with a hook at one end and a handle of some kind at the other. The hunter would fit the hook into a notch or hole in the end of a spear shaft and then, using the atlatl as an extension of his arm, he would be able to catapult the spear much farther and with much greater force than could a hunter with the unaided arm.

Early Archaic hunters found that, by adding a weight of some kind to the atlatl, they could increase the efficiency of the weapon. The first atlatl weights were simple oval or rounded stones. The toolmakers had drilled holes through them, or etched grooves around them, that allowed them to be tied securely to the shaft of the atlatl with cordage or sinew. Later Archaic artisans carefully ground and shaped them into larger and more elaborate forms. Some are so large they would have made it difficult, or even impossible, to use the atlatl as a hunting weapon. These artifacts must have served a symbolic function for the people who made them, like the unusably large "Key to the City" modern mayors sometimes present to honored celebrities. Perhaps they served as badges of honor or talismans for the people who carried them.

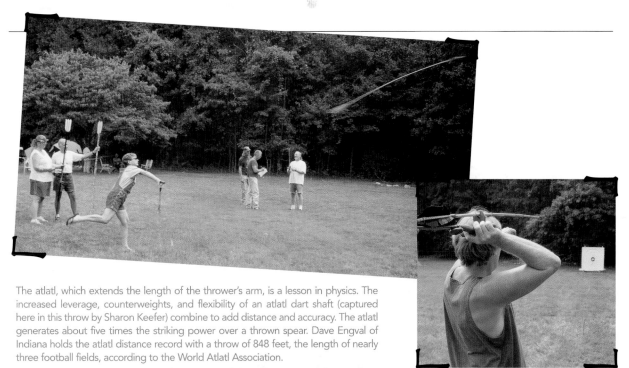

The atlatl, which extends the length of the thrower's arm, is a lesson in physics. The increased leverage, counterweights, and flexibility of an atlatl dart shaft (captured here in this throw by Sharon Keefer) combine to add distance and accuracy. The atlatl generates about five times the striking power over a thrown spear. Dave Engval of Indiana holds the atlatl distance record with a throw of 848 feet, the length of nearly three football fields, according to the World Atlatl Association.

World champion atlatlist Ray Strischek shows the accuracy of a traditional atlatl and river cane dart before a local contest at the Flint Ridge Knap In hosted by the Ohio Atlatl Association. Top competitors rarely miss the 5x5 foot target from distances of up to 32 yards.

Archaeologists begin to find artifacts called bannerstones across Ohio that date to as early as 6,000 years ago. These stones were carefully crafted to serve as counterweights for the atlatl or spearthrower. Although American Indians used a variety of stone in their manufacture, they seemed to have preferred banded slate.

Hunting is not an exact science. The hunter can do everything right and still not find an animal to kill. When an activity is critically important but fraught with uncertainty, people often turn to magic and ritual to increase their chances of success—or at least to give them some psychological comfort. For example, superstitious athletes may have a favorite pair of socks they always wear when competing, or soldiers going into battle might carry a religious symbol with them as a way of seeking divine protection. The survival of a band of hunters and gatherers could depend upon the success or failure of a hunting expedition. The proper performance of special hunting rituals might help hunters focus their attention on the task and give them increased confidence in their abilities. The oversized and beautiful atlatl weights carved from slate may have been symbolic devices used to invoke supernatural aid for hunters.

By the middle Archaic period, the dryer climate led to the expansion of western prairies into central and northwest Ohio. Less than 1 percent of Ohio's original prairie environments survive, including this pocket prairie (left) preserved in Sugar Creek Metropark, Greene County. American Indians used periodic fires to propagate prairie grasslands, an important habitat for vital resources such as the white-tail deer, woodland bison and prairie chicken.

No early Archaic burials have been found in Ohio, but three burials found in southwestern Indiana at the Jerger site indicate some similarities to Paleoindian mortuary customs, as well as some differences. Three pits found at Jerger contained burned bone, red ocher (an iron-rich mineral used as a pigment), Early Archaic spear points broken and discolored by intense heat, and beads made from animal canine teeth and small seashells. The presence of marine shells at a site in Indiana is interesting and shows us that, even at this early period, the people in this region attached importance to rare items acquired from distant lands. Individuals who possessed such unusual ornaments may have had a higher status than those who could not afford to obtain them. Finding such valuable artifacts buried with the dead suggests that the Archaic people believed in an afterlife in which their loved ones would need these items. But burying them with the dead was also a way of keeping the items rare and valuable. It also kept people from accumulating such wealth and worked to keep status differences from dividing a society based on equality. The practice of cremation may explain why archaeologists have found so few burials from this period. Even though the population of Ohio and neighboring areas was rising, there were still relatively few people living here during the Early Archaic era. Therefore, we would expect burials of this antiquity to be rare.

MIDDLE ARCHAIC PERIOD: 8,000 - 5,000 BP

The Middle Archaic period was marked by another change in the climate. Between 7,000 and 4,000 years ago, the climate of eastern North America became dryer and warmer. Prairie expanded from the Great Plains into Illinois, Indiana, and even western Ohio. Middle Archaic period sites are rare or absent from much of Ohio. The changes in climate that occurred at this time may be the reason for localized declines in population, as people abandoned traditional homelands for more fruitful regions. On the other hand, it may simply be the case that Middle Archaic sites were destroyed by erosion during subsequent periods of increased rainfall. In spite of the lack of information on the Middle Archaic period in Ohio, we can combine what we do know with data gathered by archaeologists in neighboring states to fill in our picture of life during this transitional period.

The Middle Archaic tool kit included a variety of flint spear points, knives, and scraping tools. The points had notches in the sides similar in many ways to those of the Early Archaic, but the points themselves were generally smaller. The Middle Archaic people used an increasing variety of ground stone tools, including grooved axes, atlatl weights, grinding stones, pitted stones, plummets, and net sinkers. Pitted stones are flat slabs of rock with one or more pits, or depressions, pecked into their surfaces. They may have been used as nut crackers or pigment grinders. Plummets are small, shaped and grooved stones that were suspended from lines. They may have served as weights or charms.

The Middle Archaic hunters and gatherers continued to hunt a diversity of animals and they gathered an ever-widening variety of wild plant foods. Animal bones found at Middle Archaic sites include deer, elk, raccoon, birds, turtles, and fish. Nuts became an even more important source of food —especially hickory nuts and acorns. Hickory nuts and acorns were of special importance because they were nutritious and easy to process and store. Hickory nuts are high in fats and protein, while acorns are high in fats and carbohydrates.

The Archaic peoples crafted several specialty tools, including this drill for boring holes in wood and bone, and scrapers for processing meat and hides.

⟩∞⟨

MIDDLE ARCHAIC SETTLEMENTS INCLUDE SOME RELATIVELY LARGE SITES THAT MAY HAVE BEEN occupied for several seasons as base camps. People from such a base camp formed groups to go out to hunt and fish or to gather nuts, berries, or wood for the fire. Usually, men got together with friends to go hunting. Women, with their infants snug in a sling or backpack, went as a group to a favorite grove of hickory trees or blackberry patch. Older children and the elderly might accompany one or another of the foraging parties or stay at the base camp. They could also snare small game or gather firewood. At the end of the day, all of these groups would return to camp, bringing with them whatever they had been able to forage. Successful hunters shared the meat with the rest of the band. No hunter succeeded every day, but if several groups went hunting, it increased the chances that some would find game. If everyone shared their kill, then most of the time everyone would have meat to eat. Meat was highly prized, and hunters who were consistently successful earned the admiration and respect of the band. As men did all or most of the hunting, only men could achieve this kind of status. So the seeds of sexual inequality may have been planted in these early hunting and gathering societies.

Archaeologists have found several burials dating to the Middle Archaic period in the Ohio Valley (although none have been found yet in Ohio). The increase in numbers of burials is one indication that the population continued to grow during this period. There may have been some change in the religious beliefs of the people, for the burials found from the Middle Archaic are not cremations. Whatever the cause of the greater numbers of Middle Archaic burials, being able to study the skeletons of these people allows us to get a more intimate picture of life and death in the ancient world.

Bones are living tissue that grow and change as a person ages. They are a rich source of information on a person's health, diet, growth and development, status in life, and cause of death. Generally, Middle Archaic people were healthy and well-fed, with a balanced diet. Like all hunters and gatherers, they were faced with seasons of plenty and occasional seasons of near starvation. The winter could be a particularly hard time for hunters and gatherers living as far north as Ohio. The generally dryer climate of the Middle Archaic period may have resulted in more frequent droughts and more periods when food was hard to find.

The average lifespan of a person during the Archaic was about 25 years—but this reflects the high rate of infant mortality that is sadly typical of most hunting and gathering groups. If Archaic men or women survived childhood, they had a good chance of living to the age of 35 and some people are known to have survived until the age of 60. Archaic people suffered from a variety of health problems, including arthritis, broken bones, and abscessed teeth. The hunting and gathering way of life was rich and rewarding, but it was strenuous and occasionally dangerous.

The oldest members of the band were valued and respected members of the community. Their memories preserved information that could mean the difference between life and death for the entire group. For example, if there was an especially severe drought, an elder might be able to recall how the group had survived a previous drought by using a plant not normally eaten. Before the invention of writing, the memories of people were the storehouses of the collective knowledge of the group. When an elder died, the group faced more than the grievous loss of a loved one; it was as if a library had burned.

Apart from the great respect generally accorded the elders in hunter-gatherer societies, there is little evidence of important status differences reflected in the burials of the Middle Archaic.

HOT ROCK BOILING

Dr. Ken Tankersley directs Northern Kentucky University students as they grind hickory nuts at Split Rock Conservation Park for a demonstration of an ancient American Indian cooking technique known as hot rock boiling. A pyramid fire heats basalt rocks near a shallow, fire-hardened pit, which, lined with a deerskin, will soon be filled with water. The ground hickory nuts, husks and all, are added to the water, with super-heated basalt rocks (top right), that immediately bring the brew to a boil. The nutritious hickory nutmeat and oil are scooped from the surface (bottom right). Rich in calories, this precious resource was stored for consumption during the lean winter months. Evidence of hot rock boiling extends from historic times back to the early Archaic period.

From this, archaeologists conclude that Middle Archaic groups did not have chiefs or leaders who had the authority to order people around. The people made decisions about when to move the camp to a new location or whether they should hunt or fish on a particular day by discussion and group consensus. If you disagreed with a decision, you were free to go your own way.

LATE ARCHAIC PERIOD: 5,000 - 3,000 BP

Five thousand years ago, the climate changed again. The temperature cooled somewhat, and rains came more frequently and abundantly. This is when the modern climate of Ohio became established. There was considerable environmen-tal diversity across Ohio, with unique sets of opportunities and challenges in each region. Overall, however, the resources available to hunters and gatherers were richer and more varied than ever before. The Archaic peoples responded to the increasing bounty with a population explosion. We know this because archaeologists find so many Late Archaic sites across Ohio, and often these sites are much larger than sites dating to earlier epochs. Some archae-ologists say there are only two Late Archaic sites along the Ohio River: one along the left bank and one on the right. This is an exaggeration, but it reflects the general abundance of Late Archaic sites and their apparent concentration along the major rivers of the region.

THE DAVISSON FARM SITE

Lawrence County

By Matthew P. Purtill, Principal Investigator, Gray & Pape, Inc., Cultural Resources Consultants.

Covering at least 22 acres on a high agricultural terrace in southern Lawrence County, Ohio, the Davisson Farm site represents the remains of nearly 10,000 years of prehistoric occupation along the Ohio River. The site was investigated in 2001 by archaeologists from Gray & Pape, Inc., a Cincinnati-based cultural resources management firm, in advance of a large construction project slated to destroy the site. Federal project involvement prompted archaeological research to comply with the National Historic Preservation Act, which balances historic preservation and modern development. A multidisciplinary team of archaeologists, geologists, and paleoethnobotanists was assembled to study the site, the results of which generated important new information regarding prehistoric Native American settlement and sub-sistence strategies, group organization, and technological advancement in the Mid-Ohio Valley.

Although occupied throughout most of prehistory, the site's most intensive use was during the Archaic Period, primarily between 5650 and 2650 B.P. During this time, south-central Ohio's climate was assuming modern conditions and floral communities became dominated by nut-bearing oak-hickory forests. For the first time, the site functioned as a large base camp used to coordinate a variety of tasks including hunting, collecting, food preparation, and tool production/maintenance. The dramatic increase in artifact frequency, as well as the first evidence for the construction of permanent features such as structures, drying/cooking racks, and underground earth ovens, all point towards intensified occupation over preceding times.

Davisson Farm is one of many Archaic sites found along the central Ohio River Valley. The excavations conducted here have provided archaeologists with one of the most detailed accounts of archaic lifeways in southern Ohio.

Between 3450 and 2650 B.P., there was a proliferation in the use of earth ovens across the site. Archaeologists recovered a variety of wild plant remains from these features, especially seasonally available nuts resources (black walnut, hickory, acorns) which were increasingly abundant during this time. The recovery of cultivated squash rind from several features dating to around 3300 B.P. demonstrates that Archaic groups also were beginning to experiment with plant domestication to supplement their diet. Significantly, Davisson Farm is believed to have the earliest documented use of domesticated squash in southern Ohio.

Using the season of maturity for recovered plant remains as an indicator of season of use, archaeologists determined that Davisson Farm was occupied only between the late summer through fall months, not year round. One major task appears to have been the drying and roasting of nut-foods in earth ovens for future use at off-site camps during harsh winter months. By 2650 B.P., Native American use of the site was becoming less intense and more dispersed. Artifact and feature densities decline dramatically, perhaps resulting from the shift towards increased sedentism and greater reliance on cultivated foods observed during the succeeding Early Woodland period.

Archaeologists found two artifacts called "plummets" at Davisson Farm, which are thought to be from the Late Archaic period. These plummets are made of hematite, a naturally occurring iron ore. There are a variety of interpretations on the function of these unusual objects. Many archaeologists suggest they were used as weights for fishing nets. Others believe they represent part of a throwing weapon similar to a bolas. The high degree of workmanship on several specimens, such as the one pictured to the right, also suggest they may have had a religious-spiritual significance. Plummets may have been adornments for clothing or worn like jewelry by people during important ceremonies.

One of the more startling discoveries from Davisson Farm was the recovery of three small charred fragments of twine, or rope, recovered from an earth oven dating to approximately 2800 B.P. This image is a magnified view (approximately 10x) of the largest piece of recovered twine, which was made by tightly twisting together two strands of an unidentified plant material. The twine likely was used to bind some food items during cooking. Importantly, the discovery shows the use of a textile industry at least by Late Archaic times.

EARTH OVENS
AN ANCIENT COOKING TECHNOLOGY REVEALED

The Archaic inhabitants of the Davisson Farm site began to experiment with new means to prepare food between 5650 and 2650 B.P. One effective technique involved using underground cooking pits referred to as earth ovens. Excavated between 12 and 36 inches into the hard-clay ground to provide a controlled, insulated environment, earth ovens were roughly circular and ranged between one and six feet in diameter. These features were designed to provide a steady, long-lasting heat source to cook food without direct exposure to an open flame. To generate heat, the feature typically would be lined with pre-heated rocks. In some cases, wood fires also were built directly into the feature's base as an additional heat source. Items to be cooked likely were placed directly atop the heated rock and covered with an earthen layer to fully insulate the feature. Based on several historic Native American accounts, similarly constructed earth ovens were used to roast a variety of plant, animal, fish, and shell foods. Earth ovens were often left to slowly cook their food for several days at a time.

At Davisson Farm, archaeologists identified a large number of such features (over 50 in limited work) indicating that food preparation was an important site activity. By carefully examining such features, archaeologists gain valuable insights about the types of eaten foods and what time of year groups occupied a site. Davisson Farm earth ovens, for example, yielded an abundance of fall-maturing wild-plant foods, primarily nuts (black walnut, hickory, and acorn). Coupled with an absence of spring-maturing fruits and berries (frequently found at contemporary sites), archaeologists reasoned that Late Archaic populations only visited the site during the fall months. The recovery of burned bone fragments also suggests that earth ovens were used to cook selected animal cuts in addition to plants.

An archaeological photograph and scale drawing show the remains of one of many earth ovens excavated at the Davisson Farm site. This feature was filled with fire-cracked rock and contained a small amount of nutshell and wild plant seeds.

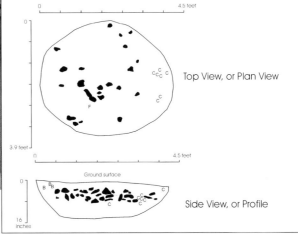

IN ADDITION TO THE GREATER NUMBERS OF SITES, ARCHAEOLOGISTS ALSO FIND A GREATER VARIETY of different kinds of sites. There are large settlements with hearths, earth ovens, deep storage pits, and middens (garbage dumps), hunting camps with a scattering of stone tools and animal bones, and small gathering sites with only a pitted stone or a handful of flint scraping tools. Also, for the first time, archaeologists find burials concentrated at particular places. These are Ohio's first cemeteries—special places consecrated to the dead. They are often located at prominent points on the landscape, such as a large hill that can be seen from a long way off.

Another new development in the Late Archaic period is the emergence of different sets of artifacts and different burial customs associated with different regions. Some of this variability undoubtedly represents the efforts of Late Archaic foragers to adapt to the regional differences in Ohio's environment. For example, the swamps of the northwest offered different opportunities than did the hills and hollows of the southeast. But some of the variability also must relate to the worldwide desire of societies or ethnic groups to highlight their distinctiveness and strengthen group solidarity by using artifacts or wearing clothes and ornaments increasingly dissimilar from those used or worn by neighbors with whom they might be in occasional conflict.

The Late Archaic people were still hunters and gatherers, but they ate a greater variety of foods and did what they could to increase the quantity of food they gathered. For example, Late Archaic hunters continued to use the atlatl for hunting white-tailed deer, but instead of individual hunters stalking or ambushing one or two deer at a time, the entire group would have cooperated in driving large numbers of deer toward several hunters waiting to spear as many as they could. They fished using a variety of nets, traps and dams so that they could get lots of fish at once. Large groups of people worked together to collect shellfish. The discarded shells from these group efforts often accumulated into large mounds.

Late Archaic foragers still gathered all the nuts they could find, especially hickory nuts. They stored the nut meat and oil as important winter foods. Small seeds rich in starch and oil became increasingly important to many groups because the nut harvest could vary so much from year to year and the growing numbers of people needed a more reliable source of food. Sumpweed and goosefoot seeds were the most important. By 4,000 years ago, these seeds made a major contribution to the diet of some Late Archaic groups. Over time, the seeds began to show physical differences in comparison to their wild ancestors, indicating that the gatherers were selecting favored varieties and even planting some of those seeds to harvest in subsequent years. In other words, the Late Archaic foragers were becoming gardeners. They also may have begun to experiment with planting squash, sunflower, and marsh elder.

The Late Archaic people did this with no thought at all of wanting to become farmers. Originally, they simply wanted to encourage the

There are literally hundreds of Archaic sites along the Ohio River, including the Zimmer site (above) excavated in 1987 before construction of a power plant in Clermont County. Archaeologists find deep pit features at many archaic sites, the remnants of storage or cooking pits.

growth of plants they relied upon as hunters and gatherers. Many of these plants would have flourished naturally in the disturbed ground of abandoned camps. The people would have noticed this when they returned to favorite camping sites. They could have encouraged the growth of preferred plants by collecting their seeds and sowing them in patches of bare ground. They then left their gardens to fend for themselves in the hope that when the seasonal cycle of movement brought the people back to that place, they would be able to gather a richer harvest of their staple foods. The economic success of this activity led to a growing population since more available food meant they could feed more people. This, in turn, meant they had to invest still more of their time and energy in these experiments with gardening. Eventually they would become dependent on their gardens, and hunters and gatherers began to settle down in one place for an entire season, or perhaps several seasons, so they could tend and weed their plantings. At some large Late Archaic sites along the Ohio River near Cincinnati, there are rows of deep storage pits where many bushels of seeds and nuts, collected in the autumn, could have been stored for use throughout the winter.

IN ADDITION TO STORAGE PITS, LATE ARCHAIC FOLK ALSO USED BASKETS AND, FOR THE FIRST time, clay pots. Pottery generally has been regarded as a hallmark of the succeeding Woodland period. Ceramic vessels certainly became much more abundant and widespread during the Early Woodland period, but archaeologists have found traces of pottery at a few very Late Archaic sites. Late Archaic potters made large vessels with thick walls and used coarse chunks of crushed rock as a temper to strengthen them. They also carved some vessels from soft stone such as sandstone and soapstone.

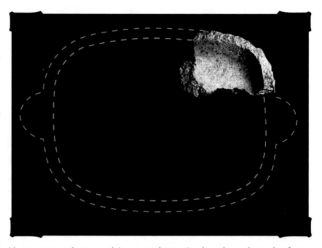

Heavy ground stone objects and steatite bowls such as the fragment above (with graphic outline of missing piece) are one clue that American Indians are staying at seasonal encampments for longer periods of time. Carved from a nodule of steatite, also known as soapstone, these thick, course bowls could weigh up to 30 pounds.

The hunters and gatherers of the Paleoindian and earlier Archaic periods did not make pottery, but it was not because they didn't know how. They would have seen clay dry and harden in the sun or by a fire and certainly understood that it could be shaped and baked into water-tight vessels. Their Paleolithic cousins in Europe had made sophisticated ceramic figurines using special kilns. The problem with clay pots is that they are heavy to carry around and easy to break if handled roughly. Hunting and gathering peoples were often on the move and had to carry all their possessions. They preferred lightweight and durable skin bags or woven baskets. If they wanted to make soup or some kind of tea, they simply heated rocks in a fire and dropped them into an animal hide container filled with water until it reached the desired temperature. Clay pots make it easier to cook and to store water or oils from nuts and seeds, but for most hunters and gatherers, their disadvantages outweighed their advantages. When people settled down in one place, they didn't have to carry all of their things around with them. Clay pots became an attractive option. The appearance of pottery vessels in the Late Archaic is, therefore, another indication that people were beginning to settle down in one place for extended periods. The reason they began to settle down is because they had started growing crops.

It is important to realize that farming didn't arise because hunters and gatherers finally figured out that seeds from a particular plant could be used to produce more of the same kind of plant. This was a fact of plant biology that hunters and gatherers already understood. According to Jared Diamond, a professor of physiology at the UCLA School of Medicine, the decision to settle down on farms and raise crops was forced onto hunters and gatherers. Diamond says this was in some respects, the "worst mistake in human history."

Settling down means limiting your options. When groups become sedentary their population explodes. Hunters and gatherers who are always on the move generally are forced to limit the number of children they have, because a mother can't easily carry more than one infant at a time. So, before they decide to have another baby, the first child must be able to walk on its own. For this reason, in most hunter and gatherer societies, women space their children about four years apart. When groups settle down in one place, women are freed from this restriction and can have children more frequently. But the resulting increase in population means that the groups consume the local resources at an increasingly rapid rate. They become more vulnerable to local catastrophes, such as droughts or floods, and health and nutrition generally deteriorate. Settled life also leads to problems with sanitation. Living sites and water supplies may become fouled with sewage, and diseases arising from polluted water or other causes spread much faster in concentrated groups of people. As if these health problems weren't enough for people to contend with, growing populations also contributed to the rise of social inequality as bosses emerged in order to organize the planting, gathering, storage, and distribution of nuts and seeds stored over the winter. A sedentary lifestyle also allowed those so inclined to accumulate

stuff they would otherwise not have been able to carry around with them. As such wealth accumulated in the hands of an ambitious few, status differences became more visible. Particularly conspicuous consumers would have attracted the jealous attention of neighbors who might resort to violence to claim a share of the wealth. Raiding and warfare became more prevalent. Few of these unfortunate consequences, however, would have been evident to the Late Archaic foragers who first opened the Pandora's Box of a sedentary farming life.

⟩∞∞⟨

PAUL SCIULLI, A PHYSICAL ANTHROPOLOGIST AT OHIO STATE UNIVERSITY, AND HIS STUDENTS HAVE conducted a number of studies of ancient Ohio skeletons from many different periods. He found that, in general, Ohio's Late Archaic people were tall and healthy. Sciulli also observed a pattern of differences in the bones of Late Archaic people, indicating that the men and women engaged in very different activities. Different activities require different sets of muscles. When a muscle is used repeatedly, the place on the bone where it is attached becomes thickened and roughened. It is likely that the differences observed by Sciulli relate to the different jobs men and women perform in most hunting and gathering cultures studied by cultural anthropologists worldwide. The men likely hunted, trapped, and fished, while the women gathered, prepared, and cooked vegetable foods. The men defended the village or went off on raiding parties, while women cared for the children and tended the homes and gardens.

Middle to Late Archaic burials also show differences in the kinds and quantities of artifacts buried with men and women. This also supports the general idea that there was a fairly consistent division of labor. Men tended to be buried with stone spear points and other hunting equipment, whereas women often were buried with other kinds

The "Ancient Ohio" Art Series
The Archaic Period
(ca 10,000-2,500 BP)

The Archaic people took particular advantage of the wide range of resources (food and raw materials) available in different seasons within their territories. At this riverside camp in northwestern Ohio, several families have banded together to prepare for the coming winter season. Men and boys fish in the river, and hollow out a log with their stone axes and fire to build dugouts in which they can travel long distances via the river systems. Some of the women grind nuts into meal and store it in baskets for food during the winter. Later, the group may split up with each family traveling to its own winter hunting camp.

Archaeological basis: Information from Archaic sites such as the Dupont, Raisch-Smith, and Weilnau. The size and configuration of the dugout is based on the Ringler dugout, discovered in a glacial bog near Ashland, Ohio. The use of stone axes, adzes and fire to hollow out the log for the dugout is based on archaeological evidence from the Ringler dugout and practices of American Indian tribes of the 17th and 18th centuries.

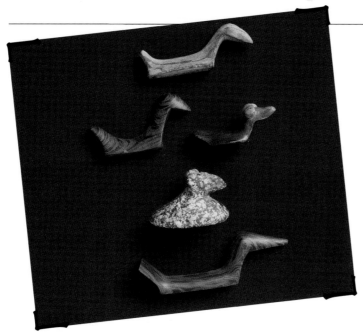

Archaeologists call them birdstones because of their resemblance to abstract bird forms, but the purpose of these enigmatic objects remains a mystery. Most are about the size of your hand and have holes drilled through the corners of the artifact at their base. Birdstones are commonly made of banded slate, but other types of stone were used. In some respects, birdstones resemble bannerstones, and also may have served as counterweights for atlatls.

of tools such as bone awls, needles, and stone scrapers. Archaeologists also find differences in the quantity and quality of grave offerings that indicate some persons had a higher status than others.

The religion of the Archaic people was an elaboration of the shamanic beliefs and practices of the Paleoindians. A Late Archaic shaman at the Williams site in Wood County cut part of the upper jaw from a bear skull, ground the edges smooth, and drilled several holes through it to fashion it into a mask. Sewn onto the hide of the bear, this sacred garment allowed the shaman to symbolically trans-form into a bear. Ritually becoming an animal in this way gave the shaman access to the spiritual powers of that animal. Such powers could be used to heal the sick or to call upon the animal spirits to aid the hunters in finding game animals. Shamans also may have officiated at important rites of pas-sage, such as marriages, births, and funerals.

During the Late Archaic period, a number of regionally distinctive burial practices developed that intensified whatever other cultural differ-ences set these groups apart from one another. For example, in northwestern Ohio, archaeologists have defined at least two "cultures" based solely on differences in their burial customs. The Glacial Kame complex is found in northwestern

Ohio and neighboring areas of Indiana, Michigan, and Ontario. These Late Archaic people buried their dead in prominent knolls formed of sand and gravel deposited by glaciers during the Ice Age. These isolated hills and ridges are called glacial kames The Glacial Kame people buried their dead in a variety of ways, but they almost always sprinkled or painted the burial with red ocher. They also included a number of artifacts with burials, including sandal-shaped shell gorgets, as well as other kinds of ornaments made from shell and polished slate, copper beads, tubular stone pipes, and elaborately shaped slate carvings called birdstones that are likely a special type of atlatl weight.

The Red Ocher complex is found in western Ohio, Indiana, Illinois, Michigan, Ontario, Wisconsin and Minnesota. Red Ocher burials are similar to Glacial Kame burials in that they often occurred on natural prominences and the bones and objects buried with the dead were coated with red ocher. But Red Ocher burials did not include sandal-shaped shell gorgets. The most typical artifact found in Red Ocher burials is the large, leaf-shaped Turkey-tail spear point made from Indiana hornstone (also known as Harrison County flint).

One of the most striking characteristics of Late Archaic burials is the increasing importance of items acquired from distant places: flint from Indiana, copper from the Lake Superior region, shells from the Atlantic Ocean and the Gulf of Mexico. Since at least the Early Archaic, certain materials from far-off places had been accorded a special importance. These things may have had a particular religious significance, but they could also serve as markers of social status. If you lived more than two hundred miles from any ocean and yet could wear an exquisitely carved ocean shell around your neck, it showed that you were a person of importance with connections to a wider world. In the Late Archaic, we find increasing evidence for social distinctions in the richness and variety of things buried with certain people.

Initially at least, these distinctions probably were based on personal achievements. The best healer, the best hunter, the best flintknapper, or weaver of baskets was accorded special respect and special privileges. But with the increasing importance of storing food and planning for the future, it may have been the best manager who earned the most privileges. And managers who could control the distribution of food eventually might find themselves in a position to institutionalize their leadership and control more than just allotments of food.

The emphasis on increasingly localized cultures with distinctive customs has a darker side. It suggests an increasing tendency for people to see the social landscape in terms of us versus them. And, indeed, conflict became more common during the Late Archaic period. For example, at the DuPont

Lake Erie began to look as it does today from the shoreline of Catawba Island State Park only recently in geologic terms. At the beginning of the Archaic period, American Indians would have seen nothing but marshland and shallow rivers in the western basin of Lake Erie. During a geologic process called the isostatic rebound, the land under Lake Erie, depressed by the massive weight of glaciers, would slowly rise. The western basin would gradually fill with water, nearing present-day levels only 4,000 years ago.

Fish biologists aboard the research vessel Grandin are using archaeological research as part of a long-term project to restore the native fish communities of Lake Erie. "Restoration plans have to have a baseline for the native fish community," says Jeff Tyson, Aquatic Biology Supervisor, Sandusky Fisheries Research Unit, Ohio Division of Wildlife. "The fish bones recorded by archaeologists in ancient American Indian middens (trash heaps) give us an idea of the variety and distribution of species in the western basin of Lake Erie." Commercial and sport fishing are a vital part of the economy in northern Ohio thanks to the productivity of Lake Erie, which often produces more pounds of fish than all of the other four Great Lakes combined.

Village in Hamilton County, two of 30 human burials had spear points embedded in their skeletons. This may not sound like a significant number, but if it means that in some Late Archaic groups two out of every thirty people would meet a violent death, then their casualty rate was higher than Americans have suffered during the course of any war. Thirty burials is much too small a sample to justify jumping to the conclusion that this ratio of deaths by violence to seemingly natural deaths was typical of the Late Archaic era, but it serves to make the point that violence was becoming a more common experience for ancient Ohioans.

As intergroup violence became more common, it offered another opportunity for status distinctions to develop into institutionalized leadership. In many societies, including our own, admired war leaders can become political leaders. Just as U. S. Grant and Dwight Eisenhower went from victory on the battlefield to become President of the United States, so an ambitious warrior of the Late Archaic might achieve some political clout through success at leading raids and killing enemies.

The Archaic period spanned a considerable length of time and witnessed profound changes in the way of life of Ohio's native cultures. Population increased, climate changed, plant and animal communities shifted. People adapted by developing new technologies and by adjusting their social arrangements. The hallmarks of the Archaic period are diversification and intensification, both in terms of the foods the people ate and in their social interactions. They hunted and gathered more different kinds of plants and animals than did their Paleoindian ancestors and they adopted tools and techniques that helped them do so more efficiently. The ways of life of Archaic groups became increasingly specialized to local conditions. Groups living in different regions became more and more different. Burial ceremonialism became more elaborate and increasingly emphasized items acquired from distant places. These trends would reach a pinnacle in the succeeding Woodland periods, but the foundation for everything achieved by those later cultures was laid by the hunters and gatherers of the Archaic.

Archaic Period Timeline
Archaeological Sites and Historical/Natural Events
(ca. 10,000-2,500 BP)

RC Years Ago (BC/AD)	Ohio	North America	World
		Upper Great Lakes flow again into Lake Erie (ca. 2,600 BP)	Persian Empire height (ca. 2,450 BP)
3,000 BP (1,200 BC)	Williams (* ca. 3,000-2,300 BP)	Sunflower first domesticated (* ca. 3,000 BP)	Polynesian settlements, Fiji/Samoa (ca. 2,950 BP)
	Rais Rockshelter (* ca. 3,100-2,700 BP)	Red Ocher cemeteries (* ca. 3,450-2,050 BP)	Zhou Dynasties, China (ca. 3,100-2,200 BP)
		Steatite bowls, widely adopted (ca. 3,500 BP)	Olmec Culture, Mesoamerica (ca. 3,200-2,400 BP)
		Glacial Kame cemeteries (* ca. 3,500-3,000 BP)	
	Madeira Brown (* ca. 3,700-3,000 BP)	Chenopodium first domesticated (* ca. 3,500 BP)	
4,000 BP (2,500 BC)	Maple Creek (* ca. 4,000-3,300 BP)	Poverty Point, LA (ca. 3,650 - 3,050 BP)	Middle Kingdom, Nile/Egypt (ca. 3,986-3,759 BP)
	Krill Cave (* ca. 4,000-3,300 BP)	Lake Erie nears present level (ca. 4,000 BP)	Babylonian, Mesopotamia/Iraq (ca. 3,990-3,500 BP)
		Indian Knoll, KY (* ca. 4,300-3,500 BP)	Knossos (Minoan), Crete (ca. 4,000-3,500 BP)
	Eppley Rockshelter (* ca. 4,400-2,500 BP)		
	DuPont Village (* ca. 4,600-4,000 BP)		
5,000 BP (3,800 BC)	Bullskin Creek (* ca. 4,700-4,400 BP)		Harappan, Indus/Pakistan (ca. 5,000-4,500 BP)
	Scioto County Home (* ca. 5,000-3,300 BP)		Stonehenge, England (ca. 5,000-3,600 BP)
		Carlson Annis, KY (* ca. 5,400-2,500 BP)	Heiroglyphic script, Egypt (ca. 5,150 BP)
			Sumarian, Mesopotamia/Iraq (ca. 5,200-4,300 BP)
			Xia Dynasty, Yellow/China (ca. 5,200-3,750 BP)
6,000 BP (4,900 BC)		Old Copper cemeteries (* ca. 6,000-3,000 BP)	Cuniform script, Mesopotamia/Iraq (ca. 5,350 BP)
			Sannai-Maruyama, Japan (ca. 5,500-4,000 BP)
7,000 BP (5,850 BC)		First evidence gourd/squash, Il (ca. 7,000 BP)	Corn cultivation, Mexico (ca. 7,000 BP)
		First "permanent" wood house structures (ca. 7,000 BP)	
			Pre Dynastic, Egypt (ca. 7,500-5,100 BP)
8,000 BP (6,900 BC)	Davisson Farm (+ ca. 8,000-2,500 BP)	Western Basin of Lake Erie marshland	Chilca Valley, Peru (ca. 8,000-4,500 BP)
	Flint Ridge (+ ca. 8,000-2,500 BP)	Warm & dry climate prevails (ca. 8,000 BP)	Ban Po, China (ca. 8,000 BP)
			Rice cultivation, Yangtze/China (ca. 8,450 BP)
			Nabta Playa, Egypt (ca. 8,500 BP)
9,000 BP (8,150 BC)	Fishing Camps, Lake Erie Islands (+ ca. 9,000-2,500 BP)	Koster-North, IL (* ca. 8,800-3,900 BP)	
		Jerger Site, IN (ca. 9,000-8,000 BP)	
		Modoc Rockshelter, IL (* ca. 9,300-7,000 BP)	
		Atlatl, widespread adoption (* ca. 9,600 BP)	
10,000 BP (9,500 BC)		St. Albans, W.V. (* ca. 9,900-7,700 BP)	Early Neolithic Era, Egypt (ca. 10,000-7,500 BP)
		Sloan, AK (* ca. 10,500-9,000 BP)	

Left margin labels: Late Archaic (ca.5,000-2,500 BP) · Middle Archaic (ca.8,000-5,000 BP) · Early Archaic (ca. 10,000-8,000 BP)

Criteria and Key
This timeline is based on published radiocarbon dates or artifact typology. The dates are listed as ca. (about) BP = Radiocarbon Years Before Present and BC/AD. The "present" is defined by convention as AD 1950, the year standards were set for reporting radiocarbon dates. The timeline includes the best information available at the time of publication. Ohio sites limited to those referenced in text or on maps.
* = based on radiocarbon (C^{14}) and other laboratory dates
+ = based on typology of artifacts and site features

The Cincinnati Tablet is one of 13 rectangular, stone and clay tablets from the central Ohio Valley that were excavated from mounds attributed to the Adena culture in the Early Woodland period. The Cincinnati tablet was uncovered in a mound just west of downtown Cincinnati in the 1841. Made of sandstone, it is about the size of a postcard (approximately 5" x 3") and incised with curvilinear designs. This and other Adena tablets may have been used as stamps for artwork or body tattoos.

THE EARLY WOODLAND PERIOD

THE

THE EARLY WOODLAND

PERIOD

Circa 2,800 - 2,000 BP

THE WOODLAND TRADITION ORIGINALLY WAS THOUGHT TO MARK THE BEGINNINGS OF THE SO-CALLED "AGRICULTURAL REVOLUTION" IN EASTERN NORTH AMERICA. ARCHAEOLOGISTS DEFINED THE EARLY WOODLAND PERIOD BY THE FIRST APPEARANCES OF DOMESTICATED CROPS, POTTERY, SETTLED VILLAGE LIFE, AND BURIAL MOUNDS. IT NOW SEEMS CLEAR THAT ALL OF THESE THINGS APPEARED AT DIFFERENT TIMES AND DIFFERENT PLACES DURING THE LATE ARCHAIC PERIOD. WE NOW UNDERSTAND THAT THE SO-CALLED AGRICULTURAL REVOLUTION WASN'T AS "REVOLUTIONARY" AS SCHOLARS ORIGINALLY THOUGHT. BUT

THE EARLY WOODLAND PERIOD STILL MARKS A CLEAR TRANSITION IN OHIO. EARLY WOODLAND SOCIETIES RELIED ON DOMESTICATED PLANTS TO A MUCH GREATER EXTENT THAN DID ANY PREVIOUS ARCHAIC GROUPS AND THEY USED POTTERY VESSELS MORE FREQUENTLY. AND WHILE SOME ARCHAIC GROUPS IN THE SOUTHEASTERN UNITED STATES BUILT MOUNDS, IN OHIO, THE EARLIEST MOUNDS DATE TO THE EARLY WOODLAND PERIOD. SO, ALTHOUGH THE TRANSITION WAS MORE GRADUAL AND EVOLUTIONARY THAN ABRUPT AND REVOLUTIONARY, THE EARLY WOODLAND SOCIETIES IN OHIO DO REPRESENT SOMETHING NEW.

Some people mistakenly refer to an Adena period as if it were the same thing as the Early Woodland period. "Adena" is actually the name of a culture as well as of a site in Chillicothe, the "type site" of the Adena culture. The "type site" is simply the site for which a culture is named. Adena was the name of Governor Thomas Worthington's estate, and a remarkable Early Woodland mound on that estate was called the Adena Mound. The Adena culture thrived in southern Ohio and neighboring parts of Indiana, Kentucky, and West Virginia during the Early Woodland period. The Early Woodland peoples of northern Ohio did not share the same symbols and practices that have come to define the Adena culture, and so we would not use that label to characterize them. In the same way, Amish groups currently living in eastern and southern Ohio have cultural practices very different from the dominant society, even though they live in the same era. This does not make one culture either "backward" or more "civilized" relative to the other; they are simply different. Anthropologists (including archaeologists) seek to understand the nature of these differences as well as the changing patterns of culture through time.

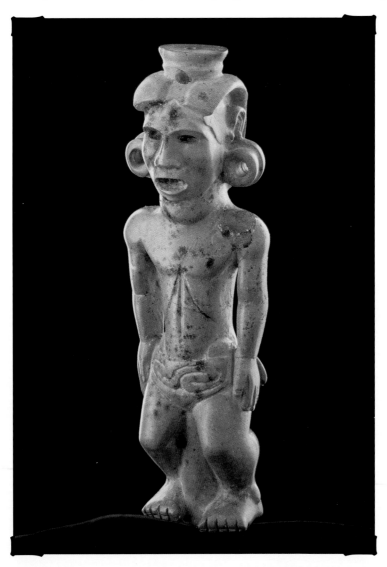

The Adena pipe is an icon of Ohio archaeology. Carved from Ohio pipestone from quarries near Portsmouth, this 8-inch tall tubular pipe is the only depiction of a complete human form from the Early Woodland period. The pipe's bowl is located between its feet. The mouthpiece is a small hole on top of the head. "We're dealing with the work of a skilled artisan," says Martha Potter Otto, Curator of Archaeology, The Ohio Historical Society. The figure is carved in ceremonial regalia: earspools, a bird feather bustle (back) and a loincloth with a curvilinear design. "It's unknown if the carving represents an actual person or an abstract shaman," says Otto. Some features are puzzling. The figure's disproportional anatomy may reflect dwarfism or simply artistic convention. His bent knees may depict dancing and his bloated neck may be a sign of a goiter.

The Early Woodland Period Tool Kit,
Circa 2,800 – 2,000 BP

The Early Woodland period marks the appearance of domesticated plants, pottery, and burial mounds in Ohio. In addition to flint knives, spearpoints, and ground stone celts (or axes), Early Woodland people also must have used wooden digging sticks to work their gardens and woven baskets to store produce, but few traces of such organic materials have survived.

Top row: (left to right) Flint knife or preform (roughed out, but unfinished spearpoint); Robbins point; Adena Stemmed point.

Second row: (left to right) Oval knife or preform; Celt (axe); Oval knife or preform.

Like their Late Archaic ancestors, Early Woodland people lived in small, dispersed communities. However, Early Woodland houses were larger and more substantial than anything built by Archaic foragers, suggesting a greater degree of permanence. A typical Early Woodland house was a circular structure between 10 and 15 feet in diameter built of log poles interlaced with twigs and probably covered with bark. Often there would be from one to five such houses in a settlement. Sometimes there could be much larger structures. For example, at the Leimbach village site in Lorain County, archaeologists excavated a series of postmolds, circular stains in the soil showing where a post had been set into the ground. The postmolds traced an arc that, if continued, would form the outline of a circular structure about sixty feet in diameter.

The Boudinot #4 site in Athens County is an example of a small Early Woodland community occupied by about 20 people. Excavators uncovered a number of features including postmolds, hearths, and roasting pits. The variety of artifacts found there reflects the variety of activities engaged in by Early Woodland folk at their homes. Archaeologists found flint spear points and knives, ground stone pestles and axes, and a few pieces of broken pottery. An analysis of the charred bits of food remains in the hearths and roasting pits indicate that nuts provided an important part of the diet.

Early Woodland people, like their Archaic ancestors, were primarily hunters and gatherers, and nuts were a storable staple of vital importance. In a good year, nuts—especially hickory nuts, black walnuts, and beechnuts—could be gathered by the bushel and stored in pits to be eaten throughout the long, lean winter. At Boudinot #4, however, archaeologists also found large numbers of small seeds in a few pits. In spite of their small size, these seeds represent a big change, if not quite a revolution. They were the remains of domesticated plants. Early Woodland people had become food producers, no longer strictly dependent on the land's natural bounty.

The importance of this achievement is not widely appreciated, probably because most of the plants in the "Eastern Agricultural Complex," which included squash, sunflower, maygrass, goosefoot, knotweed, sumpweed, and marshelder, are not important in our modern diet. The Native Americans of the Ohio and Mississippi valleys, however, should be acknowledged for independently transforming local varieties of plants into domesticated food crops. This feat was duplicated in only a handful of regions throughout the world, such as Mesopotamia, China, and Mexico.

The sunflower *(Helianthus annuus)* is one of the indigenous plants that American Indians began to domesticate nearly 3,000 years ago during the Early Woodland period. Based on ethnographic records, it's likely that women were Ohio's first plant "geneticists," selecting the seeds of the best wild plants to increase harvests in early gardens.

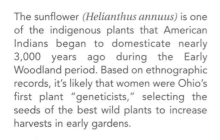

Students with an Ohio University summer field school screen dirt from test excavation units near the Conard site, an Early Woodland village along the Hocking River in Athens County.

The process of plant domestication in eastern North America probably began with women gathering fruits, nuts, and vegetables in the clearings along streams and around their campsites and villages. They would have noticed differences in the fruits or seeds that made some varieties preferable to others, and these were the ones that they brought back to the base camp for the family's meal. Some of the same places had been used off and on as campsites for generations, and many seeds had been cast aside with the garbage at these sites. The clearings in the forest made by people for their homes were ideal environments for many of these plants to thrive. So, as Archaic and Early Woodland folk returned to former camps, they often found patches of their favorite plants growing nearby.

In harvesting this fortuitously sown crop, they naturally would have selected the most favored variations and, eventually realizing what was going on, they may well have begun to uproot unwanted plants and intentionally sow seeds of their favorites before abandoning a campsite for a season or two. By continuing this process year after year, they began to shape the evolution of these selected plants. Without fully understanding the underlying processes, these women nonetheless were genetically engineering crops and, eventually, they would develop entirely new plant varieties. It was to be a momentous turning point for the Native American cultures of Ohio, yet the process was gradual and it is not likely that any individual woman would have realized that she was inaugurating a new way of life.

MANY FACETS OF EARLY WOODLAND LIFE CONTINUED MUCH AS THEY HAD FOR generations. Hunters stalked a variety of animals, including white-tailed deer, black bear, beaver, and wild turkey. Their main hunting weapon continued to be the spear propelled by the atlatl; however, the flint spear points of the Early Woodland are quite distinctive. Typically, the business end of an Early Woodland spear was a long, broad-bladed point with a rounded stem that must have been inserted into some kind of socket made from bone or wood.

American Indians began to make the first pottery in Ohio during the Early Woodland period. This large, Dominion thick pot (25" high) was reconstructed from shards excavated at the Dominion site in Franklin County. The thick walls, barrel-shape and lug handles are common features of Ohio's earliest American Indian pottery.

THE EASTERN AGRICULTURAL COMPLEX

By Dr. Elliot M. Abrams, Professor of Anthropology, Ohio University.

The Eastern Agricultural Complex (EAC) is that set of indigenous plants–squash, chenopodium (or goosefoot), knotweed, sumpweed (or marshelder), maygrass, amaranth (or pigweed), and sunflowers–domesticated by Native Americans during the Early Woodland period. Domestication involved selective management of these species that led to increased productivity, more controlled timing of seed availability, and greater ease in processing. A combination of human population increase and climatic change prompted a gradual shift towards greater collecting and eventual management of those species replacing in part nuts, and especially hickory, walnuts, and acorns.

One of the advantages of domestication is the added degree of control over the species. For example, most of the nuts were available in the fall, as were most of the EAC species. However, maygrass is available for consumption in the spring and the availability of abundant maygrass following a harsh winter would have greatly benefited the population. Further, the potential for boiling seeds, thus producing a gruel, would have contributed to the diet of infants as well as the elderly.

The distinct limitations of the EAC species are their susceptibility to failure and their very high processing costs. Unpredictable floods and frosts undoubtedly suppressed a high reliance on the EAC, and the seeds are very small, requiring high amounts of effort and time to process. Unlike regions such as the Near East and Mesoamerica, where wheat and maize, respectively, could dominate the food staples, the Midwestern United States never could rely fully on the harvest from the region's indigenous plants.

MAYGRASS

Archaeologist Jack Blosser holds stalks and seeds of harvested Maygrass in front of a fresh plot growing in the traditional garden of Fort Ancient State Memorial. "Maygrass ripens between late May and early June," says Blosser, "which means it's one of the very first nutritional supplements for American Indians in the spring."

CHENOPODIUM HARVEST

American Indians harvested Chenopodium berlandieri (or goosefoot) in the spring for its succulent greens, and again in the late fall for its nutritious seeds. Billy Wagner, Gardener, Fort Ancient State Memorial, (left) says, "It's best to harvests chenopodium seeds once they turn black after a killing frost." Wagner adds that rather than pick chenopodium seeds by hand American Indians more likely cut down and threshed entire chenopodium plants growing in fields to get enough of the plant's tiny seeds for winter storage.

CHENOPODIUM GRINDING

After removing the bitter coat, American Indians most likely ground chenopodium seeds into a fine flour for bread or a gruel for young children. The small seed of the North American variety of Chenopodium berlandieri makes it a relatively unproductive crop. Modern farmers consider chenopodium a noxious weed. However, agronomists in Colorado are experimenting with hybrids of the South American variety Chenopodium quinoa. Known as "Inca wheat," Chenopodium quinoa remains an important commercial crop in the Andes Mountains. Quinoa is sold in many health food stores in the U.S. Marketed as the super grain of the future, Quinoa's nutritional content is compared to dried whole milk.

Archaeologists spend a lot of time studying the subtle variations in stone weapon tips. Because stone doesn't decay in the soil, tools made from stone are mostly what remain for us to study. But the most time-consuming to make, and therefore the most valuable part of a spear, actually was the straight wooden shaft and any bone or wood armature or foreshaft at the end. The stone points could be replaced relatively easily—as long as a supply of flint was at hand.

Depending on where they lived, Early Woodland foragers also ate varying amounts of fish, shellfish, turtles, and waterfowl. Chemical studies on the bones of Early Woodland people indicate they ate considerable amounts of meat and, in northern Ohio around the margins of Lake Erie, lots of fish. Resources such as fish, shellfish, nuts, berries, and small animals that could be snared could be collected by groups of older folk, women, and even children. The children of Early Woodland groups undoubtedly worked hard and made important contributions to their family's livelihood. Gathering firewood would have been a daily chore for many youngsters, but they also would have had lots of time to play with their friends. They could swim together in the ponds and rivers or throw small spears at targets perfecting the skills they would need as adults.

POTTERY BECAME MORE IMPORTANT ALONG WITH AN INCREASING EMPHASIS ON DOMESTICATED plants. Early Woodland people used pots for storing seeds and cooking gruel probably much like oatmeal, but pottery vessels had lots of other uses. It may be that pottery is only indirectly connected to plant domestication. Perhaps the use of pottery vessels was made feasible simply because people had become more sedentary and didn't have to be concerned with lugging heavy and fragile clay pots from campsite to campsite. Early Woodland people, however, did not settle down in just one place so they could putter in their gardens and make ceramic pots. A sedentary life was a dangerous gamble for a people who still were more forager than farmer.

Hunters and gatherers must be free to move around, for food does not come to them, they must go to the food. For an Archaic band, if game animals became scarce in one valley, they could simply move on to the next valley, perhaps returning many years later after giving the deer herds a chance to recover. But for a Woodland group, when game became scarce in its valley, the villagers could not simply pack up and move to the next valley, because it was likely that another group already lived there. A growing population, combined with the increasingly restricted mobility of Early Woodland groups, meant that survival depended

Small shards of pottery provide archaeologists with vital clues to cultural identity. When compared to other types of pottery, the details on this shard of Leimbach-style, impressed yellow pottery from a multi-occupational village in Cuyahoga County, helps archaeologists determine the time period and cultural affiliation of a specific site feature or soil layer.

Ancient Ohio
Early Woodland Period Site Map

(ca. 2,800-2,000 BP)

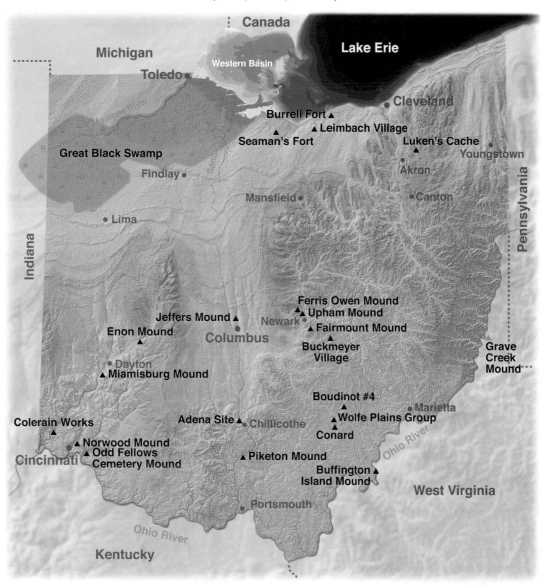

* Sites referenced in text and timelines

▲ – Ohio Archaeological Sites
▲ – Kentucky Archaeological Sites
▲ – Pennsylvania Archaeological Sites
▲ – West Virginia Archaeological Sites
● – Modern Cities

Elevation base map courtesy
Cartography & Editing Group,
Ohio Department of Natural Resources

OHIO'S FIRST TRUE POTTERY

By Thomas C. Grooms, Archaeological Transportation Reviews Manager, State Historic Preservation Office, The Ohio Historical Society.

Pottery first appears in the archaeological record of Ohio around 2,800 BP marking a significant technological shift in cooking technology. Prior to the advent of pottery, boiling was conducted indirectly by using a watertight container and placing heated rocks into the liquid slowly bringing the food to boil. This process is cumbersome, inefficient, and can leave fragments of the rock in the foodstuff. However, pottery is easily constructed, durable, and can boil liquids by direct contact with an open flame. Additional benefits of pottery include the ability to store liquid and other foodstuff within a durable, waterproof container.

Beyond the technological aspects, pottery was a medium for artistic and cultural expression. Pottery is constructed from clay, which has the capacity for great variety in form and decoration. Simple cooking vessels often displayed some type of decoration and those made for specialized functions such as ritualistic/ceremonial purposes can display decoration as well as elaborate forms. In Ohio, decorations on cooking vessels are often restricted to the incising or impressing of designs into the neck and/or rim of the vessel. In contrast, the decorations on vessels created for specialized functions can cover the entire pot. Fortunately for the archaeologist, decorations are often temporally, geographically, and culturally sensitive. These aspects of pottery allow an archaeologist to determine when the pot was made, where it was made, and who made it.

Ohio's first pottery was large, thick-walled bowls and barrel-shaped containers that displayed little to no decoration. Pottery gradually became more sophisticated, displaying thinner walls and a globular or cone-like shape. These changes provide for more efficient means of cooking.

POTTERY MAKING

Archaeologist Thomas Grooms (far left) demonstrates early American Indian pottery-making techniques and designs, including this Fayette Thick-style replica from the Early Woodland period.

POTTERY COILING

Grooms builds up the pottery wall (left) by adding coils of clay, which are then bound together with a smooth wooden paddle. The surface of the pot is then decorated with a paddle wrapped in cord. Cord-marking also has a functional purpose, making the pottery surface less slippery to handle.

Early Woodland pottery was manufactured from a mixture of clay and crushed rock called temper. Temper helps to reduce shrinkage while the pot is drying and fired thereby reducing the chances that the vessel will crack rendering it useless as a watertight container.

The most common means of constructing a vessel is by using the coiling method. This process involves the rolling of clay into long coils, stacking them upon each other, and binding the coils together. Coiling can create a variety of sized and shaped vessels without the aid of any mechanical means such as a modern potter's wheel. A cord-wrapped paddle is often used to help bind the coils together and thin the vessel's walls. Once formed, the vessel can be decorated before it dries. The clay vessel must be further hardened by fire before use to keep it from dete-riorating in water. The firing process, often done in an open pit, requires the gradual introduction of high temperatures until all water within the clay is forced out and the clay particles begin to fuse together.

Most of the beauty of Ohio's prehistoric pottery has been lost to the public due to the fragmentary nature in which it is found. However, through meticulous reconstruction of broken pieces of pottery (potsherds) some of these vessels can be restored and displayed for the public. When reconstruction is not possible archaeologists and artists are coming together and reproducing these ancient vessels in the same manner with the same materials. By reproducing the pottery archaeologists have gained a greater appreciation and understanding of how pottery was manufactured and utilized prehistorically.

POTTERY TEMPERS

A clay pot is only as good as its temper, the fire-hardened, coarse material that is ground up and added to clay to keep pottery from cracking. American Indians used a variety of different tempers (left) depending on the region and time period: (bottom) grit, chert (in wood bowl), shell (in basket), limestone (in gray bowl, and stone (in stone bowl).

POTTERY FIRING

Open pit firing gradually forces the water out of the clay vessel until the finished pot becomes hard, durable and watertight.

not on their ability to pick up and move in order to find food elsewhere, but on the ability to find ways to get more food out of each acre of the land they already occupied. Clearing the forest and planting crops was a lot of work, but it was a way to provide food for many people. Hunters were still spending a lot of time on the move tracking down deer and other game to provide meat for the village. But, like modern suburbanites who commute to their jobs, they usually returned home at the end of the day.

The earliest Early Woodland pottery vessels were large and barrel-shaped, with thick walls tempered with coarse grit made from ground-up rocks. The pots had big knobby handles, and their surfaces were scuffed up or roughened by patting the wet clay with a paddle that had been wrapped with cordage. Initially, this "cord-marking" may have been a way of making pots easier to handle without dropping them, but people soon recognized the decorative potential of these clay canvases.

Clay is wonderful because it can be shaped and decorated in any number of ways and, when heated in the fire, the forms become hard and fairly durable. Potters, like all artisans, are always looking for ways to improve their craft. They experiment with different kinds of temper, different vessel shapes, different decorative techniques, and so on. Unfortunately, pottery vessels, although relatively durable, are brittle and will break if overheated, dropped, or handled roughly. However unfortunate this may have been for the son or daughter who accidentally dropped one of their mother's favorite pots, the result was a tremendous benefit for archaeologists.

Because pots are fragile, and people are often clumsy or careless, lots of pieces of broken pottery are left at sites for archaeologists to find. Since those bits of pots are hard and durable, they will have been preserved in the ground for thousands of years. The malleability of clay gave potters the freedom to change the shape of their vessels, as well as the surface decorations they incised or impressed into their surfaces, from generation to generation. This gives archaeologists a rich record of changing pottery styles through time.

For these reasons, many archaeologists specialize in the study of ancient pottery. And many prehistoric cultures are defined partly on the basis of changes in pottery styles. Because pottery is such a sensitive indicator of cultural variation, from the Early Woodland period on, archaeologists are able to identify more refined cultural distinctions between regions. Nevertheless, the increasing differentiation of cultures evident in the Woodland period is more fundamentally explained by the varying ecological opportunities in different regions, as well as by social and cultural forces that always and everywhere have driven groups to emphasize their distinctiveness from more or less distant neighbors who were perceived as foreign and "other." This ecological and social diversification already had begun in the Paleoindian period. Differing pottery styles between regions simply became another way of advertising the already deeply felt (if largely superficial) differences between "us" and "them."

ANOTHER NEW DEVELOPMENT IN THE EARLY WOODLAND PERIOD IS THE APPEARANCE of burial mounds and other earthworks. The earliest mounds in Ohio were cemeteries, somewhat like Late Archaic cemeteries, except for the fact that Early Woodland mounds were artificial constructions whereas the glacial kames chosen for some Late Archaic burial grounds are natural features of the local geology. Therefore, the Early Woodland people were no longer simply living on a landscape, they had begun to re-shape it.

Mounds, like snowflakes, are each unique. The Early Woodland Adena culture built conical burial mounds ranging in size from the Grave Creek Mound in West Virginia, which is 70 ft tall and 240 ft in diameter, to small mounds only a few

Miamisburg Mound State Memorial is visible from several miles away as it stands high on a ridge above the Great Miami River in Montgomery County. This Adena burial mound, originally 68 feet tall and 877 feet in circumference at the base, is the second largest conical mound in eastern North America. Built in increments over several generations, Miamisburg Mound contains over 54,000 cubic yards of earth, which is enough to fill about 540 average-sized residential pools.

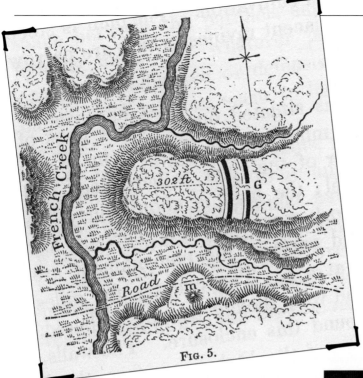

FIG. 5.

A survey map of Burrell Fort in Loraine County. Charles Whittlesey made this and about thirty other survey maps of ancient earthworks as topographical engineer for the first Ohio Geological Survey from 1837 to 1838. Burrell Fort is typical of bluff top sites documented in northern Ohio from the Early Woodland period.

Banded slate gorgets (below) are commonly found in Ohio during the Early Woodland period. About the size of an adult's hand, gorgets often have two drilled holes for suspension on a cord. Gorgets join birdstones, boatstones and pendants in a category some archaeologists whimsically call ground slate "problematicals." Their purpose remains unknown. The archaeological term "gorget" comes from the French definition of historic armor used to protect a soldier's throat. However, modern archaeologists speculate that gorgets were more likely worn as decorative ornaments for ceremonies rather than protective armor for battle.

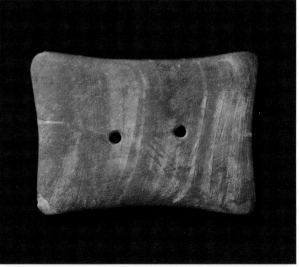

feet high. They also built circular earthen enclosures that were as large as 500 ft in diameter. In northern Ohio, burial mounds are rare. Instead, large, roughly oval enclosures or sets of walls built across a bluff top such as Seaman's Fort in Erie County are more typical.   Oval enclosures, often located on prominent hilltops, also are found at Adena sites such as the Colerain Works near Cincinnati and Peter Village in Kentucky.   These large enclosures seem to be unrelated to mortuary ceremonialism. They surrounded small villages and may have been special gathering places. Perhaps they were social and ceremonial centers serving a dispersed population, or perhaps they were defensive structures built by a particular group in response to a perceived threat. We have no evidence that warfare was widespread during the Early Woodland period, but conflict between villages may have erupted from time to time.

⋙⋘

THE BURIAL RITUALS THAT PRECEDED THE CONSTRUCTION OF A MOUND ALSO COULD BE quite varied.   Some people were buried laid out in log tombs and some were cremated. Some individ-

uals were buried with lavish offerings including shell beads, copper antlers, tubular stone and ceramic pipes, flint spear points, and tear-drop shaped flint knives, or "cache blades"; others were buried with nothing.   Some were not even buried in mounds.   The dead buried in the mounds cannot account for all the Adena people who ever lived. So, only a chosen few were entombed in mounds. The people buried in these special places must have been special themselves, but we do not know what set them apart from their fellows.

MAP OF OHIO SHOWING DISTRIBUTION OF EARTHWORKS.

The extent of the state's American Indian mounds and earthworks is seen in *Archaeological Atlas of Ohio*, a large folio compiled by William C. Mills in 1914. Mills' map shows the distribution of known prehistoric earthworks. Their cultural affiliation is not identified, but mounds are marked with dots and enclosures with an X. Since 1914, archaeologists have identified literally thousands of additional prehistoric earthworks, camps and village sites in Ohio. However, this map shows how American Indian mounds and earthworks are clustered along river valleys.

Presumably these were political leaders, mighty warriors, revered shamans, admired artisans, or family members of such important personages.

The varying ways in which the dead were treated give us clues to the social distinctions within Adena society. In general, the effort expended on a burial and the quantity and quality of stuff buried with a person are indications of the status they had when living—or status they achieved through the circumstances of their death. In addition to the grave offerings, the skeletons themselves may yield important clues about aspects of the culture and the dead person's social position.

The skulls of many of the people buried in Adena mounds exhibit a characteristic flattening of the normally rounded back portion of the skull. This cranial deformation may have been the result of the individual having been tied to a cradleboard as an infant, but the extent of flattening in Adena skulls makes it more likely that they practiced some form of intentional binding of the head to produce the desired shape. Some Native Americans of the historic era in the southeastern United States believed that flattening the skull improved your eyesight and made you more attractive to the opposite sex. Perhaps the artificial shaping of the skull was a mark of high status for the Adena.

The significance of Adena mounds goes far beyond their use as receptacles for dead people, however important the deceased person might have been. The mounds were public monuments that did more than commemorate the death of individuals. For one thing, mounds usually contain more than one body. Moreover, burial ceremonies often are not simply about showing respect for the dead.

OHIO'S CONICAL MOUNDS

There were once an estimated ten-thousand American Indian mounds and earthworks in the central Ohio Valley. Today, about 1,000 of these ancient landmarks have survived through the efforts of private landowners, local, state and federal agencies and conservation groups. Of those sites, about 73 are open to the general public or visible from public places, according to the authors of guidebook, *Indian Mounds of the Middle Ohio Valley.*

Some of the ancient earthworks that have been saved from erosion, plowing or development are conical mounds, a trademark shape of the Adena culture (ca. 2,800 to 2,000 BP). Yet, the majority of the conical mounds in Ohio have never been professionally investigated. Therefore, the exact age of these monuments, and their cultural affiliation remain unknown. Here is a small sample of the ancient conical mounds you can still see across the state.

Edgington Mound represents the difficulty in pinpointing the cultural affiliation of Ohio's conical mounds, This 16 feet high earthwork is preserved by the Archaeological Conservancy near Neville, an Ohio River town in Clermont County. The mounds classic conical shape suggests Adena culture (Early Woodland period), but a nearby village is associated with the Fort Ancient culture (Late Prehistoric period).

Jeffers Mound (20 feet high) rests on land owned by the Worthington Historical Society in Franklin County. The Jeffers Mound was part of a larger complex of earthworks. The cultural affiliation is unknown, but archaeological evidence from the 1830s and excavations near its base in the 1970s suggest it may be a Hopewell site from the Middle Woodland period.

The largest conical mound in Ohio is Miamisburg Mound State Memorial in Montgomery County. The Ohio Historical Society preserves this conical mound, which originally stood 68 feet tall, and is ascribed to the Adena culture in the Early Woodland period.

Fairmount Mound (15 feet tall) is preserved in the private cemetery grounds of Fairmount Presbyterian Church in Licking County.

Piketon Mound is a series of four conical mounds (the tallest is 25 feet high) preserved in Mound Cemetery just south of Piketon near the Scioto River in Pike County.

Odd Fellows Cemetery Mound (12 feet tall) sits in the center of the renamed Flagstone Cemetery in Newtown just east of the Little Miami River in Hamilton County.

Norwood Mound (13 feet tall) is found in Water Tower Park, which is tucked behind a residential street in Norwood, a Cincinnati suburb in Hamilton County.

Enon Mound (27 feet tall) stands in the middle of a circular drive in Indian Mound Estates, a neighborhood of the Village of Enon in Clark County.

OHIO'S CONICAL MOUNDS

Overlooked because of its famous younger brother, this low conical mound (6 feet high) is preserved on the grounds of Serpent Mound State Memorial in Adams County.

The Ferris Owen Mound (originally surveyed at 14 feet tall) is preserved within the athletic complex of Newark High School in Licking County.

A large tree shades Upham Mound (4 feet tall) which is preserved on private property but may be seen from Granville Road in Licking County.

Buffington Island Mound (20 feet tall) is part of the Buffington Island State Memorial that overlooks the Ohio River in Meigs County.

Early Woodland people often built their mounds on hilltops. Sometimes the hills chosen to serve as sites for burial mounds overlooked their villages, and sometimes the mounds were located between villages. For example, there are 11 documented conical mounds on hilltops within five miles of the Buckmeyer village site in Perry County. It appears that the mounds occupied prominent places where they could be seen by the villagers and, perhaps more importantly, by their neighbors.

According to archaeologist Berle Clay, Early Woodland mounds served as boundary markers, or "hinges" between territories. He says they were "the architectural expressions of negotiations between groups." Large burial mounds, such as the Miamisburg Mound in Montgomery County, would have shown how important the honored dead were to the builders of these mortuary monuments. They also would have been impressive demonstrations of the wealth and power of the village (or alliance of

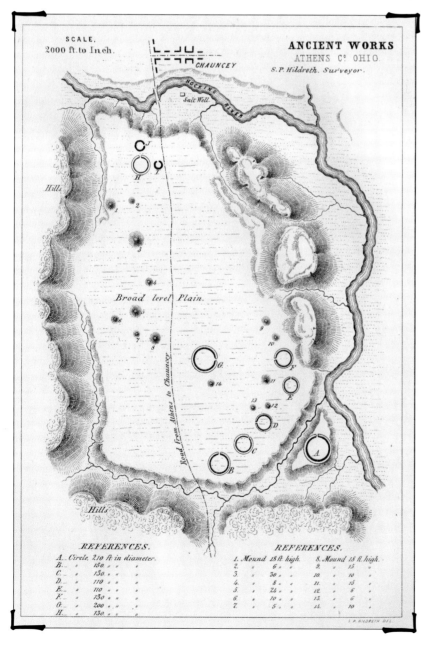

American Indians sometimes built groups of mounds and circular earthworks during the Early Woodland period. The largest such complex is known as the Wolfes Plains Group, which extended over 3-square miles on a level glacial outwash in Athens County. This survey map of the site was published in the landmark work *Ancient Monuments of the Mississippi Valley* (1848).

villages) that built them, or, since many of the largest mounds were built over several generations, of the length of time that the group had occupied the land.

Relations between villages were delicate matters. Neighbors could be a threat if they were competing for agricultural land or hunting rights. But they were also a group from which your sons and daughters might find suitable marriage partners.   Neighboring villages also could be a source of help in times when a local drought or flood caused a crop failure or a shortage of other important resources. If you could expect the neighboring village to help out in times of trouble and they could expect to receive reciprocal aid from your village, then both villages would have insurance against disaster and both would be more likely to prosper. A burial

mound between two villages would be a place where the two groups could mourn together the loss of loved ones with ties of marriage to both villages, but it could also be a traditional gathering place where they could jointly celebrate marriages and other festivals as well as peacefully resolve disputes.

Later in the Early Woodland period, mounds and enclosures were sometimes clustered together in valley bottoms, such as the group of earthworks at "The Plains" in Athens County. The greater diversity of earthworks at such locations suggests that the machinery of politics and religion was growing more complicated. Perhaps such machinery was necessary to overcome the tensions arising from formerly independent groups becoming more interdependent—from melding an "us" and "them" into a new unity.

Several remnants of the Wolfes Plains Group survive today in a residential section of the village of The Plains in Athens County. The Hartman Mound, (left) which stands 40 feet high and 140 feet in diameter at the base, is the largest remaining mound from this extensive Adena complex.

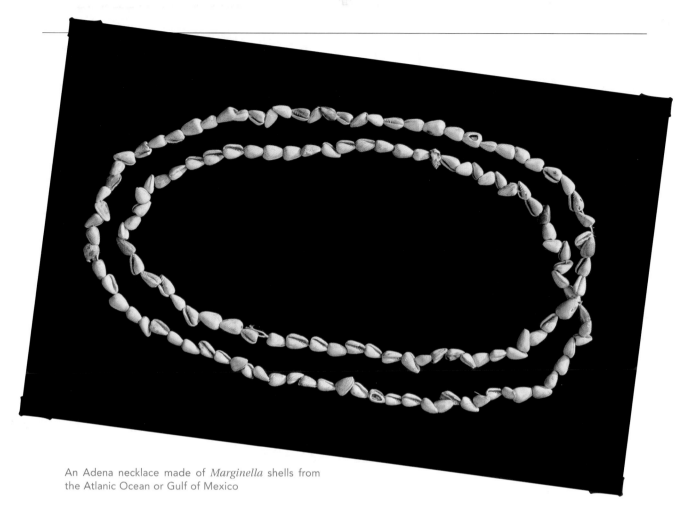

An Adena necklace made of *Marginella* shells from the Atlanic Ocean or Gulf of Mexico

The increasing importance of objects crafted from exotic raw materials was another facet of the increasing social complexity in the Early Woodland period. The exchange of rare and valuable items allowed Early Woodland groups to solidify their ties with neighboring villages. Adena people obtained copper from the upper Great Lakes, marine shells from the Atlantic coast or Gulf of Mexico, and mica from the southern Appalachian Mountains. The artifacts crafted from these materials could have been status symbols. They were highly visible indicators of wealth and of the connections the bearer had established with other peoples. And the more exotic the artifact, the more far flung the connection. Whether obtained through trade or as gifts, these objects were tangible certificates representing the good will and support of the participating groups.

THE RELIGION OF EARLY WOODLAND SOCIETIES CONTINUED TO BE BASED ON SHAMANISM, BUT we are able to enter more fully into the symbolic world of the Adena, in particular, because of the richness and variety of ritual artifacts and artistic depictions of their beliefs recovered by archaeologists. The world's most ancient religions are based on shamanism. Caves in Europe preserve paintings more than 15,000 years old that show humans transforming into animals. These paintings are remarkably similar to rock art created by shamans in southern Africa and Australia depicting their ritual transformations. Recent studies of practicing shamans by anthropologists help us to interpret the Adena artifacts and images in their proper ceremonial context.

Shamans use a variety of techniques to induce what psychologists call an altered state of consciousness. These techniques include drum-

The "Ancient Ohio" Art Series
The Early Woodland Period
(Circa 2,800 - 2,000 BP)

All human societies have ceremonies to mark important events in their lives and to express their beliefs. The Adena people occasionally constructed circular earthen enclosures to serve as the locations for ceremonies and social events. In this scene, several people are wearing wolf skins and appear to be mimicking wolf behavior, perhaps as they are enacting a clan legend or invoking the spirit of the wolf for comfort and protection. A hunter, judging from his spears and atlatl, is watching the proceedings, but the feather bustle he is wearing suggests that he will likely be joining in the events within the circle. Beyond the opening of the enclosure is the temporary encampment where the people are living. After the ceremonies and other events are concluded, they will return to their settlements scattered through the river valley.

Archaeological basis: The circular enclosure is patterned after a series of such earthworks near the town of The Plains along the Hocking River in Athens County, Ohio. Technical assistance provided by Dr. Elliot Abrams, Ohio University, who has intensively studied the Adena occupation of the Hocking River Valley.

ming, sleep deprivation, prolonged repetitive physical activity such as dancing, and the use of hallucinogenic drugs. For the shaman, such drugs are not a route to recreational stupefaction, instead they are a key that opens a doorway to a supernatural world of powerful spirits and great danger. The shaman travels to this spirit world to interact with helpful (and harmful) supernatural beings, including spirits of dead relatives and animal spirits. The shaman attempts to placate or drive off harmful spirits, who cause illness or misfortune, or call upon helpful spirits to heal an illness or lead the shaman to game. As a part of the ceremony, the shaman might put on a ritual mask to symbolize the powers of the animal spirits with whom he or she was in contact. Indeed, the shaman would ritually become that animal spirit to enable it to exercise its powers in this world.

One hallmark of the Early Woodland is the tubular pipe made from stone or clay. These pipes were likely used by shamans and other participants in rituals to smoke hallucinogenic drugs.

Inhaling the smoke produced by burning various plants, such as the potent Native American tobacco, would have helped to produce the altered states of consciousness required to initiate the shamanic experience. Other examples of Adena shamanic paraphernalia include ornamental gorgets made from parts of human skulls, beads made from human teeth, and bowls made from human skulls. These artifacts made from human bone would have been imbued with special power and the bowls may have been especially sacred and potent vessels for administering intoxicating beverages.

Archaeologists have found several examples of ritual masks in Adena burial mounds. Modified skulls of wolves, cougars, bears, and dogs, along with copper deer antlers, indicate the importance of these animals in the religious beliefs of the Adena shamans. Carvings on small stone tablets suggest Adena shamans also impersonated bird spirits. Burial 2 at the Ayers Mound in Kentucky is a particularly fascinating example of a dedicated

Tubular pipes from the Early Woodland period.

Tear-drop, biface knives or "cache blades."

shaman who was buried with his ritual garments. He was a large, rugged man who died when he was about 25-30 years old. His upper front teeth had been removed during his lifetime so that he could insert a specially shaped wolf's jaw found with his remains. This wolf jaw was part of a mask and robe that would have allowed the shaman to effectively impersonate a wolf spirit. The fact that this shaman sacrificed his own front teeth, in what must have been an exceedingly painful procedure, so that he could make a more convincing transformation reflects a strong commitment to his calling. This extreme dedication, coupled with the fact that he was buried in his ritual garb, suggests he may have been a full-time shaman rather than a part-time practitioner. This kind of specialization would represent something new in Early Woodland societies. It is an indication that the power and influence of the shaman was becoming institutionalized and that some religious leaders may have begun to exercise some political authority.

This authority likely would have been exercised primarily at the increasingly prominent and elaborate ceremonial centers. The earthen enclosures and associated structures may have been the shaman's church, temple, mosque, and hospital.

ANOTHER EXAMPLE OF POSSIBLE ADENA RELIGIOUS PRACTICES IS THE SO-CALLED "caching" of tear-drop or leaf-shaped flint blades, or bifaces. There are numerous examples of deposits of large numbers of Adena "cache blades" found generally in boggy ground. Referring to such deposits as "caches" implies that the people who left the bifaces intended to retrieve them at a later time. However, most appear to represent ceremonial offerings. The Lukens Cache is a well documented example from Portage County, Ohio. Here a farmer found 356 finely crafted ovate bifaces made from Flint Ridge flint along with the fragmentary

About 13 Adena inscribed stone tablets have been found in the central Ohio Valley, including these three from Ohio: "Berlin" Tablet (top right), "Keifer" tablet (bottom left) and the back of the "Lowe" tablet (top left). Adena tablets were often made of sandstone and inscribed with intricate designs of birds or abstract forms. They may have been used as stamps for artwork or tattoos. The smooth grooves on the back of many tablets could come from sharpening animal bone pins (center) used to create tattoos, a practice documented in many historic tribes in the eastern woodlands of North America.

Early Woodland Period Timeline
Archaeological Sites and Historical/Natural Events
(ca. 2,800-2,000 BP)

RC Years Ago (BC/AD)	Ohio	North America	World
2,000 BP (1 AD)			← Aksum, Egypt (ca. 2,001-1,900 BP)
2,100 BP (100 BC)	← Wolfe Plains Group (✳ ca. 2,100-1,700 BP)	← Anderson Mounds State Park, IN (ca. 2,100 BP)	
2,200 BP (250 BC)			← First Great Wall built, China (ca. 2,170 BP)
			← Qin Dynasty unifies China (ca. 2,221 BP)
2,300 BP (350 BC)		← Peter Village, KY (ca. 2,300-2,000 BP)	← Alexandria founded, Egypt (ca. 2,281 BP)
			← Muaryan Empire, India (ca. 2,315-2,271 BP)
			← Moche Culture rises, Peru (ca. 2,350 BP)
2,400 BP (600 BC)	← Buckmeyer Village (✳ ca. 2,400-1,800 BP)	← Grave Creek Mound, W.V. (ca. 2,400-1,900 BP)	⌐ Zapotec Culture, Mexico (ca. 2,450-1,250 BP)
			⎸ Rise of Athens, Greece (ca. 2,450 BP)
			⌐ Nok Culture, Nigeria/Sudan (ca. 2,450-1,750 BP)
2,500 BP (650 BC)		← Mt. Horeb Earthworks, KY (ca. 2,500-2,000 BP)	← Birth of Confucius (ca. 2,501 BP)
			⌐ Birth of Buddha (ca. 2,510 BP)
2,600 BP (700 BC)	← Seaman's Fort (✳ ca. 2,600-1,900 BP)	← Tchula Culture, Southeast (ca. 2,600-200 BP)	← Nazca Culture (lines), Peru (ca. 2,600-2,200 BP)
2,700 BP (900 BC)			← Nubian Kingdom rises, Sudan/Egypt (ca. 2,697 BP)
2,800 BP (1,000 BC)	⌐ Leimbach Village (✳ ca. 2,800-2,200 BP)		⌐ Zhou Court, China (ca. 2,770 BP)
	First true pottery (✳ ca. 2,800 BP)		⌐ Carthage, Tunisia (ca. 2,800-2,400 BP)
	Widespread gardening of plants in		⌐ Chavin Culture, Peru (ca. 2,800-2,150 BP)
	Eastern Agricultural Complex (✳ ca. 2,800 BP)		
2,900 BP (1,100 BC)			← Troy (Homeric), Turkey (ca. 2,900-2,100 BP)
3,000 BP (1,200 BC)	← Boudinot #4 (✳ ca. 3,000-2,000 BP)		
		← Poverty Point Culture, Southeast (ca. 3,650-3,050 BP)	

Adena Culture (ca. 2,800-2,000 BP)

Criteria and Key
This timeline is based on published radiocarbon dates or artifact typology. The dates are listed as ca. (about) BP = Radiocarbon Years Before Present and BC/AD. The "present" is defined by convention as AD 1950, the year standards were set for reporting radiocarbon dates. The timeline includes the best information available at the time of publication. Ohio sites limited to those referenced in text or on maps.
   ✳ = based on radiocarbon (C[14]) and other laboratory dates
   ✤ = based on typology of artifacts and site features

remains of a wooden bucket. The bog in which the flint tools were found had been a shallow lake in Adena times. It appears that Adena people intentionally dropped this container of artifacts into the lake, perhaps as an offering to underwater spirits. Historic Native Americans in the Great Lakes are known to have made similar offerings of artifacts to the Underwater Panther, a supernatural spirit-creature of great power. Copper pails, iron muskets, or sometimes bound dogs were dropped into lakes and rivers as offerings to ensure a safe journey or to acquire shamanic power. These flint "caches" may represent the earliest examples of this practice.

The Early Woodland period was a time of dramatic, if not revolutionary, cultural transformation. During this time, communities became more sedentary and began to use domesticated plants and ceramic vessels more widely. In addition, mortuary ceremonialism became increasingly complex. Burial mounds appeared in Ohio, sometimes associated with large, circular earthen enclosures. Early Woodland folk put more effort into acquiring artifacts crafted from exotic materials such as marine shells, copper, and mica and lavished them on their honored dead. They built most of their mounds on high hilltops overlooking village sites and apparently at the borders of their territory. Towards the end of the Early Woodland period, the people moved their centers of mortuary ceremonialism from prominent, isolated hilltops to more accessible locations in the valleys.

These trends are most apparent in the Adena culture of southern Ohio, Indiana, Kentucky, and West Virginia. The Adena culture was centered on Chillicothe with the core extending little more than 150 miles in each direction. It was a local response to local circumstances, but parallel developments were taking place in other parts of America. The increasingly elaborate mounds and ceremonial earthworks of the Adena may represent a mechanism for binding together the dispersed communities of Early Woodland hunters, fishers, gatherers, and gardeners. This complex of unifying rituals helped local groups cope with resource failures by giving them cultural connections with neighboring groups to whom they could turn for help in times of trouble. The fact that the Adena culture did not extend beyond its relatively restricted homeland suggests such an insurance policy was not necessary in surrounding regions. Perhaps the abundant resources of the Great Lakes to the north and the Mississippi valley to the west and southwest were rich enough to forestall, at least for a while, the investment in ritual unification made by Adena peoples. But the growing populations in those regions could not be supported indefinitely by the old technologies and social arrangements. Moreover, the forces that shaped the Adena culture were not static. As the villages prospered, the region's population continued to grow, as did the tensions caused by the competing interests of neighboring villages. Eventually, these forces would reach critical mass and generate an explosion at the core of the Adena heartland. Not an explosion of violence, but a spectacular florescence of art, architecture, and ritual that transformed the cultures at ground zero and sent reverberations thundering across eastern North America.

American Indians living near modern-day Chillicothe, the core of Adena Culture, would have been familiar with the varied landscape along the Appalachian Plateau such as Cedar Falls (right) in Hocking Hills State Park. By the end of the Early Woodland period, the American Indians living in Ohio were accomplished pottery-makers, mound builders and gardeners. Yet, soon, this steady stream of cultural achievements would explode into a virtual torrent of ceremonial life studied by archaeologists throughout the world.

About two thousand years ago, the American Indians living in Ohio constructed monumental geometric earthworks, exchanged exotic materials throughout North America and performed elaborate burial rituals. These are some of the traits archaeologists ascribe to the Ohio Hopewell culture. Scientists have been studying the incredible achievements of the Hopewell people for centuries, but much remains unknown including the motivation behind one of the greatest explosions in cultural expression known in ancient North America. This mural by artist Louis S. Glanzman depicts an Ohio Hopewell burial ceremony based on archaeological evidence from sites in Ohio and Illinois.

꣑4꣓

THE
THE MIDDLE WOODLAND
PERIOD

Circa 2,100 - 1,500 BP

Archaeologists who study the prehistoric past are limited to the study of things—artifacts, the physical remains of people and such structures as houses, hearths, and storage pits. We can discern glimmerings of non-material aspects of ancient cultures, such as their social, political, and religious systems, through their burial practices and their art and architecture, but the inferences we can draw from this evidence will never allow us to hear a paleoindian's prayer or ponder the wisdom in an adena shaman's parables.

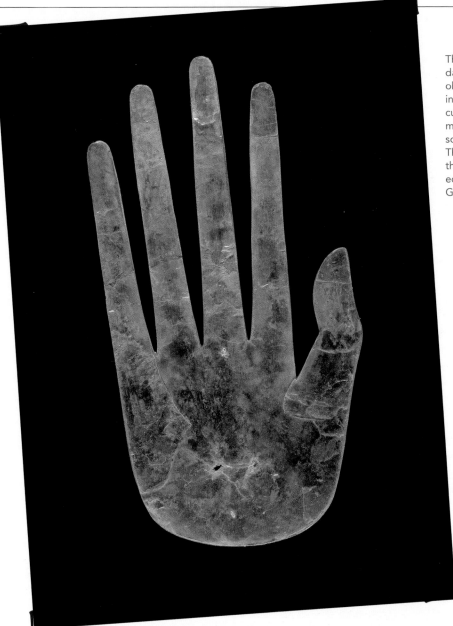

The Ohio Hopewell crafted a dazzling array of ceremonial objects out of exotic materials, including this large, open hand cut from a sheet of translucent mica obtained from a quarry in southwestern North Carolina. The mica hand cutout is one of thousands of artifacts excavated from the Hopewell Mound Group in Ross County.

THE EXPLOSION THAT MARKED THE MIDDLE WOODLAND PERIOD IS SEEN BY US AS A brilliant florescence of art, architecture, ritual, and cosmopolitan outreach that was unparalleled in North America up to that time. Its import for the people who experienced it, however, must have been primarily ideological—intellectual and emotional. The art was beautifully crafted and included naturalistic representations and abstract compositions in various media. Much of this art presented iconic images of elegant simplicity and stunning power, such as the mica or copper cut-outs of open human hands or bird talons. Such symbols must have been as richly evocative for the participants in this Hopewell culture as the Christian cross, the Islamic crescent, or the Jewish star are to modern believers; but what would these symbols mean to someone who had never read the Gospels, the Koran, or the Talmud?

A late winter snow brings out the embankments of the Octagon Earthworks, part of a massive Ohio Hopewell geometric complex built by American Indians over 2,000 years ago. Octagon Earthworks, preserved on the grounds of a golf course, is one of several ancient sites that form Newark Earthworks State Memorial in Licking County.

Ancient Ohio
Middle Woodland Period Site Map

(ca. 2,100-1,500 BP)

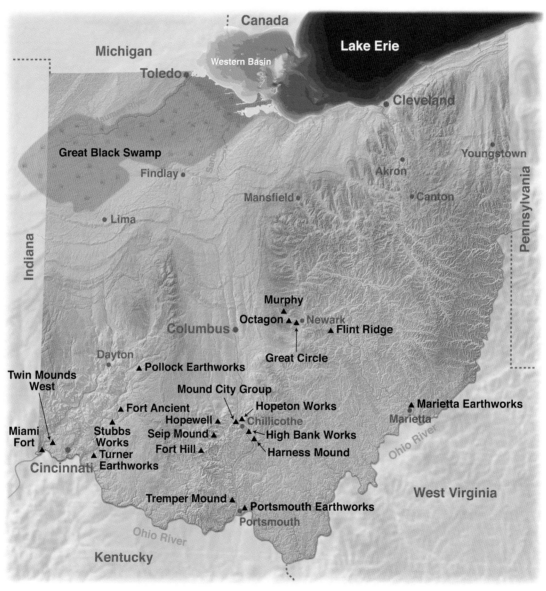

Canada

Michigan

Lake Erie

Western Basin

Toledo

Cleveland

Great Black Swamp

Youngstown

Findlay

Akron

Mansfield

Canton

Lima

Indiana

Pennsylvania

Murphy

Octagon ▲▲● Newark

Columbus ●

▲ Flint Ridge

Dayton

Great Circle

▲ Pollock Earthworks

Twin Mounds West

Mound City Group

▲ Fort Ancient

Hopeton Works

▲ Marietta Earthworks

Hopewell ▲ ▲▲ Chillicothe

Marietta

Miami Fort

Stubbs Works

Seip Mound ▲

▲ High Bank Works

▲ Turner Earthworks

Fort Hill ▲

Harness Mound

Ohio River

Cincinnati

Tremper Mound ▲

West Virginia

▲ Portsmouth Earthworks

Portsmouth

Ohio River

Kentucky

* Sites referenced in text and timelines

▲ – Ohio Archaeological Sites

▲ – Kentucky Archaeological Sites

▲ – Pennsylvania Archaeological Sites

▲ – West Virginia Archaeological Sites

● – Modern Cities

Elevation base map courtesy
Cartography & Editing Group,
Ohio Department of Natural Resources

VOYAGEUR
media group, inc.

© 2004 Voyageur Media Group, Inc.

This three-inch high sculptured human head was reconstructed from ceramic fragments excavated from Seip Mound No. 1 in Ross County in 1927. Archaeologist Richard Morgan stated in his research paper "A Hopewell Human Head" that traces of red pigment were present on the ears, lips and bottom of the object. The effigy fragments were found with a cremated human adult burial along with a miniature copper breastplate, ear spools and copper buttons. "This beautifully crafted sculpture may have been a doll's head surrounded by miniature copper accessories," according to Dr. Bradley T. Lepper, Curator of Archaeology, Ohio Historical Society. Lepper adds, "It's a wonderful depiction of an American Indian face from the Middle Woodland period and a rare opportunity to see the Ohio Hopewell people through their own eyes."

This is the archaeologist's dilemma. We can stand amid the tombs of the Hopewell people. We can touch objects of breath-taking beauty shaped by Hopewellian hands. We can walk through the remains of monumental architecture of staggering proportions and unprecedented geometrical sophistication wrought by the exertions of their minds and bodies. But the full richness of meaning behind this ritual panoply must be forever beyond our grasp. This is, of course, as true for our understanding of Paleoindian, Archaic, and Adena ceremonialism, but the frustration is more acutely felt for the Hopewell culture because, more so than in any previous period, their ritual expressions dominate the archaeological record.

The Middle Woodland period witnessed profound cultural changes in some parts of Ohio, but, in others, life went on much as it had for centuries. The new cultural developments have been subsumed under the name Hopewell, but that is not the name of any Native American tribe or ethnic group. It is an archaeological culture defined on the basis of similarities in artifacts and architecture. Mordecai Hopewell, a Confederate veteran of the Civil War, owned the farm in Ross County that included a spectacular group of mounds and earthworks that became the type site for the Hopewell culture.

In many ways, the Hopewell culture was an evolutionary development from the preceding Adena culture, and some Hopewell villages may have had neighbors who maintained an essentially Adena way of life throughout much of the Middle Woodland period. This is why the dates for the Early and Middle Woodland periods overlap somewhat. The Hopewell florescence, however, instituted cultural changes so profound and revolutionary that archaeologist N'omi Greber has characterized it as "a literal explosion."

The sparks that ignited the Hopewellian fireworks may have been struck first in southern Illinois, for that is where we find the oldest known traces of Hopewell culture artifacts. Similar artifacts and mounds and enclosures, seemingly related to the Hopewell culture, are found from southern Ontario to Florida and from Missouri to the western flanks of the Appalachian Mountains. Moreover, the Hopewell culture participated in an "interaction sphere" or, as the archaeologist Warren DeBoer prefers to call it, a "Zone of

The Esch Effigy Pipe excavated from the Esch Mound in Huron County is a rare example of a Hopewell artifact from northern Ohio. This smoking pipe may depict an alligator, frog or an unknown mythological being.

Extraordinary Travels" that reached beyond the Great Plains to the Rocky Mountains in the west and all the way to the Atlantic Ocean in the east. The fullest expression of classic Hopewell culture was, however, in southern Ohio—in the valleys of the Great and Little Miami rivers, the Scioto River, and the Muskingum River.

Surprisingly, given their proximity to the spectacular developments in southern Ohio, there were groups in northern and eastern Ohio who seem to have decided to have little to do with what they must have regarded as all the fuss and bother. So there are Middle Woodland period cultures in parts of the state whom we would not characterize as "Hopewell." For better or worse, however, the Hopewell culture dominates our view of Middle Woodland Ohio, even more so than the Adena culture did the Early Woodland period.

In spite of the vast sphere of Hopewellian influence and their far flung networks of exchange and communication, it does not appear that large groups of people moved around to any significant extent. Paul Sciulli, a physical anthropologist, and his students have studied the skeletons of Hopewell people, as well as those of Archaic and Adena people. They concluded that the Ohio Hopewell people were more closely related to the Ohio Archaic people than they were to the Hopewell people who lived in Illinois. This is an important observation, because it means that the dramatic cultural changes that define the Middle Woodland period in Ohio are not the result of a migration of people from elsewhere bringing a new way of life with them. The changes we see in the culture of these ancient Ohioans are the changes adopted by local groups in response to their changing needs. The changes that define the Hopewell culture include more elaborate burial practices, larger and more complicated earthwork constructions, the acquisition of a larger quantity and greater variety of exotic material obtained from increasingly distant regions, a more refined artistic style, and innovations in stone tool and ceramic technology.

The Ohio Hopewell crafted beautiful objects from both local and exotic materials, including these artifacts excavated in 1915 by William C. Mills, Curator of the Ohio State Archaeological and Historical Society (now The Ohio Historical Society) from the Tremper Mound in Scioto County. Clockwise from top: two platform pipes, a tubular pipe, a hollowed out beaver "boatstone," and an assortment of five stone ornaments with a reel-shaped copper ornament.

Hopewell villages typically were located in small clearings in the primeval forests of giant white oak, hickory, and other tree species depending on the particular region. The majority of known Hopewell sites in Ohio are located on the Glaciated Allegheny Plateau of south-central Ohio. This was a rich environment, situated between the Till Plains to the north and west and the Unglaciated Plateau to the south and east. Ecologists call such a boundary zone an "ecotone." Living along such a border gave Hopewell foragers ready access to the variety of resources in all three environmental zones.

A hawk flying over Middle Woodland Ohio, above the seemingly endless ocean of huge trees with their interwoven canopies riven by the larger streams and rivers, would have seen occasional scattered clearings in the forest varying in size from one to four acres. Wisps of smoke rising from some of these clearings marked the cooking

Computer graphics allow archaeologists, educators and students to take a virtual tour of an American Indian settlement as it may have looked about two thousand years ago. This depiction of an Ohio Hopewell encampment is a still frame from interactive computer animation created by designers with the "EarthWorks" project, an innovative program of The Center for the Electronic Reconstruction of Historical and Archaeological Sites (CERHAS), at the University of Cincinnati.

THE HOPEWELL TEXTILES

By Dr. Kathryn A. Jakes, Professor, Department of Consumer and Textile Sciences, The Ohio State University.

Though the archaeologists who excavated Hopewell mounds reported that they discovered textiles, they did not fully recognize the value of these fabrics. Instead the artifacts were collected without noting their relationship to specific graves or their association with other objects. Today they are dispersed in collections across the United States and Europe. Yet textiles provide clues to the technological sophistication and craftsmanship, the vast knowledge of plant and animal materials, and the social structure of the people who produced them, as well as to the cultural significance of the objects to the people that used them.

In order to make the fabrics, long bundles of fiber were extracted from plant stems and spun into yarns. The Hopewell people knew not only where to find the plants, and which plants yielded good fibers, but also the precise time to collect them so the best fiber could be extracted. These activities are likely to have been "scheduled" with groups of

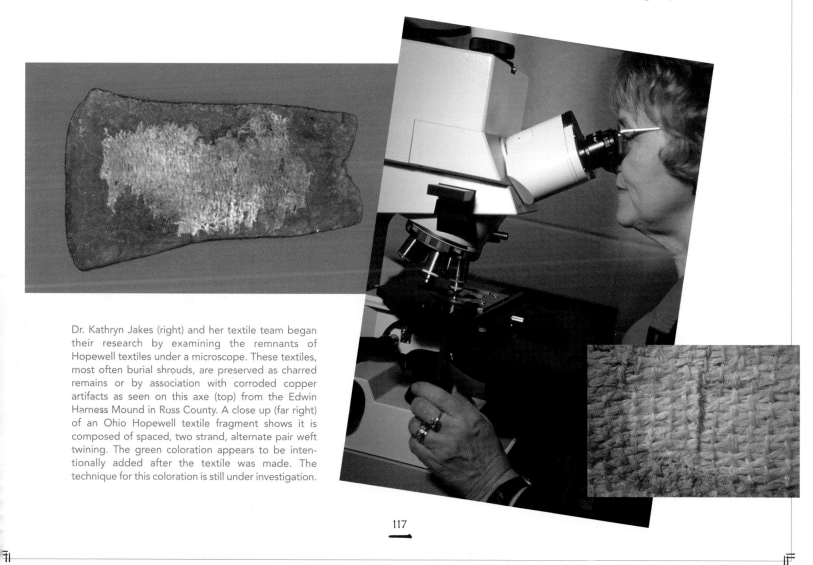

Dr. Kathryn Jakes (right) and her textile team began their research by examining the remnants of Hopewell textiles under a microscope. These textiles, most often burial shrouds, are preserved as charred remains or by association with corroded copper artifacts as seen on this axe (top) from the Edwin Harness Mound in Ross County. A close up (far right) of an Ohio Hopewell textile fragment shows it is composed of spaced, two strand, alternate pair weft twining. The green coloration appears to be intentionally added after the textile was made. The technique for this coloration is still under investigation.

THE HOPEWELL TEXTILES

people devoting time for this work in order to supply the fiber needs of the entire group. Plant materials also were used for coloring the fabrics. Some fabrics included feathers and animal hair. When first discovered, one fabric-covered copper breastplate was colored maroon, brown, and yellow but the colors quickly deteriorated after excavation. Today the object displays shades of black. Current study of the dyeing and painting methods of the Hopewell will allow us to determine which colorants were used.

Because the fiber bundles are long, thigh spinning was used to form yarns. In thigh spinning, very fine yarns can be made, without the aid of a spindle as is used in spinning shorter fibers. Originally labeled "woven," Hopewell textiles were made by complex twining of the spun yarns, in some ways similar to knotting or braiding. Fabric structures range from tight compact fabrics to open laces or nets. Each of these fabric types had a specific purpose. It has been proposed, for example, that tight compact fabrics were suitable for carrying ashes and other remains from the cremation basins to graves in the mounds. Study of textiles also has shown that while particular cremation and burial ceremonies were followed by the Hopewell people, the textiles used in these ceremonies were produced locally. There are mound to mound distinctions between them that reflect a specialization in the craft of the textile production in each local group.

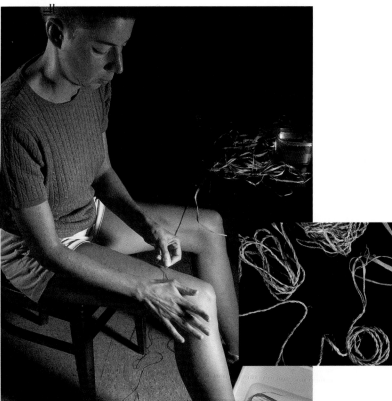

Researchers from the Department of Consumer and Textile Sciences, Ohio State University, use experimental archaeology to learn how the Ohio Hopewell made their fabrics. Christel Baldia (above) peels fiber bundles from the stems of common milkweed, one of several indigenous plants that yield long strands of fibrous material. In some cases, a rotting process or water treatment is used to aid in releasing the fibers.

Erica J. Tiedemann (right) demonstrates the art of thigh spinning. She rolls two fiber bundles against her leg to form a twisted and plied yarn. New fiber bundles are readily spliced into the free end of the yarn. Many Hopewell textiles were twined without a loom from yarns similar to these examples (far right) of thigh spun yarn made from basswood fiber.

Amanda J. Thompson experiments with combinations of dye plants such as bed-straw, and additives such as wood ash, that the Hopewell people likely used to color fibers. Controlled laboratory experiments produce a set of comparative materials to help test methods for identifying dyes in ancient Hopewell textiles.

Just as we wear clothes that reflect particular roles or status, e.g. a police uniform, a king's robe, or a white wedding dress, the Hopewell people also produced and used textiles with particular messages in mind. A set of fabrics from Seip Mound, for example, is marked in green patterns that appear to be purposely painted rather than randomly formed. These fabric pieces, which also contain rabbit hair, are thought to be part of a burial canopy and had a special significance in burial ceremonies.

Preserved due to association with copper, or because they were charred in cremation ceremonies, many of the textile fragments have been ignored because they are no longer brilliantly colored. Using the sensitive analytical methods available today, even the smallest sample of a fiber, yarn, or fabric can reveal a great deal of information. The identity of the fiber, how well it was extracted from the remainder of the plant stem, the means of coloration, and the extent of use of the textile object can be gleaned from their study. As the study of Hopewell textiles continues, more secrets will be discovered.

fires of Hopewell villages or the smoldering ashes of sections of forest recently chopped down and burned to clear the way for new gardens and villages.

The Hopewell villages were widely scattered along streams and rivers. Typically they consisted of only one or a few houses. Hopewell houses generally were squarish structures made from logs set upright in the ground. The logs were then interlaced with twigs and covered with bark or plastered with mud mixed with grass. They were usually 20 to 30 ft on a side and may have been roofed with thatch, reeds, or bark. Examples of such small villages, or "hamlets" as some prefer to call these isolated settlements, include the Twin Mounds West site in Hamilton County, and the Murphy site in Licking County. Surrounding the houses were cooking areas and other special activity areas. The trash dump or midden was usually downwind, downslope and out of sight.

ADJACENT TO THE VILLAGES WERE GARDENS IN WHICH HOPEWELL FARMERS GREW THE PLANTS of the Eastern Agricultural Complex, including knotweed and maygrass, with their starchy seeds rich in carbohydrates, and oily-seeded sumpweed and sunflower. Nearby abandoned garden plots would be overgrown with raspberry, elderberry, and sumac bushes. Hopewell women and their daughters likely tended the gardens and gathered the abundant fruits and berries, while Hopewell men and older boys hunted the deer and other animals attracted by these tasty treats, which were quite rare in the otherwise mostly closed forests. Dee Anne Wymer, an archaeologist who is a specialist in the study of the plant foods used by prehistoric peoples, argues that the Ohio Hopewell people were not just "sophisticated farmers" but also "managers of their environment."

The Ohio Hopewell used a variety of techniques and designs to decorate their coiled clay pottery. This assemblage (far left) of pottery sherds from the Middle Woodland period ranges from an undecorated Plain Jar to more stylized designs such as Plain Rocker, Dentate Rocker and Complicated Stamped to the Zoned Incised design found on more elaborate Ohio Hopewell pottery.

Some Ohio Hopewell pottery may have been made only for special purposes. This rare four-sided vessel (above), inscribed with stylized images of waterfowl, was reconstructed from pieces excavated from the "pottery mound" at Mound City, Hopewell Culture National Historical Park in Ross County.

The Middle Woodland Period Tool Kit
Circa 2,100 – 1,500 BP

The Middle Woodland period represents an intensification of the cultural practices that began in the Early Woodland. Hunting and gathering continued to be important, but gardening played an increasingly significant role in their diet.

This selection of Middle Woodland artifacts includes a large celt (axe), two spearpoints, a Chesser Notched point characteristic of the late Middle Woodland and early Late Woodland periods, and a Lowe Flared Base point, and a Hopewell flint core along with two razor blade-like bladelets driven off a similar core.

Hopewell farmers had to be able to judge when their gardens would deplete the nutrients in the soil. Before that happened, they chose a section of the forest for a new garden site and cut the bark away from the bases of the trees to be cleared. This "girdling" of the trees killed them and, after a year or two, they would be dried up hulks easier to burn and chop down. The charred stumps and many of the largest trunks were left to rot, and the farmers would sow their crops around them. A sharpened stick was the only plow the Hopewell farmers used. They gouged small furrows in the soil or just poked holes in the ashy ground to plant their seeds. This kind of farming is called "slash and burn" or "swidden" horticulture.

In many ways, Hopewell villages and their gardens were similar to those of the Early Woodland period, but there were more of them and they were becoming increasingly concentrated in the valleys of the major streams that flowed southward into the Ohio River. Archaeologists disagree about whether Hopewell people lived in these villages year round or simply used them as base camps during the spring planting and fall harvest seasons. It does seem clear that Hopewell hunters continued to range widely in their search for game animals. They hunted deer, elk, bear, turkey, and geese. Women continued to gather wild plant foods such as hickory nuts, black walnuts, butternuts, hazelnuts, fruits, and berries. Families likely worked together to catch small animals such as turtles and snakes, and fish using lines, nets, and spears.

THE TOOLS USED BY HOPEWELL FOLK WERE MORE REFINED AND SPECIALIZED THAN those used by their Adena forebears. Pottery became more commonly used and more diverse in form. Native North Americans never invented the pottery wheel, so all of their vessels were made by stacking up coils of clay and then smoothing and decorating the surfaces. Hopewell pots are thinner and generally smaller than earlier vessels, and while they still used cord-marking to roughen and decorate the surfaces of the pots, they also developed new techniques for decoration. Sometimes they incised cross-hatched patterns in the rims of the pots and used blocks of carved wood as stamps to impress designs in the sides of vessels. Common design elements included birds and ducks. The more decorated and elaborate pots were likely used only on special ceremonial occasions; it was the "good china" brought out for weddings, funerals, and special holidays.

✗✗✗

THE STONE TOOL TECHNOLOGY OF THE HOPEWELL CULTURE INCLUDED A STARTLING innovation: small, thin blades struck from specially prepared conical blocks of flint. The Hopewell people used these delicate and razor sharp knives for a variety of tasks. They are commonly found at ritual sites as well as at habitation sites. These bladelets and the special cores from which they were struck are unique to the Hopewell culture. It was a very efficient way to get the most cutting edge from the least amount of flint. Bladelets do not seem to have been set in hafts and were often used until they were worn out. They were a kind of disposable razor blade, used for a task and then thrown away.

The most common chert tools found in Ohio Hopewell sites present an archaeological puzzle. Archaeologists Bob Genheimer and Frank Cowan examine bladelets at the Geier Collections and Research Center, Cincinnati Museum Center. Excavated near the Stubbs Earthworks site, these small, narrow razor-sharp blades (about 1 inch long) are typical of the thousands of bladelets found at many Ohio Hopewell sites. "Bladelets have a standardized size and form, but their exact function is a matter of debate," says Bob Genhheimer, Curator of Archaeology, The Cincinnati Museum Center. "Use-wear studies indicate that bladelets were multifunctional tools, possibly substituting for other bifacial reduction tools during the Middle Woodland period. But, their manufacture and discard near major Hopewell-age earthworks suggest their use may be related to craft production or ritual activities."

Beyond their uniformity, what makes bladelets peculiar is the fact that this distinctive tool technology, which replaced more practical tool forms, appears and disappears with Ohio Hopewell ceremonialism. "Since they are costly to make and aren't well suited to most utilitarian purposes, I suspect their primary roles must have been within the realm of ritual activities," concludes Frank Cowan, Research Associate, Cincinnati Museum Center. "What kind of ritual purposes they served, we don't know."

The Ohio Hopewell crafted an array of personal adornments from organic materials such as animal bone, shell and teeth. This delicate swan comb made of tortoise shell is one of the few effigies of the trumpeter swan found in burial mounds, according to archaeologist Henry Shetrone. Shetrone recovered several swan combs and thousands of other artifacts during excavations of Seip Mound in Ross County from 1925 to 1928. The lower edge of the comb has a serrated edge. The fine "teeth" of the comb are missing.

Hopewell flintknappers made most of their cores and bladelets from Flint Ridge flint and a lesser number from Indiana hornstone. Flint Ridge flint, found most abundantly in Licking County, is not the best flint for making tools, but it is the most fantastically colored. It is likely that Hopewell folk chose Flint Ridge flint for their stone tools because of its many color variations, including swirling combinations of red, white, green, blue, gray, and black. And if the flint was heat-treated, that is, buried and slowly baked under a carefully controlled fire, it became easier to fashion into tools, and the colors became even more bright and vivid.

The flint spear points used by Hopewell hunters differed from those of the Early Woodland. They tended to be shorter and broader and did not have the rounded stems of Adena points. Instead they had notched or flaring stems. Hopewell hunters still used the atlatl, although there are few examples of obvious spearthrower weights such as were common in the Archaic period.

THE ART OF THE HOPEWELL CULTURE WAS beautifully crafted and included naturalistic representations and abstract compositions in various media. Important characteristics of the Hopewell artistic style included a subtle and sometimes intricate use of positive and negative space and mirror symmetry. Although most surviving Hopewell art is made from stone, ceramic, metal, the bones and teeth of animals (and sometimes humans), shells, and pearls, it is clear that these only represent the most durable of media used by Hopewell artisans. They also fashioned works of fine art from wood, textile, animal hide, fur, and feathers that have not survived except in unusual circumstances.

Hopewell art included frequent depictions of various animals, but most especially deer, bear, and assorted birds. There are representations of Hopewell shamans wearing deer antler headdresses and bear skins, so these animals must have been particularly important. Certainly the

The Wray Figurine (named after its former owner) is thought to depict an Ohio Hopewell shaman dressed in a bear cloak. Carved from limonitic schist stone, this six-inch high statue was discovered in 1881 during construction at an old rolling mill built over a large cluster of burial mounds within the Newark Earthworks in Licking County. The Wray Figurine provides archaeologists with an incredible insight into Hopewell ceremonial life. The figure is adorned with ear spools and a head rests on his lap. It's unclear if this depicts an actual decapitated head or the symbolic image of a head, such as a mask or mythological being. "The Wray Figurine may represent a shaman in the act of transforming from a human to a bear spirit," according to Dr. Bradley T. Lepper, Curator of Archaeology, Ohio Historical Society. "The hand (or paw) on the side of the head suggests the shaman is lowering the mask to complete the transformation. In many American Indian cultures, the shaman would become an animal spirit in order to heal illnesses or find game animals for hunters." In 1775, Nicholas Cresswell, while visiting a group of Delaware Indians at Coshocton, witnessed such a transformation ceremony. Cresswell wrote, "Saw an Indian Conjuror dressed in a Coat of Bearskin with a Visor mask made of wood, frightful enough to scare the Devil."

white-tailed deer was, by far, the most important game animal hunted by the Hopewell people and it may have been as revered as the bison was by the Native peoples of the Plains.

✕✕✕

A UNIQUELY HOPEWELL ARTIFACT IS THE ANIMAL EFFIGY PLATFORM PIPE. THE BOWLS OF these generally small pipes were carved into the shapes of various animals, and, in one particularly remarkable example from the Hopewell site, the platform also was carved into the shape of an animal. The bowl is a shoveler duck sitting on the back of a fish that forms the platform. Almost invariably, the animal faced the smoker and some archaeologists have surmised that the animals represented the guardian spirits of shamans. As the shamans smoked some hallucinogenic drug, such as the potent native form of tobacco, they gazed at these representations of their spirit helpers as a way of invoking their aid and protection on journeys into the spirit world.

Most of the effigy pipes come from two large collections deposited in two separate mounds, one at Mound City in Ross County and one at Tremper Mound in Scioto County. These deposits must represent important rituals during which a number of shamans collectively sacrificed or abandoned these vital tools of their trade instead of passing them on to disciples. It suggests a major rupture in the religious life of these communities; perhaps marking the end of an era—or a new beginning.

Middle Woodland Period Timeline
Archaeological Sites and Historical/Natural Events
(ca. 2,100-1,500 BP)

RC Years Ago (BC/AD)	Ohio	North America	World
1,500 BP (550 AD)			
			← Visigoths invade Rome (ca. 1,540 BP)
			← Huns invade Europe (ca. 1,580 BP)
1,600 BP (480 AD)			
			← Constantine reigns (ca. 1,644-1,613 BP)
			← Earliest Mayan calendar, Mexico (ca. 1,658 BP)
1,700 BP (320 AD)	← Fort Hill (✳ ✜ ca. 1,700-1,550 BP)		← Rise of Axum, Ethiopia (ca. 1,700 BP)
			← Huns invade China (ca. 1,730 BP)
1,800 BP (200 AD)	┌ Miami Fort (✳ ✜ ca. 1,800-1,550 BP) ├ Seip Earthworks (✳ ✜ ca. 1,800-1,600 BP) └ Marietta Earthworks (✳ ✜ ca. 1,800-1,600 BP)	← Santa Rosa/Swift Creek, South (ca. 1,800-1,200 BP)	
			← Mayan Culture, Mesoamerica (ca. 1,850-1,400 BP)
1,900 BP (120 AD)	← Turner Earthworks (✳ ✜ ca. 1,900-1,600 BP)		← Teotihuacan Sun Pyramid, Mexico (ca. 1,900 BP) ← Rome's Colloseum opens, Italy (ca. 1,920 BP)
	┌ Stubbs Works (✳ ✜ ca. 1,950-1,650 BP) └ Pollock Earthworks (✳ ✜ ca. 1,950-1,700 BP)	← Kansas City Hopewell, KA (ca. 1,950-1,200 BP)	← Volcano destroys Pompeii, Italy (ca. 1,940 BP) ← Birth of Jesus Christ (ca. 1,956 BP)
2,000 BP (1 AD)	┌ Harness Mound (✳ ✜ ca. 2,000-1,500 BP) └ Hopeton Works (✳ ✜ ca. 2,000-1,850 BP)	┌ Basketmaker Cultures, Southwest (ca. 2,000-1,200 BP) ├ Marksville Culture, LA (ca. 2,000-1,600 BP) └ McGraw Site, LA (✳ ✜ ca. 2,000-1,600 BP)	← Julius Caesar assassinated (ca. 1,994 BP)
	┌ Newark Earthworks (✳ ✜ ca. 2,050-1,550 BP) └ High Bank Works (✳ ✜ ca. 2,050-1,700 BP)	┌ Pinson Mounds, TN (ca. 2,050-1,000 BP) └ Havana Hopewell, IL (ca. 2,050-1,700 BP)	┌ Cleopatra reigns, Egypt (ca. 2,050-2,030 BP) └ Silk road opens across Asia (ca. 2,060 BP)
2,100 BP (100 BC)	┌ Hopewell Mound Group (✳ ✜ ca. 2,100-1,600 BP) └ Murphy (✳ ✜ ca. 2,100-1,700 BP)		
	← Tremper Mound (✳ ✜ ca. 2,150-1,950 BP)	← Anderson Mounds, IN (ca. 2,150-1,600 BP)	← Han Dynasty, China (ca. 2,152 BP)
2,200 BP (250 BC)	┌ Fort Ancient (✳ ✜ ca. 2,200-1,600 BP) └ Mound City Group (✳ ✜ ca. 2,200-1,750 BP)		← Moche Culture, Peru (ca. 2,200-1,200 BP)
		Point Peninsula Culture, Ontario (ca. 2,290-1,250 BP)	

Ohio Hopewell Culture (ca. 2,100-1,500 BP)

Criteria and Key

This timeline is based on published radiocarbon dates or artifact typology. The dates are listed as ca. (about) BP = Radiocarbon Years Before Present and BC/AD. The "present" is defined by convention as AD 1950, the year standards were set for reporting radiocarbon dates. The timeline includes the best information available at the time of publication. Ohio sites limited to those referenced in text or on maps.

✳ = based on radiocarbon (C[14]) and other laboratory dates
✜ = based on typology of artifacts and site features

TREMPER PIPES

In the summer of 1915, William C. Mills, curator of the Ohio State Archaeological and Historical Society, supervised the excavation of the Tremper Mound, an Ohio Hopewell burial complex located on a plateau about five miles north of Portsmouth in Scioto County. In one depository on the eastern end of the site, excavators uncovered a cache of over 500 objects; bead necklaces, stone gorgets, mica cutouts, ear spools, boatstones, animal bone, copper plates, woven fabrics and 136 smoking pipes made of materials from Ohio and Illinois. Of these, 60 were platform pipes carved into the effigies of animals, a menagerie of indigenous birds, mammals and amphibians.

In 1846, the team of Ephraim Squier and Edwin Davis excavated a similar cache of 95 animal effigy pipes from Mound #8 within the Mound City Group in Ross County. Unable to find a buyer in the United States, Davis sold most of his collection of 1,300 artifacts to the Blackmore Museum in England in 1864. This collection was then obtained by the British Museum of London. The Mound City and Tremper animal effigy pipes have a similar artistic style.

The Tremper animal effigy pipes, ritualistically broken by the Hopewell people before burial, are archived in the collection of the Ohio Historical Society. Most of the animal effigy pipes face the smoker. Evidence suggests the Hopewell used and repaired the pipes before internment. They feature a wide range of species from owls, hawks, ducks, cranes, quail, prairie chicken and the crow to toads, turtles, beaver, otter, mink, raccoon, rabbit, squirrel, porcupine, possum, fox, wolf, bobcat, bear, mountain lion and a dog. Surprisingly, only one depicts a white-tailed deer and none depict a turkey—two animals vital in their food economy. Some archaeologists believe the animal effigies may relate to clan groups or totems documented within the historic American Indian tribes of the eastern woodlands. Here are six examples of the sixty Tremper animal effigy pipes from the Ohio Historical Society.

Hawk Effigy Pipe. The artistic detail is seen in the elaborate feathers and talons of this hawk. The hawk's hollow eye sockets were probably inset with freshwater pearls. Platform length: 3.5 inches.

Dog Effigy Pipe. Portrayed in a seated, baying position, the dog is the only animal known to be domesticated in prehistoric North America. Platform length: 3.5 inches.

Mountain Lion Effigy Pipe. The mountain lion (a.k.a. cougar or panther) has elaborate eye markings and is posed sitting on its haunches. Platform length: 4 inches.

Barred Owl Effigy Pipe. There are several species of owls represented in the Tremper pipe cache, including this depiction of a barred owl whose head is turned 180 degrees to face the pipe smoker. Platform length: 3.5 inches.

Otter Effigy Pipe. Some effigy pipes portray the natural characteristics of the animal such as this otter posed with a fish in its mouth. Platform length: 3.5 inches.

Black Bear Effigy Pipe. The Ohio Hopewell had a special appreciation for both the distant grizzly bear and indigenous black bear based on the discovery of numerous artifacts of bear teeth, claws, jawbones and the Wray figurine. This effigy pipe shows a black bear with glaring eyes (inlaid with pearl or shell) and sharp teeth posed as if about to rise for an attack. Platform length: 3.5 inches.

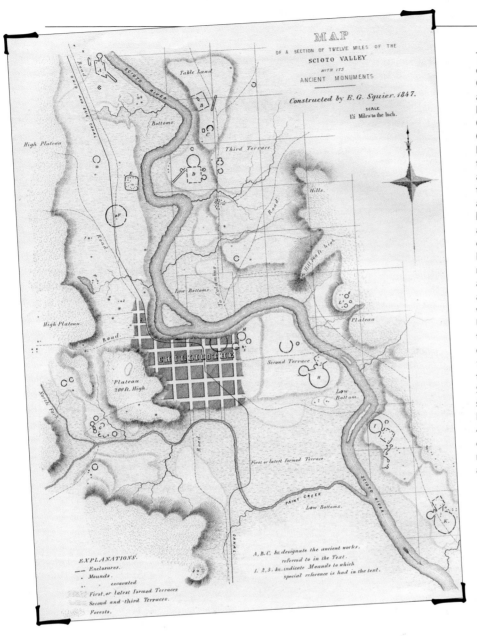

The heartland of Ohio Hopewell culture was centered on modern day Chillicothe and extended outward about 150 miles in an oblong radius. During the mid 1800s, two men from Chillicothe, newspaper man Ephraim G. Squier and physician Edwin H. Davis, conducted extensive investigations into the antiquities of the Ohio and Mississippi valleys in an attempt to answer questions as to the origin, age and identity of the people who built tens of thousands of mounds and earthworks throughout the eastern woodlands of the United States. From 1845 to 1847, this unlikely research team surveyed, excavated and gathered detailed information about the American Indian earthworks that dotted the landscape. Under the guidance of Joseph Henry, the research of Squier and Davis was compiled into *Ancient Monuments of the Mississippi Valley*, which became the first publication of the Smithsonian Institution in 1848. This survey map of "a section of Twelve Miles of the Scioto Valley" is one of 48 lithographed maps and 207 wood engravings contained in one of the most important books ever published about Ohio archaeology.

MUCH OF WHAT WE KNOW ABOUT HOPEWELL SOCIETY WE HAVE LEARNED FROM A STUDY of their burial places. These special places continued to serve as connecting links between the isolated hamlets of the Hopewell culture. Instead of uniting two or three neighboring communities, Hopewell ceremonial centers could link dozens of villages.

Indeed, some of the larger earthwork centers probably tied entire regions together and even, in a few cases, formed connections between distant regions. A "Great Hopewell Road," consisting of a set of straight parallel walls of earth, may have extended between Hopewellian Newark and Chillicothe—a distance of nearly 60 miles.

The proliferation of art during the Middle Woodland era may reflect the increasing importance of conveying social information visually. Groups from different regions who did not regularly interact and may not even have shared the same language may have needed this array of striking symbols to facilitate the communication of social role and status when they gathered at the earthwork centers to celebrate a festival or, perhaps more importantly, to negotiate alliances. Archaeologist Clive Gamble has argued that alliances between neighboring social groups served to grant both groups access to a greater variety of resources than either could marshal in their respective homelands. For hunters and gatherers, greater variety meant greater flexibility in responding to short term failures of critical local resources. Hopewell societies were becoming increasingly dependent on farming, but, in many ways, they still were grounded in the hunting and gathering way of life.

XXX

MANY PEOPLE BURIED IN HOPEWELL MOUNDS HAD LARGE QUANTITIES OF BEAUTIFUL artifacts buried with them. Some were buried with nothing. Still others were not buried in mounds at all. This certainly suggests that there was an increasing diversity in social role and status. The increasing complexity of Hopewellian society is evident in how these burials were organized. The Adena culture often buried their honored dead atop the mounds containing the bones of their ancestors. So Adena mounds grew like layer cakes, as one generation was laid to rest over their forefathers and foremothers. Hopewell burial mounds have a much more complex internal organization.

At the base of many Hopewell mounds lie the remains of large wooden-framed structures. Such structures often are called "charnel houses," but that name suggests these places were devoted entirely to the dead. There is ample evidence that many of these buildings were more like churches or temples than mere mortuaries. People were indeed cremated and buried in special crypts and altars in some of these buildings, but specially honored people also are buried beneath the stones of Westminster Abbey in London. And the entombed bones of the kings of England, along with those of luminaries such as Shakespeare, Newton, and Darwin do not make this place merely a mausoleum.

The postmold patterns that mark the outlines of especially grand Hopewell "Big Houses" typically reveal that they had separate rooms of varying size, each with their own characteristic facilities and kinds of offerings. These might represent ritual spaces designated for the use of different clans or cults within the society. At the Harness Mound in Ross County, there were three such areas and the plan of the Big House looked somewhat like the outline of a snowman. This general pattern was repeated at Seip Mound, Mound 25 at the Hopewell site, and others. This might suggest that there were three divisions, clans or cults, in Hopewell society, but all were joined under one roof.

The "Ancient Ohio" Art Series
The Middle Woodland Period
(ca. 2,100-1,500 BP)

The Stubbs Earthworks is the backdrop for this scene in which a Hopewell shaman is combining his practical knowledge as an herbalist and his connections with the spirit world to cure the illness of his patient lying on the bench. His bearskin regalia is based on the details of the Wray figurine from the Newark Earthworks, while the clothing and hair styles of the other people in the scene are taken from terra cotta figurines found at Hopewell sites in Illinois. The Stubbs Earthworks, situated along the Little Miami River in Warren County, is portrayed as it appeared in 19th century maps. The site was damaged over the years by farming, gravel quarrying, and the construction of a high school. However, archaeologists were able to investigate portions of the site before the school was built.

Archaeological basis: Technical information provided by Dr. Frank Cowan, Cowan and Associates, Cincinnati, Ohio.

THE EDWIN HARNESS BIG HOUSE

Ross County

By Dr. N'omi B. Greber, Curator of Archaeology, The Cleveland Museum of Natural History.

It was on a winter's day that I first saw the remnant of the Edwin Harness Mound. Robert Harness, whose family has farmed the area for more than 200 years, had brought me to one of his fields where I stood on his tractor and looked across a very flat stretch of ground. Here I saw the patchwork pattern that still remained from the many loads of soils carried person by person and placed over a Hopewell Big House nearly 2000 years ago. This was an amazing sight. The great mound that finally covered the wooden, multi-roomed structure had been some twenty feet high. Excavations and modern land use since 1800 had brought it down to the level I first saw. Yet, the patchwork

pattern of the remnant meant that there were still intact sections of the ancient earthen and stone construction. Possibly these sections covered charred materials and ecological samples that could now be studied using scientific techniques not available to earlier excavators. Also, at that time, even the floor plan of the Big House was not known. With Mr. Harness' permission, the Ohio Archaeological Council organized a salvage excavation for the following summer. Many volunteers helped. We found the edge of a pit dug by Ephraim Squier and Edwin Davis in the 1840s and the trench dug by Frederick Putnam in 1884. Some traces remained of Warren Moorehead's

Archaeologists and volunteers from The Cleveland Museum of Natural History conduct field excavations at Edwin Harness Mound in the summer of 1976.

An aerial view of the Edwin Harness Mound site shows the distinctive posthole pattern of the Big House. After excavations were complete, the postholes were filled with concrete (supplied by Mr. Harness) to hold their shape. The tops of these concrete forms were painted white for this illuminating aerial image.

tunnels dug in 1897. William Mills had conducted more complete excavations in 1905. We appreciated the needs of his crew when we found pieces of an empty liniment bottle in the backfill of their excavations. Most importantly, we found that we could begin to identify the original building and in situ features holding charred materials. We used water flotation techniques developed in the 1960s that enabled us to find tiny bits of charcoal and seeds. By August we knew that there was more work than could be finished in one season. Mr. Harness then graciously kept the mound area out of his planting plans. Based on the results of our first season, the Cleveland Museum of Natural History received a grant from the National Science Foundation to continue the next summer. The results that season were all we had hoped for, and more.

Specialists analyzed our finds. Botanists identified hickory as the main construction material for the Big House. Clearly, the builders had to carefully plan to have so many posts available when needed. Radiocarbon dates placed the initial building and use near the beginning of the fourth century. Food stuffs and animal bones were identified. All these were in small quantity, not as one would expect in common kitchen trash. A very small quantity of maize (corn) was found, the first in Ohio. A study of

human bones has shown that corn was not an important part of the Hopewell diet. The small quantity and its context within the remains of a small fire on the building floor indicate that this plant was more likely used in special rituals, not everyday meals. Fire was an important element in the rituals and ceremonies that took place inside and adjacent to the Big House. Most fires were small and of short duration. A different type of fire occurred in the center of the middle room where pine logs provided fuel for a fire that was kept burning for a long time. With knowledge of the Harness Big House we could give cultural and temporal context for the early excavations by restudying the museum collections curated by the Ohio Historical Society and the Harvard Peabody museums.

These and other details have been formally and informally reported to help increase appreciation of a remarkable people. All the scientific samples, soils, and artifacts recovered were donated to the Cleveland Museum where they continue to be a resource for study. For example, physical evidence of a "Hopewell Interaction Sphere" has come from a recent study by James Stotlman who has identified the local clays used to make sherds recovered from the Harness Big House. He has recognized a sherd from the same clays found at the Ice House Bottom site in Tennessee.

THE EDWIN HARNESS BIG HOUSE

A platform pipe (left) and copper breastplate (below) excavated from the Edwin Harness Mound in Ross County.

The framework of the Big House comes to life in this artist's rendering by Ellen Walters based on evidence from the posthole patterns. The Ohio Hopewell used several types of wood to build the Big House, including hickory for the main support posts.

Archaeologists have found numerous large copper axes within Ohio Hopewell mounds. The enormous size and weight of Hopewell copper axes, (one weighed over 38 pounds), suggests these objects were used for ceremonial purposes.

THE ELABORATE ARCHITECTURAL ACHIEVEMENTS OF THE HOPEWELL CULTURE STRONGLY suggest that some person or group had the authority to design the plan of the earthwork and oversee its construction. On the other hand, Hopewell villages are small, and the dwellings tend to be simple and somewhat uniform. In other words, there are no palaces or especially large houses fit for a chief, and the population was not collected together in a large town where a leader could easily exercise control over his, or her, people.

These seemingly contradictory facts suggest that although Hopewell societies were largely egalitarian, some people achieved positions of respect and power within the sphere of cults or clans. There was, however, no overarching chief, king, or caste of nobles. Leaders could suggest courses of action, they could try to persuade, cajole, or bribe followers to adopt this or that course of action, and lead through inspiration and example, but their authority was not supreme, and it is unlikely that they could compel followers to do anything they didn't want to do.

Perhaps leadership during this period was only exercised at the large social gatherings. When people dispersed to their homes, the mantle of leadership was, in effect, taken off and put into storage until the next big festival.

Men generally seem to have been buried with the greatest pomp and circumstance and so are likely to have been the leaders of Hopewellian societies, though not invariably. Certain kinds of artifacts also tend to be buried with men and not with women. For example, copper axes, which were symbolic emblems and not functional tools, ordinarily are found only with males. Warren DeBoer has suggested that these represented the awesome weapon of the mythical lords of the heavens: the Thunderbirds. Of course this interpretation is based on extrapolating the myths of historic Native Americans back into the Hopewell era, but, if he is correct, the copper axes of the Hopewell culture would have been powerful symbols of something like Thor's hammer or Jove's thunderbolts. Hopewell leaders may have carried them as badges of sacred authority.

A terra cotta (ceramic) human effigy from the Turner Mound site near the Little Miami River in Hamilton County. Charles Metz excavated the Turner Mound site in 1882 under the direction of Frederic Ward Putnam, then director of the Peabody Museum of Archaeology and Ethnology at Harvard University in Massachusetts.

IN SOME HISTORIC NATIVE AMERICAN SOCIETIES, WOMEN ALSO COULD BE IMPORTANT leaders. At some Hopewell mounds, a few women were treated royally in death, suggesting that they too had been leaders. Burial 7 in Mound 25 at the Hopewell site was a woman who, although buried alongside a man, was more richly adorned with artifacts than her consort. She was buried with copper plates under her head, hips, and knees, more than 50 copper ear spools, hundreds of freshwater pearl beads, and copper-covered buttons. These beads and buttons likely adorned finely woven textiles that did not survive the centuries of burial. The nose of this woman, along with that of her male companion, had been replaced with one fashioned of copper.

A woman buried at the Turner site in Hamilton County was, according to an analysis done by N'omi Greber, the second highest ranking individual buried at the site. She was buried with six copper ear spools (one in each hand, with the others grouped by her left shoulder), bear teeth ornaments (two of which were inlaid with pearls), a piece of galena, a marine shell, a copper ax, and several flint bladelets. She was buried on a bed of large, flat stones and the ax and bladelets were found under the stones, so it is possible they were not intended to be part of her burial offerings. Nonetheless, it was a rich trove to accompany any one person, and it is a clear indication that women could achieve positions of high status in Hopewell society.

HOPEWELL CULTURE NATIONAL HISTORICAL PARK

Ross County

By Jennifer Pederson, Archaeologist, Hopewell Culture National Historical Park.

The mounds and enclosures that dot the landscape are visible reminders of a people that lived in southern Ohio about two thousand years ago. Today archaeologists recognize the people as participating in the Hopewell culture, most notable for remarkable earthworks and exquisite artifacts. The National Park Service preserves the remnants of an ancient people at Hopewell Culture National Historical Park in Chillicothe, Ohio.

The park, formerly Mound City Group National Monument, was originally established in 1923 to preserve the earthworks at the Mound City Group. Here, a rectangular enclosure surrounds at least 23 mounds within a 15-acre area. The park grew in 1980 with the addition of the Hopeton Earthworks, an earthen complex consisting of a rectangular enclosure attached to a large circle. Legislation enacted in 1992 renamed the park and expanded

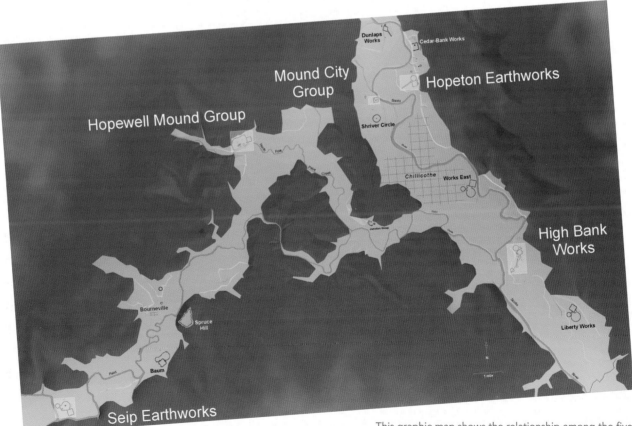

This graphic map shows the relationship among the five sites within Hopewell Culture National Historical Park, as well as about a dozen other major archaeological sites documented in Ross County.

HOPEWELL CULTURE NATIONAL HISTORICAL PARK

park boundaries to include three additional earthworks. The Hopewell Mound Group, the namesake of the Hopewell culture, spans over 130 acres and contains more than forty mounds amid two large enclosures. The circle-octagon enclosures of the High Bank Works mimic characteristics seen at the Newark Earthworks, some 60 miles distant. The tripartite construction of the Seip Earthworks, incorporating a small circle, an irregular circle, and a perfect square, is a form seen in other Ross County earthworks. In combination, these five earthwork complexes tell part of the story that was set in Ohio at the same time the Coliseum was under construction in Rome. Significantly, this park is the only federal area that protects archaeological remnants of the Hopewell culture.

The primary purpose of the park is to "preserve, protect, and interpret" archaeological remnants of the Hopewell culture, including the mounds and enclosures and associated artifacts. Without preservation, many of these earthworks might have been forever lost to encroaching development or agricultural pursuits. Information would have been destoyed about why these people built earthworks, how they hand-carried baskets of soil, and why they buried precious objects under the mounds. Fortunately, these sites have been preserved and anthropological research is currently unearthing information to provide invaluable insight about the people of the ancient Ohio Hopewell culture.

The park's headquarters, research laboratory and visitor's center are located at the Mound City Group (above) northwest of Chillicothe. Here, visitors can tour the site grounds and a small museum with exhibits and information about the park's four other archaeological sites. Two of these additional sites are accessible to the general public. The other two are closed to the public. Hopewell Culture National Historical Park's cultural resources management facility attracts researchers from all over the world. Archaeologist Jarrod Burks (right) holds a copper plate from the Mound City Group, one of over 148,000 artifacts and documents preserved in the park's repository.

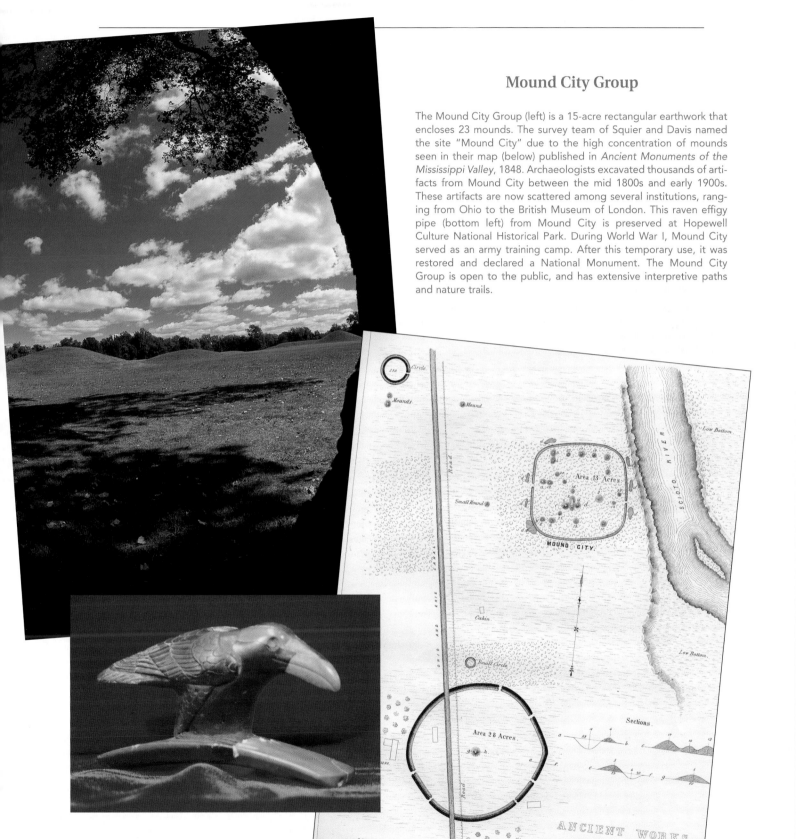

Mound City Group

The Mound City Group (left) is a 15-acre rectangular earthwork that encloses 23 mounds. The survey team of Squier and Davis named the site "Mound City" due to the high concentration of mounds seen in their map (below) published in *Ancient Monuments of the Mississippi Valley*, 1848. Archaeologists excavated thousands of artifacts from Mound City between the mid 1800s and early 1900s. These artifacts are now scattered among several institutions, ranging from Ohio to the British Museum of London. This raven effigy pipe (bottom left) from Mound City is preserved at Hopewell Culture National Historical Park. During World War I, Mound City served as an army training camp. After this temporary use, it was restored and declared a National Monument. The Mound City Group is open to the public, and has extensive interpretive paths and nature trails.

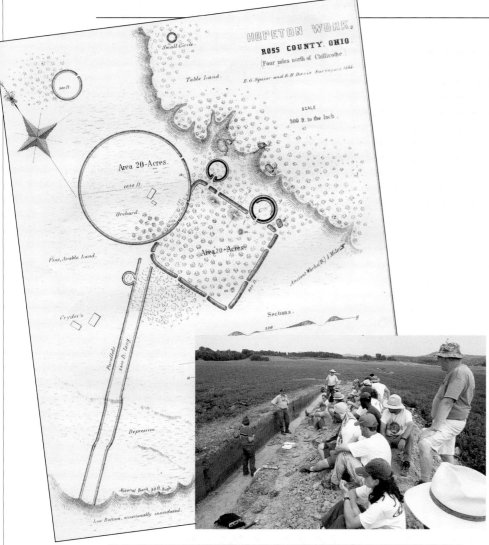

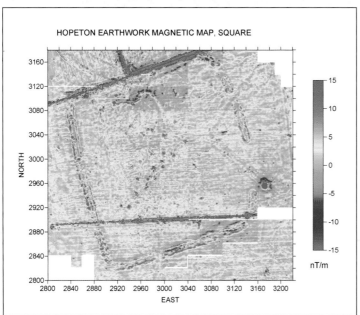

HOPETON EARTHWORK MAGNETIC MAP, SQUARE

Hopeton Earthworks

The Hopeton Earthworks is a circle and rectangular enclosure with parallel walls that stretch nearly a half-mile toward the eastern bank of the Scioto River. This 200-acre park is located just across the river from the Mound City Group. In 1848, Squier and Davis published a survey map of the site (top left) in *Ancient Monuments of the Mississippi Valley*. Beyond early surveys, little archaeological research was conducted at the Hopeton Earthworks until the National Park Service began a systematic investigation of the site in 1994. Dr. Mark Lynott, Manager, Midwest Archaeological Center, Lincoln, Nebraska, directed extensive surveys and field schools that involved archaeologists from dozens of institutions. "Although documented for over 150 years," says Dr. Lynott, "archaeology still hasn't figured out why most Ohio Hopewell earthworks were built, how they were built, or when they were built."

The investigation of Hopeton Earthworks began with a geophysical survey (magnetic) of the entire site. Archaeologists sought to identify anomalies under the heavily plowed surface, and to determine the effectiveness of this non-intrusive technology when investigating the internal structures of ancient earthworks. The geophysical survey produced a series of color magnetic maps such as this one (bottom) showing the southwest corner of the Hopeton Earthwork square. Guided by the geophysical maps, archaeologists then dug a series of trenches (center) and 2x2 meter test units to examine both the layers of wall construction and key underground features.

The investigations uncovered evidence of ritual activities—fire-clay basins, pits and fragments of ceramics, mica, bladelets, flint, stone tools and fire-cracked rock. "The Hopeton Earthworks were built with clean fill dirt carried in from outside the enclosure in a complex construction sequence over a short period of time," reports Lynott, adding, "The labor involved in moving dirt here would have been pretty substantial. We know the Ohio Hopewell weren't even full-time farmers. They were hunters and gatherers and gardeners, yet somehow managed to organize themselves to build some pretty massive earthworks. That's quite an extraordinary achievement."

The Hopeton Earthworks was nearly obliterated by farming, erosion and a large gravel mining operation. After a long legal battle, most of the site is preserved as part of Hopewell Culture National Historical Park. The Hopeton Earthworks is closed to the general public.

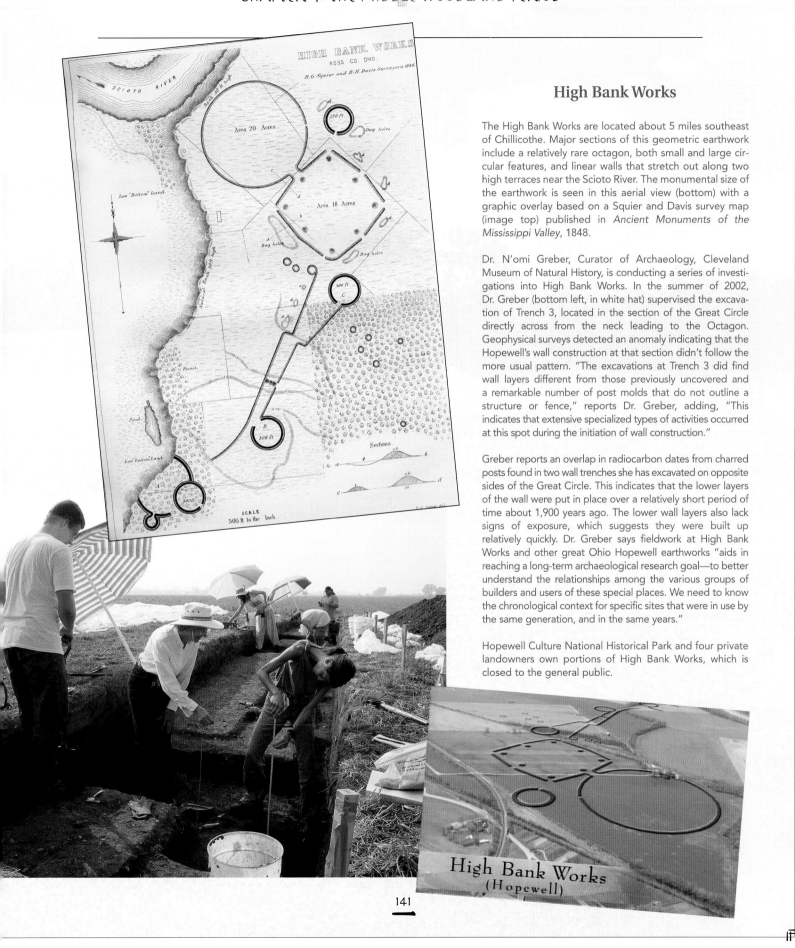

High Bank Works

The High Bank Works are located about 5 miles southeast of Chillicothe. Major sections of this geometric earthwork include a relatively rare octagon, both small and large circular features, and linear walls that stretch out along two high terraces near the Scioto River. The monumental size of the earthwork is seen in this aerial view (bottom) with a graphic overlay based on a Squier and Davis survey map (image top) published in *Ancient Monuments of the Mississippi Valley*, 1848.

Dr. N'omi Greber, Curator of Archaeology, Cleveland Museum of Natural History, is conducting a series of investigations into High Bank Works. In the summer of 2002, Dr. Greber (bottom left, in white hat) supervised the excavation of Trench 3, located in the section of the Great Circle directly across from the neck leading to the Octagon. Geophysical surveys detected an anomaly indicating that the Hopewell's wall construction at that section didn't follow the more usual pattern. "The excavations at Trench 3 did find wall layers different from those previously uncovered and a remarkable number of post molds that do not outline a structure or fence," reports Dr. Greber, adding, "This indicates that extensive specialized types of activities occurred at this spot during the initiation of wall construction."

Greber reports an overlap in radiocarbon dates from charred posts found in two wall trenches she has excavated on opposite sides of the Great Circle. This indicates that the lower layers of the wall were put in place over a relatively short period of time about 1,900 years ago. The lower wall layers also lack signs of exposure, which suggests they were built up relatively quickly. Dr. Greber says fieldwork at High Bank Works and other great Ohio Hopewell earthworks "aids in reaching a long-term archaeological research goal—to better understand the relationships among the various groups of builders and users of these special places. We need to know the chronological context for specific sites that were in use by the same generation, and in the same years."

Hopewell Culture National Historical Park and four private landowners own portions of High Bank Works, which is closed to the general public.

High Bank Works
(Hopewell)

Hopewell Mound Group

The Hopewell Mound Group is the archaeological type-site for Ohio Hopewell culture, which is named after landowner Mordecai Cloud Hopewell. Located along the North Fork of Paint Creek, Squier and Davis described this complex as "one of the largest and most interesting in the Scioto Valley." Their survey map (left) of the site entitled North Fork, Works (also known as Clark's Work) was published in *Ancient Monuments of the Mississippi Valley*, 1848. The Hopewell Mound Group is composed of a small square attached to a larger earthwork, roughly shaped like a parallelogram, with unusually thick walls that once measured 35 feet wide at the base. The survey shows more than a dozen mounds and earthworks within this enclosure, including a "D" shaped earthwork containing about seven mounds. Three of these mounds are joined together, forming an oblong mound 33-feet high and 500 feet long. Known as Mound 25, it is the largest Ohio Hopewell mound ever documented. Three major excavations of these mounds were conducted at the site between the 1840s and 1920s. These early excavations uncovered thousands of artifacts, including this copper human effigy (center) preserved at The Ohio Historical Society.

Today, archaeologists at Hopewell Culture National Historical Park avoid burial mounds. Instead, they are investigating how ancient American Indians used the space between the mounds. Archaeologists are conducting systematic geophysical surveys within Hopewell enclosures to identify underground anomalies for test excavations. This strategic archaeology has yielded some surprising discoveries. At Hopewell Mound Group, archaeologists found numerous undocumented features such as earth ovens, trash pits, and a circular ditch that is probably related to the earlier Adena culture.

In 2002, they also uncovered a long, shallow linear pit (bottom) filled with charcoal, charred wood and large fire-cracked rocks. Archaeologist Jarrod Burks reports this may be the "remains of a large bonfire built for a ceremony, feast or dance." The "bonfire" pit dates to the later stages of the Early Woodland period. Indeed, there is archaeological evidence at the Hopewell Mound Group site from the Archaic through the Late Prehistoric periods. "We're finding these Ohio Hopewell earthworks are not only more complex than previously believed," says Burks, "but were used by cultural groups other than the Hopewell over a much longer period of time."

The Hopewell Mound Group site is open to the public. It is accessible from a nearby parking and observation area and a bike trail that runs through the site. The National Park Service has acquired most of the land, and has plans for additional accommodations and exhibits.

Seip Earthworks

Seip Earthworks is one of several Ohio Hopewell complexes in the Paint Creek Valley of eastern Ross County. Hopewell Culture National Historical Park and The Ohio Historical Society preserve portions of this irregularly shaped earthwork that encloses about 121 acres. Squier and Davis documented the site's mounds and embankments in this survey map (image left) published in *Ancient Monuments of the Mississippi Valley*, 1848. The Ohio State Archaeological and Historical Society conducted excavations of the Seip-Pricer Mound from 1925 to 1928. Located in the center of the largest circular earthwork, the Seip-Pricer Mound contained over 100 graves and thousands of artifacts, including about 18,000 freshwater pearl beads (reconstructed necklace, center). The mound was then restored to the condition seen today (bottom). Seip Earthworks State Memorial, which is open to the public, preserves a rectangular section of this large Ohio Hopewell complex. Hopewell Culture National Historical Park has acquired or is authorized to acquire most of the surrounding site.

The copper, galena, marine shells, and other materials not native to Ohio that are found in Hopewell burials, reveal that they, far more than any previous or subsequent people, sought the exotic and invested such rare items with great power. Copper, for example, had been important to the Adena people and to many Late Archaic groups, but the Ohio Hopewell people obtained far more copper than any previous culture. Hopewellian earspools and celts are the most widespread copper artifacts. They have been found from eastern Iowa to western New York and from southern Ontario to northern Alabama. Hopewell craftsmen obtained the copper from the upper Great Lakes. They also obtained mica from the southern Appalachian mountains, marine shells from the Gulf Coast, and obsidian from the Rocky Mountains.

Some archaeologists have explained the presence of such material in the mounds of Ohio as evidence of trade and have referred to the region encompassed by the source areas for all of these "commodities" as the Hopewell "Interaction Sphere." If it was merely "trade," and if these things were obtained in economic transactions, what did the Ohio folks give in exchange for all of these exotic materials? There is actually very little evidence of stuff from Ohio at sites at the other end of this Interaction Sphere. One apparent exception to this curious disparity is Ohio's remarkable Flint Ridge flint. Archaeologists have found bladelets crafted from Flint Ridge flint at sites scattered throughout the Hopewell world, but those who suggest that this was Ohio's major export in a reciprocal trade network have not done their arithmetic. Typically, only handfuls of Flint Ridge flint bladelets are found at sites more than a few hundred miles from the Licking County quarries, whereas bushels of copper and mica are found in Ohio Hopewell mounds. This would hardly appear to be an indication of reciprocal exchange. Perhaps these exotic materials were intended as ritual offerings or gifts, and not goods to barter.

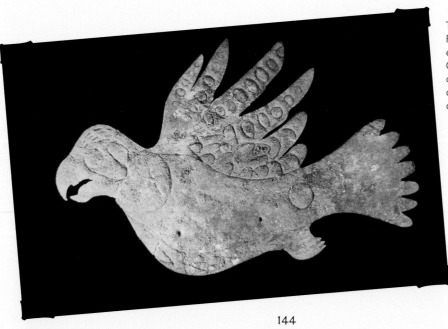

This effigy, possibly of a Peregrine falcon, was excavated from Mound City in Ross County. It was crafted from copper obtained from sources over 600 miles away along the coast of Lake Superior.

Ancient Ohio
Sources of Ohio Hopewell Exotic Materials

The Hopewell Interaction Sphere
(ca. 2.100 to 1,500 BP)

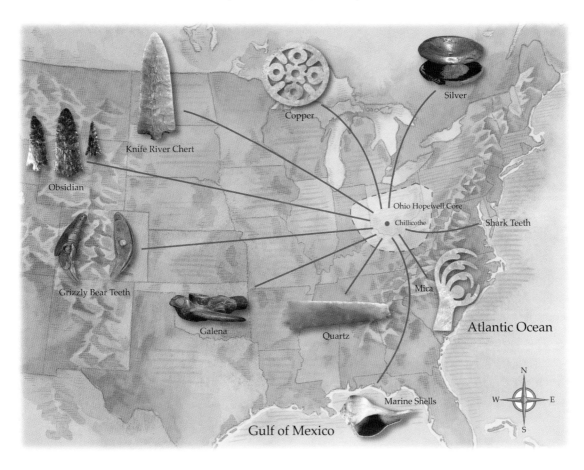

The Ohio Hopewell exchanged materials with other American Indian groups throughout eastern North America. Archaeologists have been able to pinpoint the sources for some of these exotic or foreign materials that may have been obtained through long distance travel or group-to-group trade networks. It's unknown these exotic materials were exchanged as trade goods for Ohio materials, or as a form of tribute or gifts to solidify alliances. The ambiguity underlying both the methods and motivations of this exchange network is why many archaeologists prefer more neutral descriptive terms such as "Hopewell Interaction Sphere," a concept coined by archaeologist Joseph Caldwell in the early 1960s. Interaction spheres exist when independent societies exchange material goods or information - symbols, ideas, inventions or a set of common values and religious beliefs. The Ohio Hopewell interaction sphere stretched from the Atlantic Ocean to the Rocky Mountains and the Upper Great Lakes to the Gulf of Mexico. Once obtained, Ohio Hopewell craftspeople transformed these exotic materials into beautiful ceremonial objects and personal ornaments that were often buried with individuals of high status in their vibrant society.

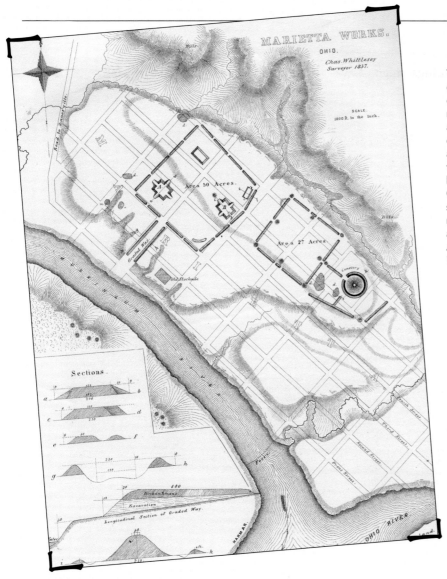

The Marietta Earthworks are located on a broad terrace near the confluence of the Muskingum and Ohio rivers in Washington County. This ancient complex of rectangular earthworks enclosing both conical and platform mounds was among the first ancient earthworks documented by Europeans traveling down the Ohio River in the late 1700s. This survey map (left) of the site was made by Charles Whittlesey in 1837, and published as Plate XXVI in *Ancient Monuments of the Mississippi Valley*, 1848.

THE STAGE FOR MUCH OF HOPEWELLIAN RITUAL AND THE REAL HALLMARK OF THEIR CULTURE was their monumental architecture. Hopewell peoples built elaborate earthen enclosures on a fantastically large scale. They built geometric enclosures on the broad terraces of southern Ohio's major rivers and more irregularly-shaped earthen walls, following the contours of flat-topped hills and bluffs, in southwestern Ohio. A significant feature of these sites, not fully appreciated until recently, is the abundance of wooden architecture that accompanied and/or preceded the construction of the earthworks.

Few traces of these monumental wooden structures remain, but archaeologist Frank Cowan and his colleagues have painstakingly uncovered hundreds of postmolds at the Stubbs Earthworks site in Warren County. The postmolds mark a variety of circular, crescentic, rectangular, and square structures. Some represent typical Hopewell houses with their hearths and earth ovens, but the archaeologists have found remarkably little household garbage associated with these sites. This suggests they represent more or less temporary housing for the large numbers of seasonal visitors to the ceremonial center. Other buildings might have been specialized craft houses, Big Houses, or gathering places for different clans or cults. One structure in particular stands out as a ritual center every bit as monumental in scale as the earthworks. Excavating in an area where a 19th century map showed the former presence of a circular earthwork, Cowan found 172 postmolds forming a circle 240 feet in diameter. The posts were the size of modern telephone poles. At some point, when this gigantic "Woodhenge" had served its purpose, the Hopewell people removed the giant posts and carefully filled in the holes with soil from other parts of the site. Finally, they mounded earth over the filled-in postholes creating a circular earthwork. Whether this marked the end of rituals at this location or simply a change in the kinds of rituals performed there is not known.

THE MARIETTA EARTHWORKS

While most of the Marietta Eathworks is associated with the Ohio Hopewell culture, some features seem to fit earlier and later American Indian cultures. The Conus Mound (top left), a 30 feet high conical mound surrounded by a circular embankment, reflects the mound building style of the earlier Adena culture. Conus Mound is preserved in Mound Cemetery along with the graves of early American settlers.

Capitolium Mound (center), one of two platform mounds, serves as the foundation of The Washington County Public Library.

The Marietta Earthworks also once held a set of parallel walls, 680 feet long and 10 to 20 feet high, that were made of earth and clay. The founders of Marietta called this feature the "Sacra Via" or Sacred Way. The Sacra Via led from the Quadranaou platform mound (preserved today as a park) to the eastern bank of the Muskingum River. The route of the Sacra Via is preserved as a narrow park (bottom, at sunset on the winter solstice) in a residential district.

STUBBS EARTHWORKS
AN OHIO HOPEWELL "WOODHENGE"

Warren County

By Dr. Frank L. Cowan, Consulting Archaeologist, F. Cowan & Associates; Research Associate, Cincinnati Museum Center.

Some archaeological discoveries happen just by plain dumb luck. Such was the case with the discovery of the great Hopewell "Woodhenge" at the Stubbs Earthworks site near the Little Miami River in Warren County.

On a chilly late September morning, Carl Doyle's backhoe scraped away the last plow-disturbed surface soil from Transect 14. With the surface soil removed, Ted Sunderhaus and I began searching for evidence of 2,000-year-old pits, hearths and postholes with shovels and trowels. We'd done this many times before during almost 5 months of steady fieldwork, a salvage project sponsored by the Cincinnati Museum Center in cooperation of the Little Miami School District. With the volunteer assistance of many archaeologists and area residents, we'd already learned much about the many kinds of wooden buildings that the Hopewell once built and used, both within and immediately surrounding what had once been a large "circle-and-square" earthwork. With only two weeks to go before the start of construction of the school, we were anxious to learn more before the bulldozers arrived. Although the surface soil in this part of the site contained no artifacts, our magnetometer survey indicated an unusual anomaly, perhaps another Hopewell house or some large ceremonial feature.

Ordinarily, we stopped backhoe work after opening up such a large transect. Subsoil "bakes out" and hardens once exposed, making it more difficult to detect subtle changes in the earth. But, Ted thought it a shame to send Carl home after only two hours of work. He suggested Carl start another sampling transect straight south from Transect 14. Our expectations for Transect 15 were low since no major anomalies appeared in the magnetometer survey of that area.

However, Ted soon noticed what appeared to be a large pit feature in the new transect, which he cleaned off and marked with an orange wire-flag. Then, he spotted and marked two more, each about 2 meters apart. As Carl uncovered yet another, Ted realized that they had hit the edge of a very long, gradual arc of huge postholes. With increasing wonderment, they continued exposing postholes until nightfall.

Over the next several days, we uncovered 172 large postholes that formed a nearly perfect circle 80 yards in diameter. The circle seemed to lie where a circular earthwork had been mapped in 1839. School district officials and the construction crew agreed to work around us as we excavated the postholes, each large enough to hold posts the size of small telephone poles. No one had ever seen this kind of wooden architecture in 150 years of Hopewell archaeology.

The Hopewell had dismantled the structure, carefully pulling the immense poles out of the ground and refilling the holes with dirt, in many cases with dirt brought from distant parts of the site. Then, they covered the postholes with a low circular wall of earth. We have now dated charcoal from several post molds, and we know that the wooden structure and its earthen replacement were built sometime between about 1,810 to 1,730 radiocarbon years ago (BP).

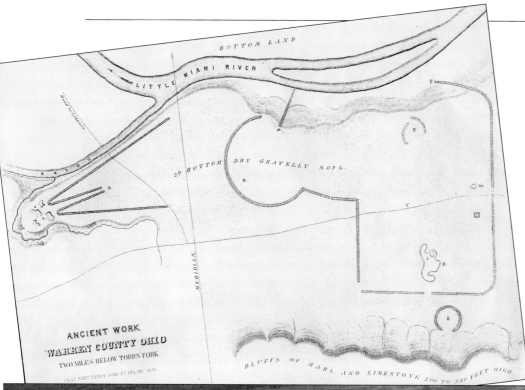

ANCIENT WORK
WARREN COUNTY OHIO
TWO MILES BELOW TODDS FORK

The magnitude of the Stubbs "woodhenge" is seen in an aerial photograph taken shortly after this circle of 172 large post molds, 80 yards in diameter, was discovered during salvage excavations in 1998. The post molds correspond to the location of an open circle embankment (figure E, lower right corner of map) marked in a survey map made by Charles Whittlesey in 1839. Most of the visible features of this massive Ohio Hopewell complex have been lost to farming, gravel mining and development.

STUBBS EARTHWORKS

Recognition that such monumental wooden architecture existed in Hopewellian times came about purely by accident. We excavated Transect 15 just because we thought it unfair to ask Carl to quit work so early one September morning. Had we placed the excavation even just four meters to the east, we would have missed this extraordinary structure entirely. Had we staked out the excavation transect a few meters to the west, we might have encountered a few large "pit features" without recognizing their alignment. For all of the science and rational logic we try to bring to archaeological excavations, pure luck and random chance still play an important part.

The salvage excavations at the Stubbs Earthworks site were conducted over two summers using high technology, heavy equipment and trowels. Archaeologists first identified features under the site during magnetometer surveys in 1998. These features were then excavated (image right) in a series of transects or long rectangular trenches. The plow zone, about 16 inches of disturbed soil, is removed with a backhoe. The archaeologists then use shovels and trowels to shave away "clean" layers of soil that hold ancient pit features, hearths and post molds. By sheer luck, the excavation team hit the edge of a circle of large post molds (right), each large enough for a modern telephone pole. The archaeologists followed the arc of the post molds until they uncovered a nearly perfect circle.

The Stubbs Earthwork "woodhenge" is depicted in this computer graphic image (center) created by designers with the "EarthWorks" project, The Center for the Electronic Reconstruction of Historical and Archaeological Sites, University of Cincinnati.

Dr. Frank Cowan reports that excavations of the post molds and radiocarbon tests have provided archaeologists with unprecedented insights into Ohio Hopewell culture. We found this 'woodhenge' underneath the only Ohio Hopewell open circle embankment ever excavated. I wouldn't be surprised if many other such embankments cover this type of earlier wooden architecture," says Cowan.

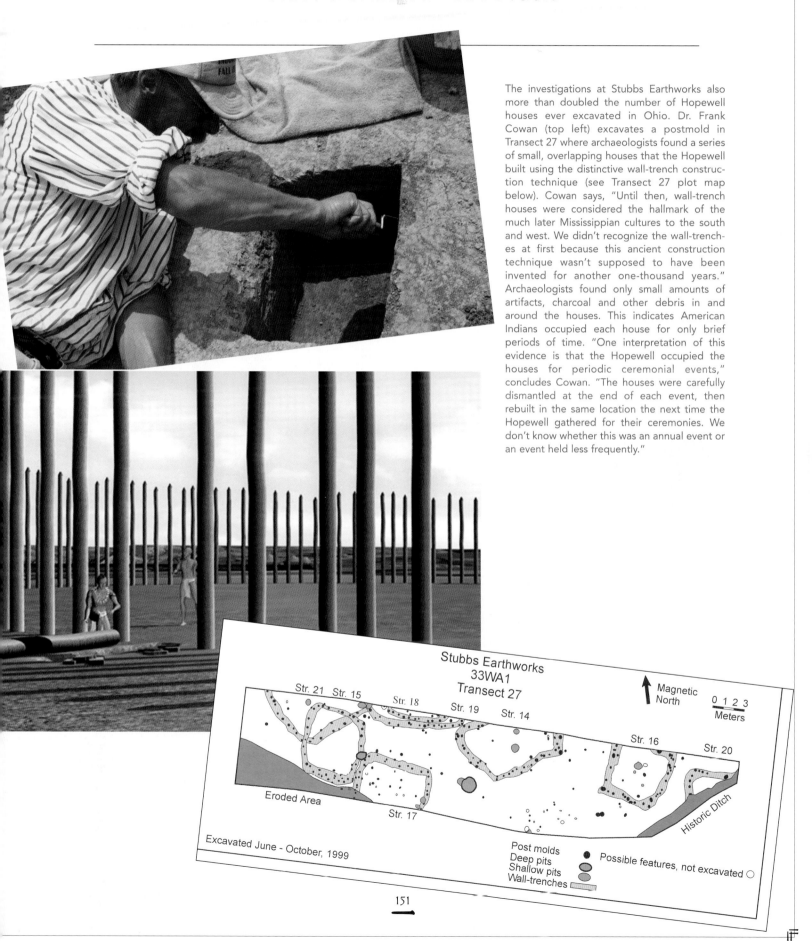

The investigations at Stubbs Earthworks also more than doubled the number of Hopewell houses ever excavated in Ohio. Dr. Frank Cowan (top left) excavates a postmold in Transect 27 where archaeologists found a series of small, overlapping houses that the Hopewell built using the distinctive wall-trench construction technique (see Transect 27 plot map below). Cowan says, "Until then, wall-trench houses were considered the hallmark of the much later Mississippian cultures to the south and west. We didn't recognize the wall-trenches at first because this ancient construction technique wasn't supposed to have been invented for another one-thousand years." Archaeologists found only small amounts of artifacts, charcoal and other debris in and around the houses. This indicates American Indians occupied each house for only brief periods of time. "One interpretation of this evidence is that the Hopewell occupied the houses for periodic ceremonial events," concludes Cowan. "The houses were carefully dismantled at the end of each event, then rebuilt in the same location the next time the Hopewell gathered for their ceremonies. We don't know whether this was an annual event or an event held less frequently."

Stubbs Earthworks
33WA1
Transect 27

Magnetic North

0 1 2 3
Meters

Str. 21 Str. 15
Str. 18
Str. 19 Str. 14
Str. 16
Str. 20

Eroded Area

Str. 17

Historic Ditch

Excavated June - October, 1999

Post molds
Deep pits
Shallow pits
Wall-trenches

Possible features, not excavated

The Hopewell culture built its most impressive geometric earthworks at the site of modern Newark on a high glacial terrace along Raccoon Creek. This huge and elaborate ceremonial complex included a Great Circle more than a thousand feet in diameter and a 50-acre octagon connected to another circle only slightly smaller than the Great Circle. The entire Newark Earthworks encompassed more than four square miles.

According to Cambridge University archaeologist Chris Scarre, author of a recent book cataloging seventy wonders of the ancient world, the complex of Hopewellian earthworks at Newark is one of only three North American sites that qualify as an ancient wonder. (The other two are Chaco Canyon in New Mexico and Cahokia in Illinois.) These earthworks were built on a scale that dwarfs many of the Old World's most famous sites. For example, the Great Pyramid of Egypt would fit comfortably within the square enclosure at Newark. The Octagon would hold four Roman Colosseums, and Stonehenge would fit within the small circular enclosure located at the Octagon's southeastern gateway. And yet, the subtler contours of the grass-covered earthen walls are less imposing and seem less impressive to our modern sensibilities.

An aerial view of the Octagon Earthworks (left) shows the embankments of this Ohio Hopewell complex preserved within a golf course in Newark. The nearly perfect circular enclosure is 1,054 feet in diameter, and covers 20 acres. The Octagon has eight walls, each measuring about 550 feet long and from five to six feet in height.

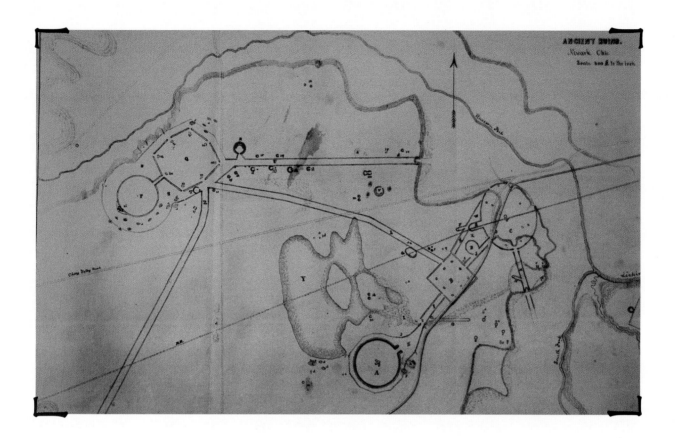

The Newark Earthworks in Licking County are one of the most complex geometric earthworks ever built by the Ohio Hopewell people. Antiquarians and archaeologists have been mapping this monumental earthwork since the 1820s. A map published by Squier and Davis in 1848 was thought to be the most accurate survey of the entire site. Recently, archaeologists re-discovered a map made by the Salisbury brothers in the 1860s. James Salisbury, a local physician and inventor of the Salisbury steak, and his brother Charles prepared this survey map for a book that was never published due to the Civil War. The Salisbury map languished in the archives of the American Antiquarian Society in Worcester, Massachusetts. In the 1990s, Ohio archaeologists recognized the importance of the Salisbury's survey, drawn just before agriculture and development obliterated most of the remaining features of the Newark Earthworks. Today, The Ohio Historical Society preserves three portions of this massive complex as The Newark Earthworks State Memorial - the Octagon Earthworks, the Great Circle Earthworks and the Wright Earthworks.

The Newark Earthworks originally sprawled across a low plateau nearly surrounded by three streams. Since 1800, however, the cities of Newark and Heath have expanded across this rich landscape plowing over and engulfing the monumental geometry. But, while much of Newark's ancient grandeur has been lost, significant portions are preserved in public parks, backyards, and wood lots. The most important surviving remnants are the Great Circle and Octagon Earthworks.

FORT ANCIENT STATE MEMORIAL

Warren County

By Jack K. Blosser, Site Manager, Fort Ancient State Memorial, Ohio Historical Society.

Situated 245 feet above the Little Miami River in southwestern Ohio's Warren County is Fort Ancient State Memorial, the largest prehistoric hilltop enclosure in the United States. Constructed over 2,000 years ago by Mound Builders using small basket loads of soil, it is estimated to have taken approximately 400 years (ca. 100BC-AD 290) to complete the 18,000 feet of earth walls within the 100 acre complex.

Visitors to the memorial will see many archaeological features including crescent mounds, stone faced mounds, stone pavements, reconstructed stone circles and rings, and small ponding areas. Nearly 2.5 of the 3.5 miles of earthworks are still visable throughout the site. Archaeologists estimate that Fort Ancient is composed of approximately 553,000 cubic yards of soil, which translates to 200

miles of commercial grade dump trucks, placed end for end. Visitors can also walk over three miles of hiking trails throughout the site, look at two beautiful overlooks of the Little Miami River Valley, or possibly take in an afternoon lunch in the picnic area.

The first documentation of Fort Ancient can be seen in the *Portfolio* magazine of Philadelphia, PA, published in 1809. Archaeologists and surveyors visited the site throughout the 19th Century but the first systematic excavation of the site occurred from 1887-1890 by Warren King Moorehead who convinced the state to make the site the first state park in 1891.

Over the years there has been several interpretations as to how the site functioned. One reference suggested the site was used to ward off mastodon attacks, while another suggested

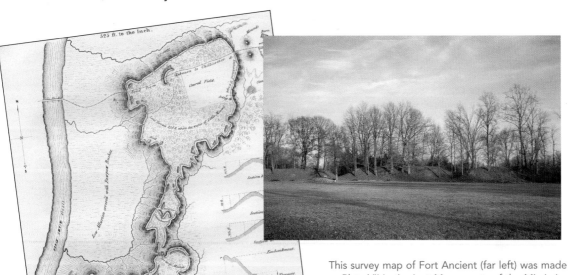

The earthen walls of Fort Ancient run nearly 3.5 miles along a plateau above the Little Miami River. The highest walls (left), up to 23 feet tall, are found where the landscape flattens out at the northeastern side of the North Fort.

This survey map of Fort Ancient (far left) was made by John Locke and published as Plate VII in *Ancient Monuments of the Mississippi Valley*, 1848. Locke's supplementary map (bottom right corner) shows a set of parallel walls that extended more than 1,350 feet from the Twin Mounds just outside the northeastern gateway to a small mound outside the main earthwork.

the site was used for prehistoric sporting events and competitions. Although many early archaeologists thought Fort Ancient was used as a military outpost, the site is now viewed as a major ceremonial complex where hundreds of people gathered at specific times of the year to hold social and ceremonial observances.

One of the most interesting archaeological components is the evidence of archaeoastronomy. There are four small circular, stone faced mounds approximately 512 feet apart that form a nearly perfect square. By watching the sun and the moon rises that occurred within the "U" shaped gaps within the walls, the Hopewell people had the ability to have ceremonial and social observances at specific times of the year. It seems that the sun was used for annual events while the moon was used in conjunction with a decadal event.

Today visitors can walk through Fort Ancient's museum with a 9,000 square foot exhibit space that spans nearly 15,000 years of Ohio Valley prehistory. A reconstructed prehistoric garden that depicts crops grown over the last 2,000 years is connected behind the museum. Children can also play in a 1,000 square foot hands on area in the Sprint Center for Learning.

Fort Ancient contains many features, including stone-capped mounds reconstructed from archaeological evidence. One stone-capped mound (above), in the North Fort is thought to be the sighting post for tracking important solar and lunar alignments.

About 10,000 students visit Fort Ancient each year through organized field trips. This popular education program combines staff and volunteer instruction with interactive tours of the site museum, traditional garden, a reconstructed house and grounds. Fourth-grade students from Kilgour Elementary School in Cincinnati complete a scavenger hunt in the museum (bottom right), and learn about ancient technologies (top right) by throwing a safe replica of a spear using an atlatl. In the winter, Fort Ancient has an innovative "distance learning" program that connects site staff and educational resources to classrooms across the state.

THE POLLOCK WORKS

Greene County

By Dr. Robert V. Riordan, Professor and Chair, Department of Sociology and Anthropology, Wright State University.

Pollock is a hilltop earthwork located in Greene County, Ohio that was built during the Middle Woodland period. Its embankments, which are between 1-3 meters high, were formed of earth and stone and are situated on the west and north-west sides of an oval-shaped 12-acre limestone plateau. The plateau is naturally bounded by cliffs between 3-15 meters high around the rest of its perimeter, so the artificial walls serve to complete the isolation of the enclosed acreage from its immediate environment. The waters of Massie's Creek flow along the north side of the site, 7 meters below the embankments. They emerge just west of the plateau from between the vertical rock walls of a scenic gorge.

The site is owned and administered by the Greene County Department of Recreation, Parks and Cultural Arts. It is located within Indian Mound Reserve, a wooded park of over 160 acres that also contains the 10-meter high Williamson Mound, several rockshelters that were used as campsites since Archaic times, and numerous historic archaeological resources. The site has been investigatied by staff and students from the Field School in Archaeology of Wright State University since 1981.

Many years of archaeological work at Pollock have revealed a great deal about it, and by extension about other Hopewell hilltop enclosures. One major datum is that its construction appears to

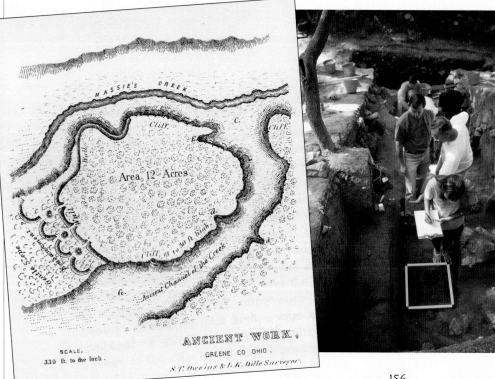

This survey map of the Pollock Works (left) by S.T. Owens and L.K. Dille was published as Plate XII, No. 3, in *Ancient Monuments of the Mississippi Valley*, 1848.

The Pollock Works is the most thoroughly studied Ohio Hopewell hilltop enclosure. Since 1981, Dr. Robert Riordan (blue shirt left), has conducted a field school here with archaeology students from Wright State University, and dozens of volunteers. This extensive research led to the discovery of wooden architecture within the earthen walls of the southwestern gateway. The entire complex was built in at least five major stages over a period of about 225 years.

The Indian Mound Reserve preserves the Pollock Works and the Williamson Mound (left), a 28-foot high conical mound built in the style of the Adena culture. The Pollock Works and Williamson Mound are accessible from public nature trails.

This computer graphic depicts the Pollock Works as it may have looked after the Ohio Hopewell constructed a wooden and plaster stockade along a barrier wall and bluff top edge about 1,820 to 1,722 years ago. The north gateway and central gateway are seen in this frame from an animation created by the "EarthWorks" project, The Center for the Electronic Reconstruction of Historical and Archaeological Sites, University of Cincinnati.

have involved five major stages that began in the first century A.D. The first three stages resulted in the building of the barrier wall that first served to isolate the hilltop acreage by connecting the creek bluff with the cliff to the south. The central and northern gateways were formed as part of this construction. The earthwork is believed to have been built to satisfy the unknown ritual needs of its builders, creating a special (sacred) space within which they may have conducted activities that were meaningful to them. A second major discovery at the site has been the remnants of a timber and mud-plastered stockade that was built in the late second century A.D., on top of the barrier wall sections and on what was until then the previously-unaltered edge of the bluff that overlooks Massie's Creek. This construction seems to have radically transformed the place, possibly to satisfy newly-risen defensive needs. Then, within a few years of its construction, this structure was burned and allowed to collapse toward the earthwork's interior. The smoldering remains were then immediately covered by a final mantle of soil that was added to the top of the barrier wall sections, and also deposited to form the meter-high perimeter embankment that overlooks Massie's Creek. It is thought that the destruction of the stockade may have signaled the rededication of the earthwork to its original purpose(s). While limestone was used to face the exterior of the barrier wall embankments during each construction stage, a limestone pavement was constructed on the exterior of the central gateway during the fifth and final stage.

After about A.D. 225-250 no further architectural changes seem to have been made, and the Pollock Works was sometime thereafter abandoned by its builders. The reasons for this have not been determined.

The Great Circle is the best preserved of all the large geometric earthworks built by the Hopewell people. Walking amid the trees encompassed by the walls of this huge enclosure, the visitor might almost forget that she is surrounded by a 21st century Ohio city. That same sense of timelessness is not possible at the Octagon Earthworks, since it serves as the grounds for a modern golf course, but here too the monumental Hopewellian geometry is remarkably intact.

NEWARK'S GREAT CIRCLE

The Great Circle encloses 30 acres and measures 1,200 feet in diameter, the length of almost four football fields. This massive Ohio Hopewell earthwork has walls ranging from five to fourteen feet high, a deep interior ditch, and a large gateway facing the northeast. Historically, the Great Circle served as a fairground, horserace track, army training camp and amusement park until transferred to The Ohio Historical Society in 1933. The site was then restored to its present condition as a public cultural park.

In 1928, The Ohio Historical Society excavated Eagle Mound, a low central mound that was found to cover the site of a Hopewell Big House. In 1992, archaeologists excavated a section of the Great Circle Gateway to determine how and when the walls were constructed. Initially, the builders erected a series of small mounds to lay out the extent of the circle (graphic, bottom). Then, they dug the ditch and the embankment (graphic, top). Finally, they obtained bright yellow-brown earth from deep pits. This special earth was deposited between the crest of the existing dark-brown embankment and the edge of the ditch.

"The Ohio Hopewell may have filled the interior ditch with water to create a sacred circle," according to Dr. Bradley T. Lepper, Curator of Archaeology, The Ohio Historical Society. "No other enclosure within the Newark Earthworks contains an interior ditch. The Great Circle may have required specialized features for the ceremonies performed here over two-thousand years ago."

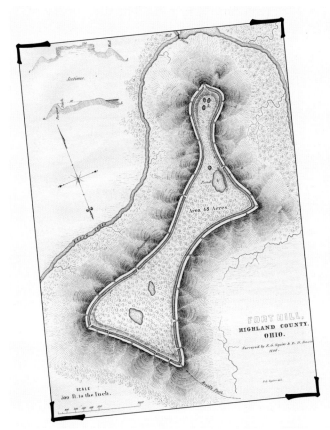

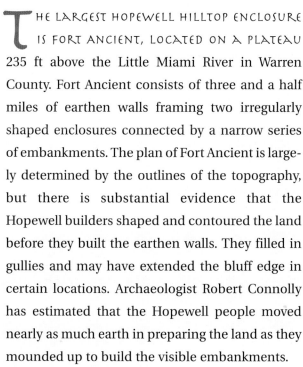

FORT HILL STATE MEMORIAL

Fort Hill State Memorial is a 48-acre hilltop enclosure situated high above Brush Creek in Highland County. Squier and Davis made this survey map of the site (right) in the 1800s.

Fort Hill is protected within a nature preserve. Trails lead up to and around this hilltop enclosure whose crumbling earth and stone walls are overgrown with trees, similar to the state of most ancient American Indian earthworks when first surveyed. In January of 1934, aviation pioneer Dache Reeves took an aerial photograph (above) of Fort Hill that shows the 1.6 mile long walls following the contours of the ridge.

THE LARGEST HOPEWELL HILLTOP ENCLOSURE IS FORT ANCIENT, LOCATED ON A PLATEAU 235 ft above the Little Miami River in Warren County. Fort Ancient consists of three and a half miles of earthen walls framing two irregularly shaped enclosures connected by a narrow series of embankments. The plan of Fort Ancient is largely determined by the outlines of the topography, but there is substantial evidence that the Hopewell builders shaped and contoured the land before they built the earthen walls. They filled in gullies and may have extended the bluff edge in certain locations. Archaeologist Robert Connolly has estimated that the Hopewell people moved nearly as much earth in preparing the land as they mounded up to build the visible embankments.

Although the hilltop enclosures often are called "forts," such as Fort Ancient and Fort Hill, it is extremely unlikely that this was their intended function—or at least their sole purpose. The Fort Ancient site, for example, is simply too big and there are too many openings in the walls for it to have served as an effective defensive structure. Archaeologist Robert Riordan has studied the Pollock Works in Greene County and discovered that this enclosure may have been used as a fortification for a brief period. Riordan found the burned remains of a palisade buried beneath a portion of the embankments. But Pollock and the other hilltop enclosures seem to have been predominantly ceremonial centers much like their more obviously geometric incarnations on the broad terraces of the major river valleys.

OHIO ARCHAEOASTRONOMY

By Dr. Ray M. Hively, Professor of Physics and Astronomy, and Dr. Robert L. Horn, Professor of Philosophy (emeritus), Earlham Collage.

Archaeoastronomy is an interdisciplinary inquiry, which seeks evidence of astronomical knowledge among the artifacts of ancient societies. Where there are no written records, the first approach to the question of what, if any, astronomy a given society practiced, is to ask whether any remains of their architecture show preferred orientations on unique horizon rise or set events: most notably the extreme (north or south) rise and set points of the sun and moon. Such preferred orientations might serve significant ritual or calendrical purposes.

What is a 'preferred orientation' on a unique horizon rise or set event? The first consideration is the geometry of the earthen and/or stone architecture of the site. The geometry itself must point out a position on the local horizon. A circle alone suggests no horizon orientation. A straight wall suggests two opposite orientations. Once it is established that what is evident on the ground today is what the Hopewell builders designed more than 1500 years ago, the major linear features of the construction can be tested against astronomical tables which list the known rise and set times of sun, moon, and planets for any date and location.

Let us take the Newark earthworks as an example. The most prominent linear feature of the Newark works which has survived destruction is the long symmetry axis of the Observatory Circle and Octagon. Here a line more than 2800 feet long drawn from the Observatory Mound, through the avenue connecting the Observatory Circle and the Octagon, to the gate at the opposite vertex of the Octagon falls on the north lunar extreme, the north-most rise position of the moon in a cycle which repeats every 18.6 years. This is enough to suggest, but only to suggest, that the Hopewell builders oriented the circle-octagon to the north maximum moonrise. Such a single orientation, taken by itself, might well be an accident. Establishing the likelihood that such an alignment was intentionally built into the structure requires more evidence.

Dr. Ray Hively (right, on right) and Dr. Robert Horn, (right, on left) spent many hours pouring over historical surveys and documents on the ancient American Indian earthworks of the Ohio Valley. Some of the Ohio Hopewell geometric earthworks that are preserved today were restored after archaeological excavations or other uses in the early 1900s. Hively and Horn had to take these historic modifications into account before examining any ancient earthworks for astronomical alignments.

The Ohio Hopewell built the Octagon Earthworks on a monumental scale. One possible reason for the massive size of these geometric earthworks is that long, straight embankments (far right) provide longer sight lines that increase the accuracy of astronomical alignments.

When we study the design of the Newark circle and octagon we find clear signs of geometrical knowledge. Four vertices of the octagon form a square whose side matches the diameter of the associated circle. The four remaining vertices fall at the intersection of circular arcs with a radius equal to the diagonal of that square. Slight but noticeable deviations from this plan have been incorporated to align four of the octagon walls with the lunar extreme rise and set points. Octagonal symmetry has been combined with knowledge of the eight lunar extremes to build a structure, which displays five of those extremes on its symmetry axis and walls. Computer studies of alignments to be found in randomly constructed octagons show that the probability of such a combination of alignments and distortions arising by chance alone is less than one in a million.

Further features of the Newark site support the view that Hopewell builders chose preferred orientations on lunar extremes. At High Bank Works, near Chillicothe, perhaps for reasons connected with the local environment, the only other Hopewell circle-octagon earthwork is rotated 90% relative to the north maximum rise point. Yet here both lunar and solar extremes appear to have been marked.

Current evidence is insufficient to know in detail what the Hopewell intended with works such as Newark and High Bank. Sophisticated archaeological study of Hopewell geometric earthworks might establish whether other Hopewell sites repeat these lunar and solar orientations, and/or incorporate orientations to other celestial events on their local horizons.

The High Bank Works (below) has design elements that are closely related to the Octagon Earthworks in Newark. The diameters of each circle are the same. Moreover, the main axes are oriented at precisely ninety degrees to one another. High Bank Works, seen in this graphic overlay based on a Squier and Davis survey map, also encompasses the eight rise and set points of the moon that define the 18.6-year lunar cycle. However, unlike Newark's circle and octagon, High Bank Works also includes alignments for the summer and winter solstices (not shown).

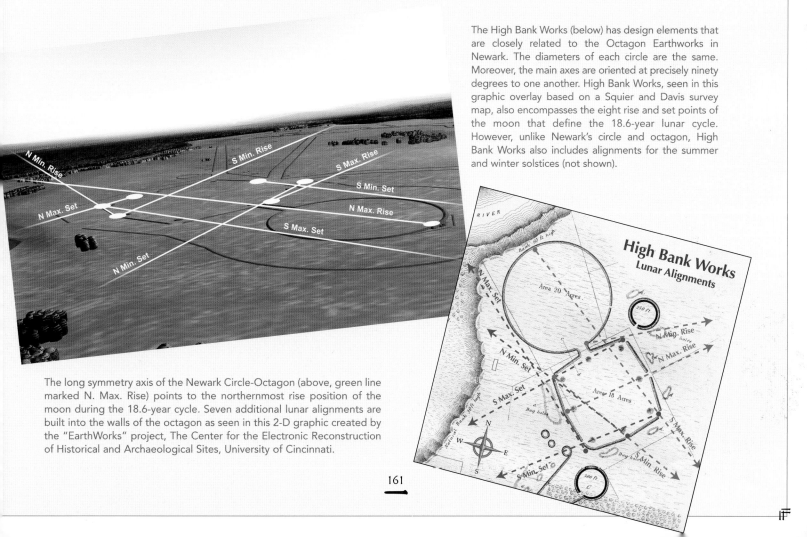

The long symmetry axis of the Newark Circle-Octagon (above, green line marked N. Max. Rise) points to the northernmost rise position of the moon during the 18.6-year cycle. Seven additional lunar alignments are built into the walls of the octagon as seen in this 2-D graphic created by the "EarthWorks" project, The Center for the Electronic Reconstruction of Historical and Archaeological Sites, University of Cincinnati.

EARTHWORKS

By John E. Hancock, Project Director, EarthWorks, The Center for the Electronic Reconstruction of Historical and Archaeological Sites, University of Cincinnati.

Founded in 1995, the Center for the Electronic Reconstruction of Historical and Archaeological Sites (CERHAS) is an interdisciplinary research and production laboratory in the College of Design, Architecture, Art, and Planning (DAAP) at the University of Cincinnati. CERHAS's research in advanced multi-media and digital imaging is applied particularly to educational, museum, artistic, and architectural treatments of vanished cultural resources.

The invisibility of the ancient Ohio Valley earthworks is likely a major reason for their steady, two-century-long decline in the public imagination. Many have been destroyed, but even those that remain, like Fort Ancient or the Newark Octagon, are hard to completely see or understand. Computer reconstructions and new multi-media approaches have enabled CERHAS to create photo-real, moving animations over the cleared,

John Hancock, Project Director, "EarthWorks," (bottom left) discusses computer animation of the Turner Earthworks site with designers in the CERHAS lab.

EarthWorks designers created this computer animation of the Turner Earthworks in stages. First, they studied historical survey maps, written accounts and archaeological research related to this Hopewell enclosure along the Little Miami River in Hamilton County. These data, dimensions, measurements and archaeological evidence, is then applied to a wire frame model (top left) with topographical landforms based on a modern USGS quadrangle map. Finally, designers add textures and colors (top right) that bring this 2,000 year-old American Indian earthwork to life.

"EarthWorks" computer animation of sites such as the Hopewell Mound Group (above) is proving to be a valuable research tool for archaeologists, allowing them to see ancient sites in various stages of their original development and from multiple perspectives.

restored earthwork sites—probably the only way that their uncanny scope, beauty, and precision can be visualized "as they existed in the imaginations of their builders," to use Roger Kennedy's wonderful phrase. Besides the old survey maps, aerial photos and the latest field data from archaeological investigations are used in the development of the models. CERHAS's exhibitions and publications also feature an interactive format with multi-media content segments distributed throughout re-created landscapes, inviting the audience to explore freely and discover a variety of stories. That variety includes viewpoints, including interviews, from archaeolo-gists, architects, artists, religion scholars, astronomers, historians, Native American leaders, and others, reflecting the idea that our understanding is an open, evolving process and that no specific discipline or knowledge-tradition "owns" either the earthworks or the truth.

All other ancient cultures who hold a place in the public imagination do so by virtue of vivid, shared images of their architectural monuments (think: Parthenon, Pyramids, etc). CERHAS seeks to provide the equivalent for these ancient native cultures, on whose sacred ground much of middle America has been built, so that they might take their rightful place in the public consciousness.

THERE WAS A SOPHISTICATED GEOMETRY UNDERLYING HOPEWELLIAN MONUMENTAL architecture. Hopewell architects and engineers built nearly perfect circles and squares to precise dimensions. For example, the circle connected to the octagon at Newark is 1,050 feet in diameter. Astronomer Ray Hively and philosopher Robert Horn have shown how this unit of measure was integral to the plan of the Newark Earthworks. The distance between Newark's two largest circles and between the centers of its octagon and square are both precisely six times the diameter of this circle. The only other circle joined to an octagon is at the High Bank Works south of Chillicothe in Ross County. That circle has exactly the same diameter. William Romain identified this same unit of measure in a total of 24 Hopewell earthwork sites. He also showed that many Hopewellian earthworks share a variety of less obvious geometric relationships. When superimposed upon one another, a number of the largest circles, squares, and octagons, from Newark to Chillicothe to Marietta, seem to "nest together in one interrelated design."

These similarities hint at connections between widely separated Hopewell centers. There is even evidence to suggest that at least some of the Hopewell earthworks were connected by parallel-walled roads, such as the "Great Hopewell Road," that may have linked Newark and Chillicothe.

The alignments of certain Hopewell earthworks also encode the apparent movements of the sun and the moon. Hively and Horn have determined that the two great octagonal enclosures that are connected to circular earthworks at both Newark and Chillicothe are aligned to points on the horizon that mark the major risings and settings of the moon through a cycle that takes 18.6 years to complete. Romain found that the parallel walls leading from Marietta's large square down to the Muskingum River, as well as the long set of parallel walls extending from Hopeton's circle and square to the Scioto River, both are aligned to the setting sun on the winter solstice.

Observatory Mound sits outside the southwestern edge of the circle at Newark's Octagon Earthwork. This twelve foot high, loaf-shaped mound may have served as a viewing platform for Ohio Hopewell astronomers who likely charted the complex, 18.6-year lunar cycle within the sophisticated architecture of this geometric enclosure.

STUDIES OF THE EARTHWORKS INDICATE THAT THE HOPEWELL BUILDERS HAD A REMARKABLE understanding of mathematics and geometry, a deep knowledge of astronomy, a common unit of measure, and reliable methods of surveying. It also indicates the Hopewell people did not lay out their earthworks in a haphazard manner. They built them according to a predetermined plan that incorporated the cyclical movements of sun, moon, and perhaps the planets and stars as well. One of the most incredible things about the monumental architecture of the Hopewell culture is that the builders accomplished all of this with the simplest of tools. They used sharpened sticks, antler picks, bone and shell hoes, and baskets carried on their backs to build uncounted miles of intricate earthen walls one basket load at a time.

Why did they do it? N'omi Greber has written that the earthworks are symbols "written upon the landscape." This is certainly true, but they were not just "symbols"—they were likely conceived to be more like machines. The giant enclosures were enormous engines of ceremony and ritual intended to do something. They not only symbolized the cosmos, they may have allowed the Hopewell shamans to draw on the energies of the cosmos. And, as somewhat standardized symbols, they could be "read' or understood by the disparate peoples who sometimes traveled great distances to participate in the rituals and political negotiations that took place at these earthwork complexes.

The huge spaces encompassed by the earthworks are in striking contrast to the small, scattered Hopewell villages. The earthworks were places where people from many villages came together to join in ceremony and celebration. Our archaeological view of the Hopewellian world is unavoidably dominated by the dead, but their experience of the earthworks was full of life. They buried their honored dead in mounds at these sacred places, but the mortuary ceremonies were reaffirmations of the ties that bound neighbors together. A primary reason for bringing large numbers of otherwise dispersed people together would be to find suitable marriage partners. The exchange of marriage partners between villages would insure the perpetuation of the population and avoid the genetic perils of inbreeding, but it also would establish close alliances between groups. Hopewell leaders solidified these alliances with gifts. The alliances were not primarily military, although the evidence from the Pollock Works indicates that warfare may have flared up at times. On such occasions, groups with strong ties to neighbors would have had a considerable advantage over more isolated bands. The principal advantage of such alliances lay in granting allied groups access to a broader range of resources.

A copper panpipe from the Hopewell Mound Group in Ross County.

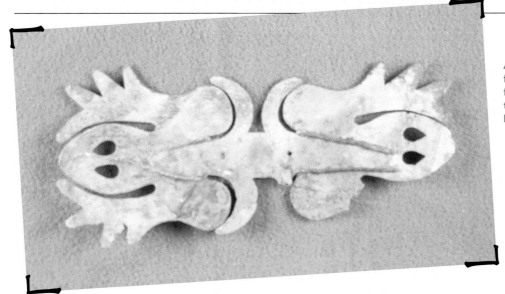

A copper cutout in the form of a two-headed frog or salamander from the Rutledge Mound in Licking County.

THE THINGS THAT THE HOPEWELL PEOPLE EXCHANGED WERE THE TANGIBLE TOKENS OF their friendship. As the historian Daniel Richter has observed for the historic Iroquois Confederacy, words of peace and gifts of peace were inextricably linked: "together they demonstrated and symbolized the shared climate of good thoughts upon which good relations and powerful alliances depended."

The Hopewell culture, however, was unique in the extraordinary scale of cosmopolitan interaction. The distances involved preclude the idea that such contacts were strictly for the purpose of building alliances to hedge against local crop failures and occasional hostilities among neighbors. And the continuing biological distinctiveness of local populations indicates that mates were not being widely shared across such geographic distances. There is another factor, or another level of complexity, at work. People did sometimes travel extraordinary distances to participate in special ceremonies and to acquire exotic materials, but they seem always to have returned to their homes.

The great earthworks of the Hopewell culture may have been, in part, pilgrimage centers like Mecca or the Vatican. People may have come to these places from across the Hopewell world bearing offerings or tribute to the spirits conjured by these architectural wonders of the world. Large numbers of houses of diverse form surrounded the Stubbs Earthworks. Frank Cowan interprets these as housing for visiting groups. Near the Murphy site, only a few miles from the Newark Earthworks, there is a habitation site with an abundance of bladelets and other tools made from Indiana hornstone. This may represent the encampment of a group visiting from the vicinity of the quarries in Indiana. Perhaps individuals or groups journeyed to the earthworks in fulfillment of a religious vow. Perhaps they came in thanksgiving for a healing or other blessing. The characteristic Hopewell art, such as copper ear spools or mica cutouts, could have served as passports understandable by people who may not have spoken the same language. Hopewell pilgrims or travelers carrying such distinctive badges may have identified themselves as members of a particular cult or religion entitling them to the respect and protection of their distant brethren.

When the pilgrims returned to their distant homes, they brought back epic tales of their journey. They would have awed and entertained their less adventurous friends and family members with stories told around the campfire of the wonders they had seen and the outlandish peoples they encountered. Often, they brought back tokens signifying that they truly had ventured into the lands beyond—perhaps a handful of gloriously-colored flint bladelets as a tangible reminder of their spiritual odyssey. Such things would have been viewed as objects of great power and the people who had journeyed to find them and bring them back to the village must have achieved thereby some notoriety and influence. Traveling into the unknown and returning with a special blessing is the hero's mythic quest. And such heroes would have been responsible for initiating contacts between widespread groups and for spreading the Hopewellian "gospel."

The Hopewell "explosion" produced prodigious architecture and unprecedented efforts of exploration and interaction with distant peoples. Southern Ohio may not have been the epicenter of this cultural revolution, but the Adena heartland north of the Ohio River witnessed the most spectacular florescence of Hopewell culture. Extravagant quantities of art and exotic materials gathered from the ends of the Hopewell world became concentrated in the great ceremonial centers in southern and central Ohio. And shards of Flint Ridge flint were scattered like so much shrapnel across much of eastern North America.

Archaeologists may never be able to reconstruct the historical circumstances that led to southern Ohio's predominance in Middle Woodland ritual, architecture, and art, but it may have involved the vision and charisma of a particular man or woman who was able to capture the collective imagination of large numbers of people—someone like Mohammed, Buddha, or Christ.

However it began and whatever it meant to individual Hopewell people, one reason for the success of the Hopewell culture is that its elaborate ritual machinery facilitated the maintenance of social and political alliances between widely dispersed groups. Periodic gatherings of people at ceremonial sites allowed parents to identify potential wives and husbands for their children. Ties of marriage would become political ties between groups. When those groups gathered at ceremonial centers and worked together to create magnificent ceremonial earthworks, they strengthened their sense of unity. Moreover, they must have amazed themselves with what they were able achieve by working together.

Stone rings, carved and polished with incredible precision, from the Hopewell Mound Group in Ross County

The low embankments that enclose the Mound City Group shine in the sun at Hopewell Culture National Historical Park in Ross County.

THE HOPEWELL CULTURE PROSPERED FOR SIX CENTURIES. WE STILL ARE SEARCHING FOR THE answer to why it eventually collapsed. One theory is that it fell victim to its own success. The people prospered and villages grew in size. They began to deplete their local resources at a faster rate. The need to establish ever wider networks of alliance became greater. Some of the larger regional centers may have begun to vie with one another in their attempts to outdo each other's achievements. Groups with more allies could draw upon a larger labor pool and so were able to build more impressive earthworks. These, in turn, may have attracted more pilgrims leading to alliances with more groups as well as with more distant groups. Hopewell farmers intensified their cultivation of local plants building up large amounts of storable food to feed the hundreds of people who gathered to build the giant earthworks. The planning and management of large-scale earthwork construction, the proper distribution of the food surplus, the delicate negotiations necessary to maintain the alliance network, and the direction of military operations when those negotiations failed, all required leaders. As this political authority became more centralized, local villagers may have begun to feel that they were breaking their backs growing extra crops and building more and larger earthworks so that some jumped up headman could collect more gee gaws to flaunt before his social inferiors. Their strong commitment to social equality may have asserted itself in a peasants revolt before the leaders were in a position to solidify their authority.

Whatever the cause, the peoples of the Ohio Valley abandoned the grandiose ceremonial architecture of the Hopewell culture. The succeeding Late Woodland cultures became more inwardly focused. They withdrew into their villages, rejecting the cosmopolitan extravagance of the Hopewellian elite. They discarded many of the hallmarks of Hopewell culture, such as animal effigy platform pipes, Flint Ridge flint, and the more exotic elements of the "Hopewell Interaction Sphere," and allowed the great earthwork centers to become overgrown. Some may have continued to visit these sacred spaces longing for the good old days when young people had a proper respect for the spirits, but such visits would have grown more and more infrequent as the older generation passed away. Within a few hundred years, the earthworks may have become enigmatic and magnificent vestiges of a mythical antiquity peopled by impossibly grand heroes like Achilles, Beowulf, and King Arthur.

A mica cutout in the form of a human head from the Turner Mound in Hamilton County.

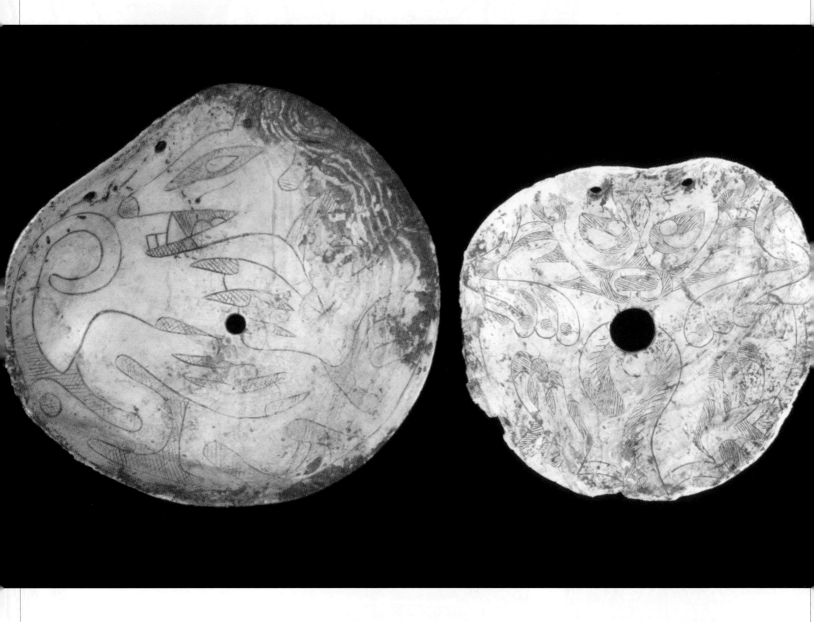

The transition from the Middle to the Late Woodland period presents a cultural enigma. Archaeologists find relatively few examples of artistic expression in artifacts after the phenomenon of Ohio Hopewell culture. These two inscribed, marine-shell gorgets are rare examples of artworks from the Late Woodland period. The Fairfield-style gorgets, recovered during salvage excavations at the Newtown Firehouse site in Hamilton County, are thought to depict a opossum (left) and a mountain lion (right). "Whatever the metaphysical purposes of art, they were not being served in the Late Woodland societies of the mid-Ohio Valley," according to archaeologists Mark Seeman and William Dancey, authors of "The Late Woodland Period in Southern Ohio: Basic Issues and Prospects."

ᴈ5ɛ

THE
LATE WOODLAND
PERIOD

Circa 1,500 - 1,100 BP

The idea of progressive evolution has dominated our ideas about culture history for more than a century. And why not? Throughout that period, science and technology have brought many of us ever faster cars, bigger airplanes, smarter computers, and longer and healthier lives in which to enjoy these new and constantly improving goods and services. What lesson of history could be clearer? From the stone age through the copper, bronze, and iron ages, human cultural evolution has been one long ascent up the ladder of progress. The idea that progress is the natural way of things is so deeply ingrained in our consciousness that when we are confronted with clear evidence that, for much of human history, things didn't get better and often they got considerably worse, we reject these episodes as aberrations and skip over them to get on with the "real" story of the march of progress.

THE LATE WOODLAND PERIOD IS ONE SUCH NEGLECTED EPISODE OF NATIVE AMERICAN culture history. The authors of a recent synthesis of Late Woodland archaeology characterize the transition from the Middle Woodland to the Late Woodland as a "true 'collapse.'" In a short span of time, people ceased building monumental ceremonial centers, they drastically reduced their production of art, they acquired far fewer exotic materials, and their interaction spheres contracted to small territories surrounding villages that often were themselves surrounded by stockade walls. The Hopewellian Big Bang explosion had reached its limits and collapsed in a Big Crunch. Ohio's Late Woodland period witnessed the response of local people to this dramatic social upheaval. It is not a story of progress, but is instead a story of survival and adaptation.

><><

THE LATE WOODLAND PERIOD OFTEN IS DEFINED BY THE END OF ALMOST EVERYTHING that marked the Middle Woodland period, but such a definition obscures the fact that it also marked a new beginning. The Late Woodland period witnessed profound changes in technology and social organization that were anything but simple reversions to pre-Middle Woodland ways of life.

In spite of the Hopewellian collapse, the population continued to grow rapidly throughout the Late Woodland period. There was a shift towards larger villages that were dispersed more widely across the landscape rather than just along the major rivers. Late Woodland villages could cover as much as ten acres and include several houses surrounding an open plaza at the center of the village. The Lichliter village near Dayton consisted of twelve or thirteen circular houses. Some were quite large and may have been communal winter houses. Others were much smaller and may have been the summer homes for individual families. A common feature of Late Woodland villages was the large earth oven, probably used for cooking meals for large groups.

Late Woodland villages were larger and more permanent than Middle Woodland villages. People lived in these villages throughout the year and for several years at a time. The archaeologist Michael Shott estimates that the Childers site, a Late Woodland village located along the Ohio River in West Virginia across from Gallia County, may have had as many as one hundred and twenty residents and they may have lived in that village for about twenty years. As a result of living in one place for so long, they built up larger middens, or trash dumps.

Often the Late Woodland people surrounded their villages with stockade walls or deep ditches. The Water Plant site in Franklin County, for example, consisted of eleven clusters of artifacts, interpreted as households, partially encircled by a ditch. The most plausible interpretation of such ditches and stockades is that the builders were afraid their neighbors, or marauders from elsewhere, might attack them. That these fears were justified is indicated by increasing numbers of burials of men and women skewered with flint points.

Ancient Ohio
Late Woodland Period Site Map

(ca. 1,500-1,100 BP)

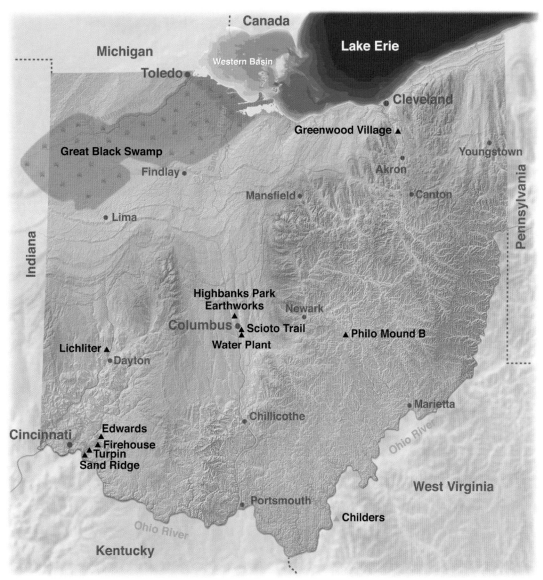

* Sites referenced in text and timelines

▲ – Ohio Archaeological Sites
▲ – Kentucky Archaeological Sites
▲ – Pennsylvania Archaeological Sites
▲ – West Virginia Archaeological Sites
● – Modern Cities

Elevation base map courtesy
Cartography & Editing Group,
Ohio Department of Natural Resources

© 2004 Voyageur Media Group, Inc.

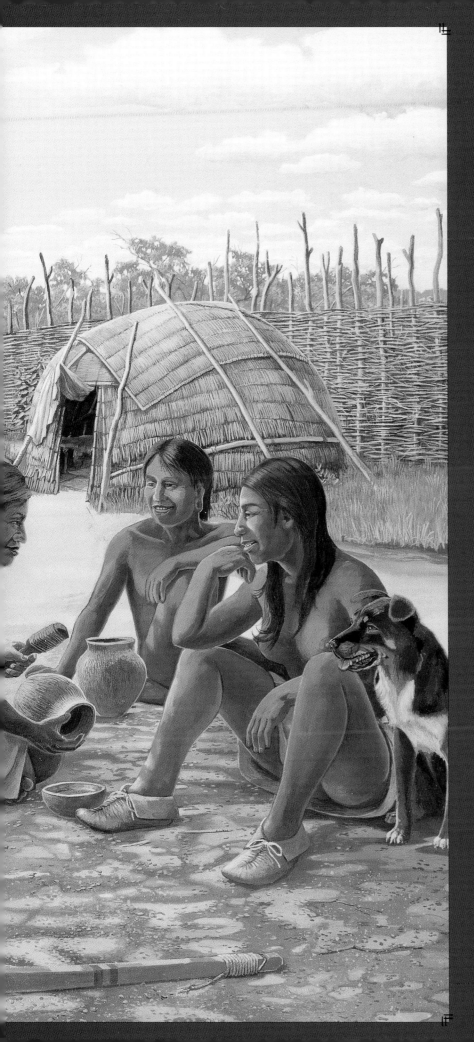

The "Ancient Ohio" Art Series
The Late Woodland Period
(ca 1,500-1,100 BP)

The lives of the Late Woodland people revolved around their villages such as this one situated along the Scioto River in central Ohio. There the people raised crops such as squash, sunflowers, and other seed-bearing plants. Hunting was still an important occupation for the men and boys, although they were now shifting from spears to the bow and arrow as their main weapon. For the women and girls, making pottery and weaving were probably frequent tasks. Unlike pottery, most woven textiles, baskets, and mats have not been preserved. However, they were probably important commodities for clothing, containers, and household furnishings. Dogs, such as the one here, probably accompanied the Paleoindians, the Archaic people, and Early and Middle Woodland societies as well. Besides assisting in hunting and providing security, the animals were likely also appreciated for their companionship.

Archaeological basis: Evidence from the Water Plant and Zencor/Scioto Trail sites in Franklin County and the Lichliter site in Montgomery County

Domesticated squash (*Cucurbita pepo*), a component of the Eastern Agricultural Complex, remained an important food source for American Indians living in Ohio during the Late Woodland period. Archaeologists debate whether squash was introduced to the region from the tropics of Mesoamerica, or was propagated independently from wild gourds (ancestors of green and yellow squash) that grew along river valleys in the eastern woodlands of North America.

The people who lived in these large Late Woodland villages supported themselves with more intensive farming and hunting, but the way of life of Late Woodland peoples varied regionally. Around the margins of Lake Erie, for example, hunting, gathering, and especially fishing continued to make the most significant contributions to their diet. In central and southern Ohio, on the other hand, Late Woodland folks spent surprisingly little time and effort fishing. At the Turpin site in Hamilton County, ninety percent of the animal bones are deer whereas only two percent are fish, even though Turpin is located in a rich floodplain environment where fish should have been abundant.

Early Late Woodland foragers collected nuts in large quantities, especially hickory nuts, black walnuts, and acorns. Nuts declined rapidly in importance, however, as domesticated plants became more of a staple. Late Woodland farmers practiced the same general kind of slash and burn farming as did their Middle Woodland predecessors, but they did so on a much larger scale. Based on the diversity of tree species represented in the charcoal of Late Woodland hearths, Dee Anne Wymer has determined that the Late Woodland people were clearing large sections of forest and dramatically altering their environment. Instead of moving their villages frequently to allow old garden patches to fully recover a mature forest growth, Late Woodland farmers would return to plots that had been fallow for only a decade or two, which is not enough time for a mature forest to redevelop.

Late Woodland farmers grew all the plants of the Eastern Agricultural Complex in their gardens with a particular emphasis on maygrass, until about 1100 BP. when the importance of maygrass declined. They harvested large quantities of seeds and stored them in pits to provide food for the winter. They also cultivated squash, gourds, tobacco, and some maize. Squash is particularly abundant at Late Woodland sites and maize became more important as maygrass declined. By the end of the Late Woodland, maize would be their most important crop.

THE WATER PLANT SITE
Pickaway County

By Dr. William S. Dancey, Associate Professor of Anthropology, The Ohio State University.

I clearly recall the moment when I began to realize that the Water Plant site had been home to a Late Woodland period nucleated community in the 6th century A.D. By studying distribution maps I learned that my initial expectation was wrong. My original hypothesis was that the dense scatter of artifacts covering this 7 acre plot of cultivated land represented the remains of episodic, seasonal encampments. However, the maps were showing something different, a set of clusters containing artifacts of the same period and functional diversity. Furthermore, the clusters were contained within a prehistoric ditch the dirt from which, although flattened today, probably was used to make an embankment. Newtown Cordmarked pottery along with Chesser Notched projectile points dominate in the clusters and argue that they accumulated at the same time. Radiocarbon dating and cross dating place the occupation between A.D. 500 and 600 (ca. 1500 BP). Nothing of this nature had been previously reported in central Ohio for the post-Hopewellian era so its discovery created some excitement, and still does.

WATER PLANT SITE
(Defined by arrows)

The ancient ditch and/or embankment that surrounds the Water Plant site along Big Walnut Creek is still visible in this ASCS aerial photograph taken in June of 1957. This semi-circular enclosure is a distinctive feature of Late Woodland villages, which Dr. Dancey interprets as the remnants of defensive structures. Archaeologists often use aerial images to study prehistoric sites, including a huge archive of aerial photographs taken by the U.S. Department of Agriculture's Agricultural Stabilization and Conservation Service since the late 1930s to monitor American farmlands and crops.

THE WATER PLANT SITE

In addition to the nearly identical ceramic and projectile point styles, the clusters also contain a common set of functional types, including pestles, mauls, and chipped slate disks. Each one contains a complete array of chipped stone tool-making debris from chert cobble to finished product. Most also include products and by-products of a ground slate tool and ornament manufacturing industry. Anvil stones were found in all clusters and may have been used in chipped and ground stone tool-making. Excavation of a small area on the southern edge of the village unearthed evidence of cooking pits and post-molds that may be from dwellings. Trash, including broken pots, was thrown in several of the pits. No other style but Newtown was represented. Functionally, Newtown vessels are tall, broad, thin-walled, wide-mouthed jars decorated only by vertical cord-marks and occasionally by trailed diagonal lines on the neck. By their size and shape, it would seem that they were either storage or cooking vessels, though the kinds of tests necessary to decide have not been done.

Water Plant is one of Ohio's most thoroughly investigated Late Woodland sites. Archaeologists from Ohio State University conducted extensive fieldwork here in 1980. The test pits and post molds from a possible circular structure in this photograph (below) show evidence of some of the earliest, year-round American Indian settlements in Ohio.

These two pottery sherds from the Water Plant site are decorated with the Newtown Cordmarked design commonly seen in Late Woodland pottery from central Ohio.

One of the most exciting discoveries at the Water Plant site was the charred remains of domesticated plants along with nuts and berries in the fill of the excavated cooking pits. Maygrass, goosefoot, and erect knotweed are prominent; maize is absent. Given that the site appears to represent the permanent home of a nucleated community, it is tempting to wonder if indigenous domesticates had become the staples of a full-scale agricultural subsistence strategy by this time.

The 600-year period between the eclipse of Hopewell mortuary ceremonialism (ca. A. D. 400) and the emergence of maize agriculturalists (ca. A.D. 1000) normally is viewed as a conservative time. Water Plant, and other sites like it across the Midwest, show that, to the contrary, exciting things were happening during the Late Woodland period.

Dr. William Dancey works with students Rachana Bhatt, Heather Cox, and Chris Brown who are re-analyzing materials excavated from the Water Plant site in the 1980s. Laboratory analysis is a vital part of archaeology. "The real hard work begins in the lab," says Dr. Dancey. "For every hour of fieldwork, archaeologists typically spend about twenty hours in the laboratory carefully washing, measuring, cataloguing and photographing thousands and thousands of cultural materials."

PALEOETHNOBOTONY

By Dr. Dee Anne Wymer, Chairperson and Professor, Department of Anthropology, Bloomsburg University.

A new field and laboratory technique, paleoethnobotany, has literally revolutionized archaeology. Paleoethnobotany is the study of preserved plant remains from archaeological soils (or deposits). In the late 1960s archaeologists became interested in a better understanding of the diet of ancient peoples and soon discovered that charred fragments of plants were still present in the soils that made up the fill of trash pits, floors of houses, and prehistoric activity areas. Organic material, such as fruit pits, seeds, corn cobs, and firewood, will preserve if they become "carbonized" - this refers to a light charring of the material which burns off the organic component normally decayed by bacterial action. If the soil is left largely undisturbed these fragmented portions of plant remains can preserve for thousands of years.

Today, archaeologists typically collect soil samples from archaeological features, such as hearths or trash pits, to process for paleoethnobotanical investigations. The first step entails using water to separate the charred material from the soil and allowing the plant remains to dry. The plant specialist then sorts the material under a microscope, identifying the specimens and counting and weighing the results. The most common plant categories identified include wood charcoal from fires, nutshell, seeds from fruits, crops, and weeds, as well as tubers and squash rind.

Most paleoethnobotanists are trained in both fields of archaeology and the ecological sciences. Paleoethnobotanists typically visit or participate in site excavations from which samples will be analyzed in the laboratory. A sample that took merely a few moments to collect in the field can take up to several days to completely analyze under the specialist's microscope. The results of the analysis will be used to address research questions focusing on the diet of the prehistoric inhabitants and reconstructing past environments. A recent emphasis has also included the investigation of the ceremonial use of plants in ancient societies.

What's in a seed? Paleoethnobotonists can determine much about ancient lifeways by studying preserved plant remains, including the seeds of sunflowers and other domesticated flora. These sunflowers were grown in a reconstructed Eastern Agricultural Complex garden (circa A.D. 200) designed by Dr. Wymer at the Great Circle Earthworks, Newark, Ohio.

Paleoethnobotanical soil samples are drawn from the sediment of such archaeological features as this firepit (left) from the Murphy site—a Hopewell habitation site in central Ohio.

Archaeologists use flotation to separate plant remains from soil. Botanical materials (right) float out of the dirt matrix into a special cloth. These materials are subsequently dried and analyzed in a paleoethnobotanical laboratory.

A close-up of 11,000 year-old seeds from the stomach contents of the Burning Tree mastodon, Licking County. The upper central dark seed is a water lily *(Nymphaea)* and the lighter-colored seed in the center is a swamp buttercup *(Ranunculus).*

A reconstructed Late Woodland pot (Newtown Cordmarked, 15.5" high and 48" in widest circumference) from the Zencor site in Franklin County.

Late Woodland pottery consisted largely of simple, wide-mouthed jars with thinner walls than the pots of the Middle Woodland period. The pots were mostly grit-tempered and decorated with cord-marking. Typically, the potters applied the cord-marking in a pattern of vertically-oriented ridges on the outer surfaces of the pots. The thin walls, grit temper, and roughened surfaces allowed the pots to be used for cooking liquids at higher temperatures and for longer periods of time. This improvement in cooking soups and gruel made it possible for the Late Woodland folk to get the most out of their food. They could boil deer bones to draw out the grease and make a more nutritious porridge from the seeds of the Eastern Agricultural Complex. Well-cooked gruel could be fed to infants allowing them to be weaned at an earlier age. Since prolonged breastfeeding lowers a woman's fertility, early weaning meant women could have more children in the course of their lives. This would have contributed to the rapid growth of population during this period.

Late Woodland stone tools were simpler and more practical than the tools of the Middle Woodland. Late Woodland people used whatever chert was handy to make simple flake tools. The naturally sharp flakes required little modification to perform most jobs and they were tossed away after one or two uses. Hunters in the earliest phases of the Late Woodland period used simple notched and stemmed spearpoints, but by 1200 BP. the bow and arrow had been introduced into the Ohio Valley. This new weapon was brought to America from Asia about 4,000 years ago and it revolutionized hunting techniques. It also made it easier for people to kill one another. The new "arrowheads" were simple, triangular points chipped from whatever flint was at hand.

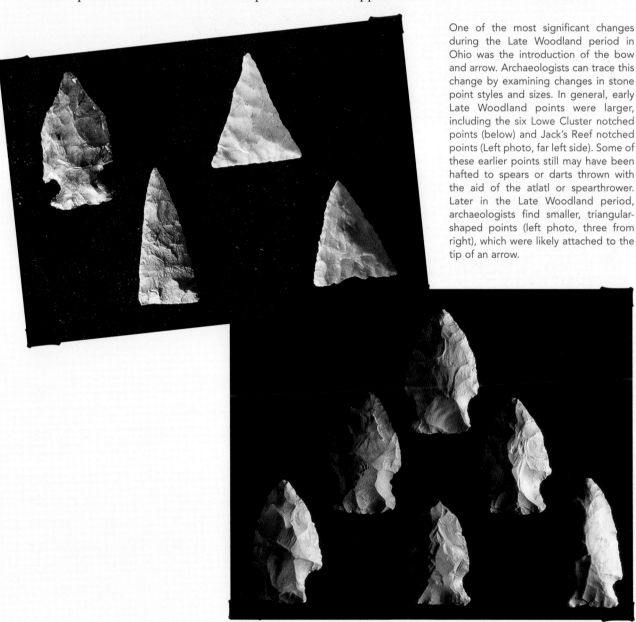

One of the most significant changes during the Late Woodland period in Ohio was the introduction of the bow and arrow. Archaeologists can trace this change by examining changes in stone point styles and sizes. In general, early Late Woodland points were larger, including the six Lowe Cluster notched points (below) and Jack's Reef notched points (Left photo, far left side). Some of these earlier points still may have been hafted to spears or darts thrown with the aid of the atlatl or spearthrower. Later in the Late Woodland period, archaeologists find smaller, triangular-shaped points (left photo, three from right), which were likely attached to the tip of an arrow.

THE WOODLAND BOW AND ARROW

By Donald A. Miller, Archaeologist, ASC Group, Inc.

The subject of the bow and arrow in the Late Woodland period is a complex topic containing elements of several sciences. In its simplest form, a bow is a piece of wood that is spanned by a string attached to either end. The string is held onto the upper and lower limbs by nocks. The limbs of the bow store energy when the string is pulled back (drawn). When drawn, the back of the bow (that part facing the target) is under tension, while the belly (that part of the bow facing the archer) is under compression. When an arrow is placed on the string and then drawn and released, the energy stored in the limbs is transferred through the string to the arrow sending it downrange toward the target.

Although no examples of bows used by the Late Woodland people of Ohio are known to exist, several historically documented bows from the eastern Woodlands have survived to this day. One of the best known is the Sudbury Bow which was collected in the 1600s in Sudbury, Massachusetts. This particular style of bow is known as a self bow. Self bows depend on the elasticity of the limbs to propel the arrow. Wood choice was important to the design. Several wood types native to Ohio provided adequate tensile strength and compressive tolerance to make self bows. Those woods include hickory, ash, elm, and black locust.

The bow and arrow offers several improvements over the atlatl. First, although the atlatl exhibits a powerful punch on impact it is relatively slow when compared to an arrow. Second, an arrow can be shot from many positions including kneeling, standing, sitting, and even lying down, while an atlatl must be thrown from a standing position to achieve maximum velocity. Many arrows can be carried on a hunting excursion with greater ease than the large and cumbersome atlatl darts. Finally, several arrows can be launched in succession providing numerous shot opportunities at fleeing game animals when compared to the time it takes to load and throw an atlatl dart.

Experimentation with replicated archery tackle indicates that the goal of the Late Woodland archer was not an immediate kill shot like modern archery, but it was just to hit the animal with the arrow(s) and then to let the animal run away to expire due to blood loss. The animal could then be easily tracked and recovered. Late Woodland people were excellent trackers. Unlike today, they did not have the issues of crossing fences and property boundaries to recover their game.

The white-tail deer was the primary quarry for American Indian hunters during the Late Woodland period, but small mammals and game birds such as these wild turkeys also were an important part of the food economy, helping American Indian family groups survive lean winters in Ohio.

Archaeologist Don Miller (left) demonstrates his replica of a self bow, which is based on the 1660 Sudbury bow from Harvard's Peabody Museum in Cambridge, Massachusetts. The energy to propel the arrow is stored within the limbs of the bow when drawn.

A completed self bow and an unfinished stave are displayed (above) by traditional craftsmen at the annual Flint Ridge Knap-In. Eastern Woodland self bows were made of strong, elastic woods such hickory, ash, elm and black locust.

Archaeologists find evidence that American Indians occupied Ohio's upland rockshelters such as Ash Cave in Hocking County (above) during the Late Woodland period. Don Miller, archaeologist says this evidence may reflect a growing population. "The rockshelters were probably used as seasonal base camps for small hunting parties, most likely composed of men," says Miller.

LATE WOODLAND PEOPLE ALSO OCCUPIED CAVES AND ROCKSHELTERS TO A MUCH GREATER extent than previous peoples. Archaeologists have found Late Woodland artifacts in nearly every rockshelter they have investigated in southeastern Ohio. They have interpreted most of the rockshelter sites as the remains of temporary hunting camps. The number and widespread distribution of these sites provides more evidence of how intensively Late Woodland hunters were combing the landscape for deer and other game.

Many of the rockshelter hunting camps were winter occupations. It is likely that some people left the large villages to spend the winter in sheltered valleys hunting deer. This would have been a help to the older folks and others who stayed in the village, since their food supply would largely be limited to the nuts and seeds that they had been able to store up during the autumn harvest. If some groups left the village for the winter, then there would be more food available for those who stayed behind. Moreover, if the people who stayed behind moved in together into a larger communal house, then it would take less firewood to meet the cooking and heating needs of the village. The hunters would have brought fresh meat back to the village throughout the winter, but by staying away on extended hunting trips they would have been helping to conserve the resources of the village.

Archaeological investigations of caves and rockshelters also have contributed to our understanding of the richness of Late Woodland material culture. Excavations in dry rockshelters reveal textiles, basketry and gourd containers, moccasins, and other leather garments and bags giving us a glimpse of a variety of technologies not usually preserved at such ancient sites.

IN ADDITION TO CHIPPED STONE SPEAR POINTS AND TRIANGULAR ARROWHEADS, THE LATE Woodland hunters also used sharpened antler tines to tip their weapons. Late Woodland farmers used axes and fire to clear their fields, digging sticks, limestone hoes and thick, chipped stone picks for tilling their fields. They used ground stone slabs and pestles for grinding up seeds and nuts. Women, children, and the older folks likely tended the fields while parties of men went off in search of game, but such a division of labor was not followed with absolute rigidity. Certainly the women could have snared small game and hunters who failed to kill a deer would not have returned home empty-handed. They might have filled their bags with nuts or at least brought back firewood.

The shift from small hamlets occupied for a few seasons to larger villages occupied for several years necessitated numerous changes in social organization. Villages became more inwardly focused and contact between villages became more infrequent. The growing sense of "us" versus "them" intensified to the point where walls and ditches became necessary for protection. Some archaeologists suggest that the differences between groups during this era indicate the beginnings of a sense of tribal identity.

The introduction of the bow and arrow also may have contributed to the big changes in their social system. This new technology may have increased the efficiency of hunters, allowing villages to become more self-sufficient. Groups may have felt that they no longer needed the goodwill of neighbors as a hedge against shortfalls in resources. Indeed, those neighbors may have been

The Late Woodland Period Tool Kit
Circa 1,500 – 1,100 BP

Some archaeologists see the Late Woodland period as a time of dramatic cultural decline. Others consider the changes that define this era as successful accommodations to the social challenges imposed by larger and more stable villages and an increasing dependence on domesticated crops.

This selection of Late Woodland artifacts includes a series of four spearpoints: two Chesser Notched points (left, bottom), carry-overs from the late Middle Woodland period, and two Jack's Reef Corner-Notches points (left, top). These may be the first true "arrowheads" in Ohio as the bow and arrow was introduced into this region during the Late Woodland period.

Additional Late Woodland artifacts include a Jack's Reef preform/knife (bottom, middle), a granite pick (center), and a chipped slate disc (top, right).

American Indians developed an array of specialized tools during the Late Woodland period, including these artifacts from the Water Plant site in Pickaway County. (top) Drills used to bore holes in wood and shell. (middle) A notched axe used to cut wood. (bottom, left to right) a serrated scraper, a spoke shave and a knife.

seen increasingly as a threat to the security of the village. The hunters from neighboring villages would have been competing for the same deer; and encounters between hunting parties from rival villages may have erupted into open hostilities.

Studies of deer bones from Late Woodland and Late Prehistoric sites show that, over time, the deer being hunted were getting smaller. This is one indication that the Ohio deer population was under severe stress from intensive hunting. Deer were a critical resource for all of Ohio's ancient peoples. They provided not only meat, but also hides for clothing and bone and antler for a variety of tools. Just as modern nations are willing to go to war over access to oil, ancient peoples would have been willing to fight over access to deer.

American Indians constructed a few earthworks during the Late Woodland period, including these embankments (below) preserved on a ridge above the Olentangy River in the Highbanks Metro Park in Delaware County.

Archaeologists can learn how American Indians made stone points by examining each stage of development in the life of an artifact. These five artifacts (above) from the Water Plant site show a point reduction sequence from the blank chert (left) to a finished point (right).

Villagers still would have faced the problem of finding mates for their young people who were not close relatives. As hostilities between groups increased, the opportunities for peaceful interactions, including the exchange of marriage partners, would have declined. One solution to this problem, adopted centuries earlier by the Romans in their dealings with the neighboring Sabines, was to dispense with the tedious formalities of negotiation and courtship by forcibly abducting young women from other villages. There is evidence for this practice at the Late Woodland Riviere aux Vase site in southeastern Michigan. Archaeologists studying the burials from this site found that 15 females and five males, almost ten percent of the population, had injuries to the head and face. The unusually high proportion of battered young women suggested to the investigators that Late Woodland groups in this area raided neighboring villages to obtain young women for mates.

THE LATE WOODLAND PERIOD IS MARKED BY THE ALMOST TOTAL ABANDONMENT OF THE art and ritual that were so characteristic of the Hopewell culture. There are a few isolated examples of continuities such as the elaborately engraved marine shell gorget from the Firehouse Mound in Newton, Ohio bearing a very Hopewell-like opossum design. Also, the cut and polished jaws of mammals sometimes are found with Late Woodland burials, almost always burials of men. The absolute rarity of such objects, however, indicates that there was a great reduction in the need to convey information visually. Even the stone tools used by Late Woodland people tend to be simple and practical things banged out of whatever chippable rock was available locally. Clearly, this emphasis on quick and dirty practicality means the tools were not being used in displays of social status. Evidently, the majority of social contacts during the Late Woodland era were between members of the same village who knew each other quite well. There must have been few occasions when people from different villages came together to participate in common rituals or festivals. This is further indicated by the fact that the ceremonial heart of the village was no longer a monumental earthwork shared with neighboring groups. It was, instead, the plaza at the center of the village.

✕✕✕

THE HONORED DEAD WERE NO LONGER BURIED AT CORPORATE CEREMONIAL AND social integration centers. Late Woodland villages had their own cemeteries. Often these were clusters of small, stone burial mounds located close to the village.

There was great variety in the treatment of burials throughout Late Woodland Ohio. Archaeologists have discovered extended burials, bundle burials, and cremations. Some Late Woodland groups buried their dead under small stone mounds, others entombed loved ones in stone cysts, while still others dug simple graves in middens. This may seem to us like simply throwing out the bodies with the garbage, but the Late Woodland people may not have viewed middens as nasty refuse dumps. From a practical standpoint, the soil of middens would have been relatively easy to dig into, even during the winter when the ground was frozen. Perhaps the midden burials are the remnants of people who died in the winter. Generally, Late Woodland burials include very few grave offerings.

Some groups or cults buried certain individuals in already antique Hopewell earthworks. This became even more common after 1300 BP. These

In 1988, archaeologists from The Cincinnati Museum of Natural History (now Cincinnati Museum Center) conducted salvage excavations of stone-capped mounds that were uncovered during construction of a residential subdivision. Known as the Hawkins Ridge site, volunteer Al Adamson (above) holds a survey scale next to one of several stone-capped mounds documented at this Late Woodland site in Hamilton County. Bob Genheimer, Curator of Archaeology, Cincinnati Museum Center reports, "the stone-capped mounds were later additions to a complex of earthen mounds dating to the Early Woodland period." The investigations at Hawkins Ridge are important, says Genheimer, because "they show changes in mortuary practices, but a continuity of use by American Indians over a long period of time."

so-called Intrusive Mound burials usually included offerings of red ocher, antler harpoons, platform pipes, and granite picks. By burying their dead in these earthworks, these Late Woodland groups must have been attempting to make a symbolic connection between themselves and these landmarks of ancient grandeur.

The variability in the ways Late Woodland people buried their dead suggests two things. First, differences between villages and regions confirm the pattern of regional diversification already evident in other factors such as use of resources and styles of artifacts. Cultural practices diverge when groups are isolated from one another and especially when they choose to emphasize the ethnic uniqueness of "us" versus "them." Second, differences between individuals in the same village may indicate the presence of different religious cults with varying burial practices or differences in the status of the individuals. Persons with higher status generally are buried with more elaborate treatment than are persons of lower status.

Status during the Late Woodland period likely was earned by being a good hunter, gifted healer, wise counselor, or a mighty warrior. The continuing importance of shamans as religious practitioners is suggested by the presence of elbow pipes carved from limestone and sandstone. The carved animal jaws also may be shamanic talismans, but such items are rare and there is no uniformity in their design or patterns of use.

✕✕✕

YET ANOTHER INDICATION OF THE CONTRACTING SPHERE OF INTERACTION BETWEEN groups is the marked decline in the numbers of items crafted from exotic raw materials. Archaeologists have found some small mica mirrors and a few marine shell gorgets at Late Woodland sites and these must have been treasured status symbols. After 1300 BP, there is a bit more evidence of exotic raw material making its way into Ohio, including some steatite and marine shells from the east coast. Although highly valued by Late Woodland peoples, the fact that such items are so rare in Ohio indicates that they did not serve as important ceremonial linkages between networks of cooperating villages. Such things had been the cogs and gears that ran the complex social machinery of the Hopewell culture, but during the Late Woodland period they had become tokens of more modest and, perhaps, more particular alliances. Social groups do not exist in a vacuum and villages undoubtedly made common cause on occasion for a variety of reasons. A local crop failure or the appearance of a particularly aggressive band of raiders could have led to joint action by two or more groups, but during the Late Woodland, such cooperative efforts seem to have been quite temporary.

A team of archeology students survey rockshelters near Twinsburg in Summit County. Led by professor Linda Whitman, University of Akron, field surveys such as this allow archaeologists and government officials to determine how future development may impact archaeological and historical sites.

The Late Woodland period was a time of dramatic change. Middle Woodland societies were faced with problems they could not overcome without a radical transformation. Initially, there was a change from small, dispersed villages that cooperated in elaborate rituals at monumental ceremonial centers to larger, more permanent villages that not only ceased cooperating with one another, but seem to have been in competition for agricultural land, hunting grounds or other scarce resources. Most villages of this era came equipped with a defensive wall or ditch and an increasing number of individuals seem to have died a violent death. Somewhat later there was a technological change from the spear and atlatl to the bow and arrow. This innovation increased the efficiency of hunters and deer meat became more important in the Late Woodland diet. The bow and arrow also made it easier for Late Woodland people to kill one another. Finally, the most dramatic change involved the increasing importance of maize in the diet of the Late Woodland people. This led directly to the transition marking the end of the Late Woodland and the beginning of the Late Prehistoric period.

The Late Woodland period was a time of transition as American Indians embraced new customs, new technologies and the advent of early agriculture on fertile lands in river valleys, including the floodplains along the Little Miami River seen here near its confluence with the Ohio in Hamilton County. Yet, bigger changes were just around the bend as inland waterways delivered unprecedented cultural influences from distant European explorers and colonists during the last prehistoric period in Ohio.

Late Woodland Period Timeline

Archaeological Sites and Historical/Natural Events
(ca. 1,500-1,100 BP)

RC Years Ago (BC/AD)	Ohio	North America	World
1,000 BP (1,070 AD)			
		← Anasazi build pueblos, Southwest (ca. 1,050 BP)	
			← Vikings settle Greenland (ca. 1,080 BP)
1,100 BP (950 AD)			
	← Highbanks Park Works (✦ ca. 1,150-650 BP)		← Songhayi Kingdom rises, West Africa (ca. 1,150 BP)
		← Parkline Site II, W.V. (✳ ca. 1,170-1,020 BP)	← Charlemagne reigns, Europe (ca. 1,179-1,136 BP)
1,200 BP (830 AD)	⌈ Greenwood Village (✳ ca. 1,200-1,100 BP) ⌊ Bow & arrow, widely adopted (ca. 1,200 BP)	← Colington/Cashie Cultures, N.C. (ca. 1,200-430 BP)	← Moors invade Spain (ca. 1,210 BP)
			⌈ Early Maori reach New Zealand (ca. 1,250 BP) ⌊ Islam sweeps northern Africa (ca. 1,250-1,150 BP)
1,300 BP (750 AD)		← Coles Creek Culture, Southeast (ca. 1,300-1,000 BP)	⌈ Tang Dynasty rises, China (ca. 1,332 BP)
	⌈ Cole Culture (✳ ca. 1,350-750 BP) ⌊ Western Basin Tradition (ca. 1,350-750 BP)	← Riviere aux Vase Culture, Great Lakes (ca. 1,350-1,050 BP)	⌈ Mayan height, Central America (ca. 1,350 BP) ⎱ Bantu migration, Southern Africa (ca. 1,350 BP) ⌊ Tiahuanaco Culture rises, Bolivia (ca. 1,350 BP)
1,400 BP (640 AD)		← Effigy Mound Culture, Midwest (ca. 1,400-700 BP)	⌈ Birth of Muhammad, Mecca (ca. 1,380 BP)
	← Scioto Trail (✳ ca. 1,450-1,175 BP)	⌈ Basketmaker Culture, Southwest (ca. 1,450 BP) ⌊ Childers, W.V. (ca. 1,450-1,250 BP)	⎱ Buddhism state religion, China (ca. 1,412 BP) ⎱ Angles/Saxons settle England, (ca. 1,450 BP) ⌊ Fall of Roman Empire (ca. 1,470 BP)
1,500 BP (550 AD)	← Water Plant (✳ ca. 1,500-1,250 BP) ⌊ Sand Ridge (✳ ca. 1,510-1,080 BP)		⌊ Tomb of Emperor Nintoku, Japan (ca. 1,475 BP)
	← Turpin (✳ ca. 1,550-1,250 BP)		← Teotihuacan city of 250,000, Mexico (ca. 1,550 BP)
1,600 BP (480 AD)		← Weeden Island Culture, FL (ca. 1,600-1,200 BP)	← Jin Kingdom begins, China (ca. 1,599 BP)
			← Gupta Dynasty, India (ca. 1,650-1,400 BP)
1,700 BP (320 AD)	← Philo Mound B (✳ ca. 1,700-1,600 BP)		
1,800 BP (200 AD)			
	Lichliter Village (✳ ca. 1,850-1,350 BP)		

Late Late Woodland Period (ca. 1,300-1,050 BP)

Early Late Woodland Period (ca. 1,500-1,300 BP)

Criteria and Key
This timeline is based on published radiocarbon dates or artifact typology. The dates are listed as ca. (about) BP = Radiocarbon Years Before Present and BC/AD. The "present" is defined by convention as AD 1950, the year standards were set for reporting radiocarbon dates. The timeline includes the best information available at the time of publication. Ohio sites limited to those referenced in text or on maps.
  ✳ = based on radiocarbon (C¹⁴) and other laboratory dates
  ✦ = based on typology of artifacts and site features

SunWatch Indian Village in Montgomery County is called the "Colonial Williamsburg of American prehistory" as one of the finest reconstructed ancient American Indian villages in the United States. The establishment of corn agriculture allowed about 200 to 250 people to live in this Fort Ancient farming village year round during its peak about 800 years ago. SunWatch is laid out like a giant calendar. Solar alignments mark two key agricultural dates—spring planting (on or about April 20) and summer harvest (on or about August 20). At sunrise on these dates, the shadow cast from a large pole in the central plaza (photo of summer harvest mark) crosses a hearth just inside the entrance to the largest structure, the "Big House."

∃6∈

THE
LATE PREHISTORIC
PERIOD

Circa 1,100 - 400 BP

Many of the dates archaeologists have chosen to demarcate one cultural epoch from another seem to become, on closer examination, somewhat arbitrary points on a continuum of cultural change. Certainly, there are important differences that distinguish the Paleoindian period from the Archaic, the Early Woodland from the Middle Woodland, and so on. But the changes reflect, for the most part, gradual processes and not transformative events. Therefore, assigning a particular date to mark the transition from one period to another can be problematic and misleading. For example, sites occupied at these pivotal points in prehistory often are difficult to assign to one period or the other since they may have characteristics of each. The changes that define the Late Prehistoric period, however, were truly revolutionary and they appear in the archaeological record of southern Ohio as an abrupt transformation at about 900 BP. In brief, these changes included a shift to larger and more permanent villages, changes in the form and construction of ceramic vessels, changing ritual practices, increasing evidence for institutionalized leaders, and a dramatic increase in the use of maize as a staple food. The last named change definitely is not the least important. Indeed, the rise of maize agriculture may have been the engine driving the changes in other aspects of Late Prehistoric culture.

The Native peoples of Highland Mexico first domesticated maize (or corn as it is called by most modern Ohioans) and it, along with beans and squash, fueled the great civilizations of the Mayans and the Aztecs. Maize, beans, and squash often are called the "three sisters," for each has nutrients the others lack and they thrive when grown together in the same field. Calling them "sisters," however, suggests each was equally important in the Late Prehistoric diet when, in fact, corn was queen and her two "sisters" were more like handmaidens.

Maize was passed from village to village and eventually made its way into the Ohio Valley during the Middle Woodland period. Maize was, however, a tropical plant and it took time for North American farmers to develop a strain that could thrive in the colder climate of the Upper Midwest. It was not until the very end of the Late Woodland period that maize became a staple crop in this region.

The people of eastern North America acquired their Mexican corn by way of the Mississippi Valley and the transfer of seeds undoubtedly was accompanied by information concerning how and when to plant, harvest, and prepare the new crop as well as rituals appropriate to each stage in the process. Some archaeologists call the Late Prehistoric period the Mississippian period, because they believe that this dramatic cultural transformation involved far more than the importation of new kinds of seeds and rituals. Some think the sweeping changes that mark this era were initiated by an influx of people from the Mississippi Valley who overwhelmed the existing Late Woodland groups.

The importance of the "three sisters" (corn, beans and squash) is demonstrated each season in the traditional garden at Fort Ancient State Memorial in Warren County. The year this cornucopia was photographed, the harvest was bountiful. But, torrential spring rains and a summer drought completely destroyed the garden the following year. "If this crop had failed 600 years ago, a lot of people in the village would have died over the winter," says Billy Wagner, Gardener, Fort Ancient State Memorial.

Decades of archaeological research, however, have shown that the changes were, for the most part, local evolutionary developments and not a revolutionary "Mississippification" of Ohio Valley societies. In other words, Ohio's Middle to Late Woodland peoples adopted and adapted "foreign" elements (such as maize) into their culture and these innovations led to inevitable changes of various kinds. Foreigners from the Mississippi Valley did not conquer or otherwise come to dominate the cultures of the Ohio Valley. Archaeologists indicated the importance of this change in our understanding by discarding the old "Mississippian" label for the more neutral designation of "Late Prehistoric."

Ancient Ohio
Late Prehistoric Period Site Map

(ca. 1,100-400 BP)

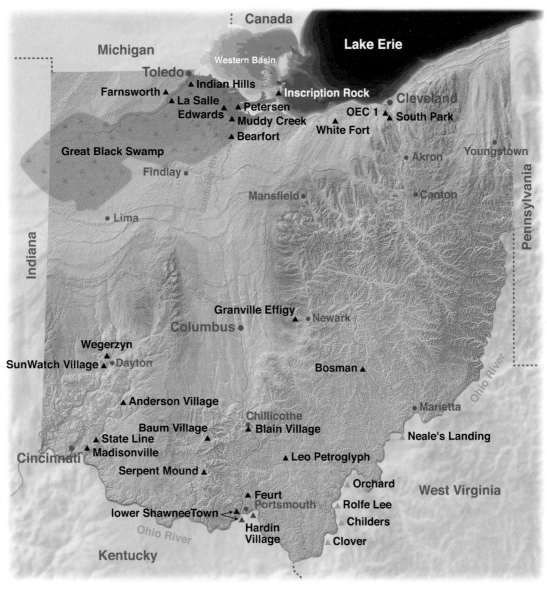

Canada

Lake Erie

Michigan

Western Basin

Toledo

Farnsworth ▲

▲ Indian Hills

▲ Inscription Rock

Cleveland

La Salle ▲

▲ Petersen

OEC 1 ▲

▲ South Park

Edwards

▲ Muddy Creek

White Fort

▲ Bearfort

Great Black Swamp

Akron

Youngstown

Findlay

Pennsylvania

Mansfield

Canton

Lima

Indiana

Granville Effigy

Newark

Columbus

Wegerzyn

SunWatch Village ▲ ● Dayton

Bosman ▲

▲ Anderson Village

Marietta

Chillicothe

Baum Village

▲ Blain Village

▲ State Line

Neale's Landing

● Madisonville

Cincinnati

▲ Leo Petroglyph

Serpent Mound ▲

Orchard

West Virginia

▲ Feurt

lower ShawneeTown

Portsmouth

▲ Rolfe Lee

Childers

Hardin Village

▲ Clover

Ohio River

Kentucky

* Sites referenced in text and timelines

▲ – Ohio Archaeological Sites
▲ – Kentucky Archaeological Sites
▲ – Pennsylvania Archaeological Sites
▲ – West Virginia Archaeological Sites
● – Modern Cities

Elevation base map courtesy
Cartography & Editing Group,
Ohio Department of Natural Resources

© 2004 Voyageur Media Group, Inc.

This is not to say that there were no migrations of people into or out of Ohio during this period. Physical anthropologists Paul Sciulli and James Oberly have determined, from their studies of ancient skeletons, that while there is a clear biological continuity in Ohio from the Archaic through the Late Woodland periods, significant differences show up in their sample of Late Prehistoric human remains. For example, the people who lived and died at the Madisonville site, located near Cincinnati, were quite distinctive and may represent a group of people who migrated to Ohio from elsewhere during the Late Prehistoric period.

Many of the cultural influences that shaped Ohio's Late Prehistoric period did, indeed, come from the Mississippi Valley and spread eastward, from village to village, up the Ohio Valley and then northward up the Ohio's major tributaries. The rivers were natural transportation corridors and many of the largest villages were clustered along their banks. As a result, the first groups in Ohio to adopt the Late Prehistoric way of life lived in southwestern Ohio, to be followed later by central, eastern, and northern Ohio within one or two centuries. The idea that cultural change flowed across Ohio in only one direction is, however, overly simplistic. Many of the changes that shaped the Late Prehistoric cultures of northern Ohio were more closely tied to what was happening along the shores of the Great Lakes than to developments in the Mississippi Valley.

EACH OF THE REGIONAL LATE WOODLAND POPULATIONS RESPONDED IN THEIR OWN WAYS to the challenges and opportunities of the times and each developed their own increasingly distinctive cultures. In southwestern, southern and parts of central Ohio, archaeologists recognize the Fort Ancient culture, confusingly named for the earthworks in Warren County we now know to have been built by the Hopewell culture. The Monongahela culture occupied far eastern Ohio and much of neighboring Pennsylvania, while the Sandusky culture and Whittlesey culture developed along the western and southern margins of Lake Erie, respectively.

Archaeologists study artifacts and recognize cultures on the basis of similarities and differences in sets of artifacts. The artifacts that are most important for recognizing the appearance of Late Prehistoric cultures, and for distinguishing regional differences among the various groups, are pottery vessels, usually found in fragments that, perplexingly, almost never seem to fit together to make a whole pot. Pottery is so important to archaeologists because prehistoric people made lots of it, shaped it and decorated it to suit changing fashions, and frequently accidentally broke their creations into bits that they left lying about because they were no longer of any use to anyone—except archaeologists.

The ceramics of the Late Prehistoric period in Ohio generally are thinner than Woodland period pottery and much of it was tempered with ground-up shells. The vessels often are large, plain jars used for cooking or storage. In some regions of Ohio, many of the jars have lug or strap handles and some are decorated with a variety of regionally-distinctive incised and stamped patterns. The diverse forms of the vessels and the designs incised and stamped upon these clay canvases were

Greater regional differences are seen in the diversity of pottery styles during the Late Prehistoric Period, including these two reconstructed pots from southern Ohio. A guilloche design decorates the pot on the right (width 4.5", height 4.5", circumference 13") from Anderson Village, a Fort Ancient site along the Little Miami River in Warren County. A simple cordmark design graces this Madisonville-style pot on the left (width 5.5", height 5", circumference 18").

Madisonville site artifacts show the skills of Fort Ancient craftspeople (right, clockwise): an igneous stone celt; a bone effigy carved into the form of a deer or heron; a red catlinite pipe; and a pottery sherd decorated with a salamander.

among the ways Late Prehistoric peoples expressed their ethnic identity. Ceramic art increasingly became a way of broadcasting the differences between "us" and "them." Whereas Hopewell art conveyed a sense of unity among far-flung groups who shared certain beliefs and cooperated in various ritual endeavors, Late Prehistoric art appears to have been aimed at a local audience. The shared symbols helped to unify the local group by emphasizing their distinctiveness from the potentially hostile "others" who lived in surrounding regions and whose raiding parties occasionally threatened villagers who strayed too far from the safety of their towns.

The Late Prehistoric Period Tool Kit
Circa 1,100 – 400 BP

The Late Prehistoric period witnessed an agricultural revolution as maize, a plant originally domesticated in Mexico, became a staple crop for Ohio's growing population. The diversity of tools shown
here reflect greater specialization in the way American Indians made their living, and the fact that
more organic materials such as animal bone and shell survived Ohio's acidic soils

Top row (left to right): Madison point; Levanna point; Fort Ancient point; Bone point
Second row (left to right): Shell hoe: Bone fishhook; Flint knife; Chipped flint celt.
Third row (left to right): Notched stone (net weight)
Bottom row, (left to right): Bone beamer (used like a draw-knife to scrape hides)

THE LATE PREHISTORIC STONE TOOL KIT WAS MORE UNIFORM ACROSS OHIO. IT WAS invariably dominated by small, triangular flint arrowheads and larger, triangular knives, chipped from whatever flints were available locally. Large, tapering groundstone axes were essential for clearing the forest, and hoes made from large, perforated shells were used to work the fields.

The Late Prehistoric tool kit included a variety of additional items made from bone and antler, including awls, gorges, fishhooks, and harpoon heads. It also must have included an even greater variety of tools shaped from wood, fiber, leather, feathers, and other perishable materials, but archaeologists seldom are able to recover such items.

There is little evidence for trade during the Late Prehistoric period, although a few exotic items occasionally made their way from one village to another. Containers and ornaments carved from marine shells are found at many later Late Prehistoric period sites; but most Late Prehistoric groups either chose not to invest the energy needed to acquire foreign things, or were prevented from doing so on a regular basis. It may be simply that the importance of such exotic paraphernalia lay in conveying social information between groups. As opportunities for peaceful intergroup communication declined, so too did the need for the expensive symbols used in that interaction.

THE LATE PREHISTORIC PERIOD BEGAN WITH A TRUE AGRICULTURAL REVOLUTION. MAIZE, combined with beans and squash, became the primary focus of the economy, almost completely replacing the plants of the Eastern Agricultural Complex. The revolutionary impact of the shift to maize farming was felt, and can be measured, in the bones of the people. Diana Greenlee, while a graduate student in archaeology at the University of Washington in Seattle, examined the chemical composition of bones from hundreds of adults from 69 Late Woodland and Late Prehistoric period sites in the Ohio Valley. She found a dramatic and abrupt shift in diet from little or no maize to mostly maize at around 1,050 BP.

Several studies have shown that many Late Prehistoric groups came to depend on maize for fifty to seventy-five percent of their diet. Maize can feed more people per acre of cultivated ground than any of the plants of the Eastern Agricultural Complex, but it is lacking in protein and important vitamins. An abrupt shift to a diet dominated by such a productive, but nutritionally incomplete, food was likely necessitated by the need to feed a rapidly growing population. The strategy was a success, for the population continued to grow, but the overall health of Late Prehistoric villagers declined. People suffered chronic malnutrition from the high carbohydrate diet made worse by occasional crop failures caused by a late spring or early autumn frost, droughts, or flooding. As a result, Late Prehistoric people were shorter than their ancestors and were less able to withstand infectious diseases. The sugar content of the corn, combined with the coarse grit added to the meal from the stones used to grind it, caused a variety of dental problems including cavities, worn teeth, and abscesses. Common health problems observed in Late Prehistoric skeletons include arthritis, tuberculosis, yaws, and a number of diseases related to various vitamin-deficiencies.

Indian Point Park preserves a series of three embankments built across a narrow peninsula high above the confluence of Paine Creek (above) and the Grand River in Lake County. These Late Prehistoric earthworks were surveyed by Charles Whittlesey whose map (right), "Ancient Works 3 miles East of Paineseville," was published in *Descriptions of Ancient Works in Ohio, Smithsonian Contributions to Knowledge, Volume III*, in 1850.

The average life expectancy for Late Prehistoric men and women was as low or lower than it had been for any of Ohio's prehistoric peoples. W. C. Mills reported that 92% of the 127 skeletons recovered from the Baum Village site in Ross County had died before the age of 50; and 56% had died before reaching the age of 30. At SunWatch Village in Montgomery County, life was even grimmer. Fifty-five percent of the burials recovered in the excavations (conducted prior to 1990) were children under the age of 6, and researchers have identified only a few individuals older than 35 years of age. In one report, the analysts observed, "virtually all SunWatch villagers show some sign of pathology. Arthritis and dental disease have been found in all individuals above 15 years of age."

Evidence for warfare, or at least escalating violence between communities, is common at Late Prehistoric period sites. Many villages are enclosed by palisades and, in northeastern Ohio, they tend to be built upon high bluffs. Late Prehistoric cemeteries yield evidence for why the walls were necessary. At Blain Village in Ross County, a burial mound enclosed the remains of seven people of varying ages. Perhaps it was a family group that died together in a single event. Four of the people had arrow points lodged in their skeletons indicating the violent nature of the event. At SunWatch Village, one man was buried with arrow-points in his chest. Animal tooth marks were present on many of his bones. Evidently, he was caught outside the walls of the village, killed, and left exposed to scavengers. Eventually, his family or friends found his remains and brought them home for burial.

The threat of violence was by no means constant, however, and many communities seem to have escaped the worst ravages of warfare. At the State Line site, in Hamilton County, archaeologists found projectile points embedded in only three of 390 burials.

Late Prehistoric villages were like almost any small community of farmers: everyone worked. The men likely cleared the fields and hunted game. The women probably did the planting, weeding, harvesting, and grinding of the corn, while the children helped out and also watched the fields to keep off marauding crows and deer. The village dogs undoubtedly helped with this job and, as thanks for their efforts, often ended up in the cooking pot.

The Late Prehistoric diet included more than just maize and the occasional dog. Hunters still sought game in the surrounding forests and gatherers still collected hickory nuts, black walnuts, and other wild fruits and berries. The most important game species were deer, elk, and black bear. Turkeys also were important and, at some sites, such as SunWatch Village, there is evidence that the villagers kept turkeys in pens. Late Prehistoric people, at various times and places, also hunted or snared raccoons, squirrels, turtles, and birds. For some groups, especially those living along the shores of Lake Erie, fish was a major food source. Late Prehistoric people fished using a variety of lines, nets, and traps. Groups living along rivers also collected mussels.

Late Prehistoric villages varied widely in size and structure, but generally they were larger and more permanent than any Late Woodland village. Many had between one to five hundred residents, but the population would vary with the season. Some families would disperse to winter hunting camps, but return in time to help with the spring planting. Spreading people out during the winter was a good strategy for saving the village's stores of food and firewood. The young men and women who went off enjoyed their privacy and lived off the scattered game animals far from the village's normal hunting grounds.

Late Prehistoric villages may have been occupied for 20 to 30 years at a time, but, by then, the fertility of the soils would be depleted, all of the firewood within a mile of the village would have been gathered and burned, and garbage, including human waste, may have accumulated to the point where it was more than just a nuisance.

Many Late Prehistoric villages were laid out in a regular community plan. SunWatch Village, for example, was built in a series of concentric circles. The heart of the village was an open plaza where people gathered for festivals, rituals, or public meetings. It also would have been a safe place for the village children to gather for games and sports. The village cemetery ringed this plaza. The people buried their loved ones in graves there, some of which they covered with limestone slabs. They may have placed their cemetery here so as to include the dead in the ongoing life of the village. On the other hand, it may have been a way of protecting the graves from being violated by hostile neighbors.

The "Ancient Ohio" Art Series
The Late Prehistoric Period
(Circa 1,100 to 400 BP)

Growing crops, specifically corn, beans, and squash, provided a predictable food supply that allowed Late Prehistoric people to settle in fairly permanent villages. This village, patterned after the SunWatch village site along the Great Miami River south of Dayton, Ohio, illustrates the variety of activities typical of mid-summer. The crops are well established just outside the stockade. From time to time rotted posts in the stockade had to be replaced, although fire-hardening the ends helped slow the process of decay. Bundles of prairie grass made good roofing material, although it, too, had to be replaced periodically. With more people living together for extended periods of time, the community had to find ways to deal with common concerns and to resolve disputes peacefully. No doubt such problems were presented to the elders of the community who determined the final outcome by consensus. Such a group has convened on the village plaza.

Archaeological basis: Village plan and activities based on evidence from SunWatch village; information from Sandy Yee.

SUNWATCH INDIAN VILLAGE AND ARCHAEOLOGICAL PARK

Montgomery County

By Sandra Lee Yee, Archaeologist, International Archaeological Research Institute, Inc. Guam; and former Site Manager/Site Anthropologist, SunWatch Indian Village and Archaeological Park.

About 800 years ago, a group of people of the Fort Ancient culture established their village along the Great Miami River just south of Dayton in Montgomery County. Following typical practices of their culture, they located in a pocket prairie with adjacent river and forest environments for use in housing, hunting, fishing and farming. The villagers, numbering between 200 and 250 inhabitants at their peak, farmed and lived here for about 20 years before picking up and moving to a new location.

Their village was laid out on a concentric circular plan, with the outer ring comprised of a wooden post stockade encircling three acres. The posts were native hard woods spaced approximately two feet apart, and interwoven with flexible branches to form a semi-solid barricade to protect the villagers from outside threats, keep pets and small children within, as well as delineate their community boundaries. Immediately within the stockade, the rectangular houses were constructed in a concentric ring, with their long axes parallel to

Archaeologists were able to accurately reconstruct SunWatch Indian Village because of extensive excavations that revealed postmolds (top right). Once plotted, the postmolds indicate about 25 houses had been built around the central plaza over a period of about 20 years. Archaeologists soon realized this 800-year old village was laid out to serve as a giant calendar. American Indians raised large allignment poles (left, reconstructed) in the center of the plaza that mark key agricultural dates. "You can't be a successful farmer unless you can 'control' time," says J. Heilman, Curator of Anthropology (Emeritus), Dayton Society of Natural History. "At SunWatch, the whole focus is on the 'control' of time for the harvest and planting of corn."

the adjacent stockade. These houses averaged 16 feet deep by 20 feet long. The largest, the ceremonial Big House, was approximately 20 by 30 feet. The next concentric ring in the village layout consisted of the storage and trash pits in the general household work areas in front of the houses. The final ring contained the burials, most of which were covered by ground level limestone slabs. The core of the village layout held the calendar post complex in the central plaza.

House construction consisted of vertical hardwood posts set into the ground. These posts were lashed together with flexible branches every 1-2 feet above the ground to support a thin "lath" of prairie grass. This lath was then plastered over with a daub consisting of local clays with chopped grass temper for strength. Daub on the inside and outside of the grass lath walls provided a very comfortable cool house in the summer and good insulation in the winter. The roof, framed with hardwood logs, was covered with thatching of local prairie grass, specifically the preferred Big Bluestem grass.

Many storage pits were dug about 3 feet deep for each household and lined with sticks and grass to keep the dried foods preserved and safe for consumption throughout the year. When the pits were

SUNWATCH INDIAN VILLAGE AND ARCHAEOLOGICAL PARK

SunWatch houses were built for the change of seasons. Andy Sawyer, Site Manager/Site Anthropologist, SunWatch Indian Village, stokes a small fire (right) inside the Solstice House to keep visitors warm for an annual overnight on December 21st. "The houses at SunWatch can get as much as 30 degrees warmer than the outside air in winter when continually occupied and a small fire is maitained inside the structure," says Sawyer. The grass thatch lath and daub walls, and the high roof also serve as a natural air conditioner, keeping the interior relatively cool during the summer.

American Indians at SunWatch coped with lean winter months by storing corn and other foods in numerous underground pits located between the central plaza and the outer ring of houses. The efficiency of these storage pits is shown in a cross section (above) on display in the SunWatch museum. The typical storage pit (about 3 feet in diameter and 6 feet deep) was lined with mold-resistant bluestem grass, which was anchored in place by a wooden framework. The bottom was lined with small poles and dried skin. American Indians then stacked dried corncobs around the outer wall, before filling the center with shelled corn. An average-sized storage pit could hold about 30 to 40 bushels of shelled corn for as long as one year.

emptied, they became the convenient location for trash disposal, which was covered over when full. These excellently preserved pits gave archaeologists wonderful insights about life at SunWatch, for they contained evidence of the foods, tools, and relationships that existed here 800 years ago.

The burials discovered at SunWatch gave a wealth of information on the health, stature, and status of individuals. There is evidence that the heavy reliance on corn in the diet had negatively impacted their health and life.

The central ceremonial plaza/calendar pole system was the inspiration for the modern name, SunWatch. It was discovered that these poles and the whole village were laid out as a giant sun calendar. The planting and harvesting days were marked by the passing of the rising sun's light across the central calendar pole and casting a shadow into the Big House and across its hearth.

This occurred on the date in April when corn could be safely planted without risk of frost, and again in August when it would be ready to harvest, for the Green Corn or Busk Ceremony.

Life at SunWatch was intimately tied to agriculture. Their village was surrounded by crops composed of the "three sisters" of native agriculture—corn, beans, and squash.

The villagers were organized along maternal lines, with women remaining in their mother's family area upon marriage, and their husbands moving in with them. This matrilocal society governed house location, property allocation, and other aspects of everyday life.

People at SunWatch produced beautiful art in their pipes, pottery, and stone work. The environments provided a fine mix of deer, elk and turkey from the forests and prairie, as well as their own agricultural produce, and fish and clams from the river. Transportation and trade occurred along the river system as well as the overland trails.

Archaeologists recovered an array of tobacco pipes at SunWatch Indian Village. Made of banded slate, the "wolfman" pipe (upper center) is the most intriguing. The pipe's bowl is carved into the form of a wolf. The stem side on the right depicts the profile of a human face.

The cemetery was encircled by a work area revealed today by the remains of hearths, cooking pits, and scatters of artifacts. Here groups of men and women worked to prepare food, mold pottery, mend tools, weave baskets, and do the many other chores necessary to keep the village running smoothly. Family and friends would also gather here to sit and gossip or tell stories around the fire. This area was the community's kitchen, family room, entertainment center, and workshop.

Beyond the work area was the circle of houses. Archaeologists estimate that there were 25 to 30 houses at SunWatch Village; though these may not all have been occupied at the same time. The houses generally were rectangular and ranged in size from 16 to 22 feet wide by 19 to 30 feet long. Most of the structures were homes to extended families of between six and 16 people including parents, children, grandparents, and maybe an aunt or uncle along with their spouse and children.

In contrast, the Sandusky culture village of White Fort in Lorain County appears to have had two types of houses: a rectangular lodge more than 30 feet long and a smaller, circular dwelling. Brian Redmond, the archaeologist in charge of the White Fort excavations, compared this to Kickapoo villages of the 17th and 18th centuries. The Kickapoos lived in large, bark-covered longhouses during the summer months and switched to small, round, mat-covered houses during the winter.

The outer limits of many Late Prehistoric villages were defined by a wall. A wooden palisade, built on an earthen embankment with ditches on either side, surrounded White Fort. The palisade surrounding SunWatch Village was 420 feet in diameter and built from more than 1,300 posts. Villagers ventured beyond the walls to fetch water, tend the garden, gather firewood, hunt for game, fish, collect nuts, and do a variety of other things, but at the end of the day they returned to the safety of the walls. The palisade represents an architectural expression of a growing sense of estrangement felt by the disparate communities of Late Prehistoric Ohio. Since the Paleoindian period, people had recognized and maintained distinctions between themselves and those they perceived as "others." The groups were, however, small, fluid in composition, and interdependent. By the Late Prehistoric period, these communities were no longer as interdependent. Frequently, they were in direct competition and, occasionally, in bloody conflict with one another.

THE GROWING SENSE OF SEPARATENESS WAS NOT LIMITED TO FEELINGS TOWARD GROUPS on the other side of the palisade. Within communities, there was an increasing division of people into social classes. For example, the houses at SunWatch Village were grouped into recognizable neighborhoods of varying social status. The largest houses with the largest storage pits and the graves with the richest offerings were on the west side of the village. The differences were not great, but they do suggest the emergence of more formalized village leaders whose status was reflected in greater material wealth.

THE WHITE FORT SITE

Lorain County

By Dr. Brian G. Redmond, Curator and Head of Archaeology, Director of Science, The Cleveland Museum of Natural History.

Archaeologists have been hard at work in northern Ohio for more than 70 years. And like their counterparts in southern Ohio, these scientists have documented a record of prehistoric cultures that extends back 11,000 years to the end of the Ice Age. Since 1995, I have directed the excavation of one particularly informative Late Prehistoric period settlement along the Black River of Lorain County known as White Fort.

Our work at White Fort has uncovered the well-preserved remains of village life during the fourteenth century AD. Among the most common discoveries are shallow pits that Native Americans used to build fires and prepare foods of different kinds. Deeper pits were used to store the harvest of maize, beans, and squash, as well as hickory nuts, walnuts and other wild foods. Eventually all these pits were fill with everyday trash or "midden" soils

The White Fort village, as depicted in a line drawing by artist Kirk Olmstead, shows the relationship of several key structures: a small mat-covered hut (right), a large rectangular house (center), a low "pit" house (left), and the sturdy wooden stockade that surrounded this 700-year old Sandusky village along the Black River of Lorain County.

THE WHITE FORT SITE

Archaeologists from The Cleveland Museum of Natural History spent five seasons excavating the White Fort site, which has yielded hundreds of objects such as these four triangular arrowheads (left), a black bear jaw fragment (above, bottom), and two bird-bone beads (top).

that contained lots of animal bones, pottery sherds, clam shells, charred plant remains, and even fire-cracked rock left over from hot-rock methods of cooking. The bone remains reveal that foods such as elk, deer, and fish were popular. The thousands of pottery sherds from White Fort indicate that all families constructed earthenware jars for cooking and storing foods. One reconstructed vessel illustrates the elongated, round-bottomed shape of these very useful household items. Nearly all the pottery bears a distinctive "dentate" stamped design that is typical of Sandusky Tradition groups at this time.

We have found the traces of wooden post walls, which once outlined rectangular houses that were about 15 feet wide and 30 feet long and undoubtedly housed several related families. We suspect that these were summer lodges since they had open ends to allow air-circulation during the warm months and were probably covered in thin bark sheets. Our work also uncovered the foundation of one circular house that measured 15 feet in diameter. This structure was most likely the home of a single family and, given its sturdy construction with large posts, this house could have been used as a winter dwelling in the fashion of cattail mat-covered houses used by historic Indian groups in the Great Lakes. In 2002, we found the remains of one other kind of structure used by the White Fort villagers. This was a shallow pit house that had a sloping, trench-like entrance and was probably covered with a dome-shaped roof. Based on comparisons with historically recorded groups in the Great Lakes region, these pit houses could have been used as cold-season sleeping quarters for a small family, ceremonial sweat-lodges, or even menstrual huts used by young women of the village.

One of the most intriguing features of White Fort is the extensive log stockade that surrounded the entire living area. Our excavations uncovered soil stains from as many as eight rows of deeply set posts, which must have towered ten to fifteen feet above the houses of the village. The presence of such a formidable barrier points out that warfare was prevalent during this period. Thus, archaeology reveals that life along the Black River more than 600 years ago was at times rich and full but never without danger.

Most of the White Fort pottery was decorated with the Mixter Dentate stamped design. Archaeologists recovered one nearly complete pottery vessel at the White Fort site (above), which has been reconstructed into its original form (right).

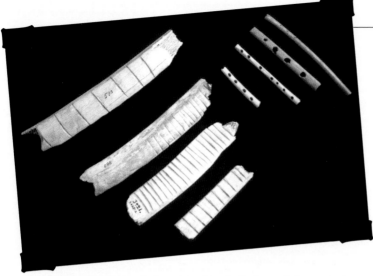

Late Prehistoric farmers made a variety of tools (below) such as hoes, picks, shovels and rakes by hafting hard blades to sturdy wooden handles. The wooden handles are long gone, but the blades survive, including these elk antler spades (left) and freshwater shell hoes (right) from the Madisonville site in Hamilton County.

American Indians created a variety of musical instruments from animal bone (above), including small flutes made from hollow bird bones (top) and rasps made from the ribs of bison and deer (left).

The archaeologist Patricia Essenpreis studied the burials from Anderson Village in Warren County and compared them with the burials from SunWatch Village. She concluded that leadership at these sites was in the hands of one or two older men. At SunWatch Village, one man had been buried with a pipe and a headdress made from a wolf's jaw and shell beads. Another older man was buried with a pipe and a shaman's medicine bundle. At Anderson Village, one older man also was buried with a pipe and medicine bundle. While hardly extravagant, these special offerings set these men apart from the others buried in the village cemeteries. Seventy-five percent of the burials at SunWatch Village, by comparison, had no grave offerings at all.

Greenlee's study of the chemical composition of Late Prehistoric skeletons identified a few men and women at southwestern Ohio sites who had more balanced diets than their neighbors. In other words, while almost everyone else was eating mostly maize for breakfast, lunch, and supper, a few people were getting access to meat on a more regular basis. It is possible that these indi-

viduals were the leaders of these Fort Ancient culture villages, but this seemingly obvious interpretation is complicated by the fact that Greenlee found that these individuals were not always the ones with the richest grave offerings. Here, as in tribal societies everywhere, there was a complicated relationship between the privileges and responsibilities of community leaders.

✕✕✕

UNDERSTANDING THE ORIGINS OF SOCIAL INEQUALITY IS ONE OF THE MOST INTERESTING questions in all of prehistory. Why should any group of people with a tradition of independence allow one member of the group to lord it over all the others? Actually, there were a number of things happening during the Late Prehistoric period that may have made the rise of such institutionalized leaders almost inevitable.

The increasingly sedentary way of life of Late Prehistoric people must have led to increasing social friction between the people forced to live together for long periods of time. People had become less free to vote with their feet and they had to find ways to get along with one another without resorting to violence. Giving a few respected elders the authority to resolve disputes may have eased such social pressures.

Increasing competition between groups for farmland or hunting grounds might have led to violent interactions and eventually warfare between villages. A leader would be required to organize defensive measures, such as the construction of a palisade wall, and direct offensive actions against the groups who threatened the security of the village.

A growing population, combined with increasing restrictions on a group's ability to move, made it necessary for people to produce enough crops during the growing season to feed the village throughout the entire year with some to spare for possible shortages in next year's harvest. The need to produce this surplus of food may have required a leader to organize the necessary labor as well as to distribute the food.

THE INCREASING COMMITMENT TO AN AGRICULTURAL WAY OF LIFE WOULD HAVE led to a need for specialized knowledge of the seasonal calendar so that the corn would be planted neither too soon or too late in the year. Astronomical knowledge, already an important part of Hopewell rituals, was adapted to the special requirements of maize agriculture. The Late Prehistoric people developed a solar calendar for determining the timing of planting and harvest and the various religious rituals and festivals that accompanied these pivotal points in the seasonal cycle. The shaman, always a respected member of the society, may have taken on new leadership responsibilities in Late Prehistoric societies.

The farmer's life, even more so than the hunter's, was fraught with uncertainty. After the back-breaking toil of clearing a patch of forest and planting the seeds saved from the previous year's harvest, the farmers could only wait. If the spring rains were too heavy, the fields would flood and the crop would be washed away. If there was a prolonged drought, the plants would wither under the August sun and there would be no crop. The farmer could do everything right and still lose an entire harvest to the seemingly random fluctuations in rainfall. In such circumstances, when the lives of their families depended on factors that could not be controlled through planning or their own hard work, many people have turned to various supernatural powers for aid and comfort. If gods or spirits brought the rain or withheld it according to their whims, then perhaps offerings to those beings might compel or persuade them to act in a reciprocally generous manner. Shamans had, for generations, called upon spirits to aid them in the hunt. Now they adopted new ceremonies centered around the planting and harvesting of their crops. Such ceremony provided a measure of psychological comfort and security to believers, but the ritual calendar also provided a solid framework of dates for planting and harvesting that was carefully attuned to the seasons.

SunWatch Village, for example, had a gigantic cedar post planted at the center of the village plaza. Twice a year, on April 29th and August 19th, the rising sun cast the pole's shadow through the doorway and across the hearth of the largest house in the village, referred to by the archaeologists as the Big House. These dates framed the peak growing period of maize 800 years ago, when the climate was a bit warmer than today. April 29th marked the beginning of the reliably frost-free season and by August 19th the corn would have been ready for the historically-documented "Green Corn Festival."

In the historic era, the Green Corn Festival was a time of thanksgiving and religious renewal for the tribal societies of the Eastern Woodlands. The village was cleansed and purified and all the fires were extinguished, to be re-ignited with the first rays of the sun on the following morning. Perhaps such rituals were a part of the religious life of the Late Prehistoric villagers. A pit excavated at the Blain Village site contained burned corn, black walnuts, and other vegetable matter along with artifacts interpreted as the remains of a medicine bundle. The archaeologists who studied the site suggest this pit is evidence for a Fort Ancient Green Corn Ceremony.

Many of our contemporary holidays and religious festivals have their roots in an agricultural calendar. Christmas, for example, occurs at about the time of the winter solstice. At SunWatch Village, the rising sun on the winter solstice (December 21st) cast the shadow of SunWatch Village's center post along the truncated edge of one of the houses and through the doorway and across the hearth of another specialized house structure. Sandra Lee Yee, former manager and site anthropologist, said "...the entire village was a sun calendar."

THE LATE PREHISTORIC BIG HOUSE, KNOWN PRINCIPALLY FROM THE FORT ANCIENT cultural area, was quite different from the earlier Hopewellian version, though each served as the hub of religious life for their respective cultures. The Hopewell Big House often was a very large structure with different lobes, or chambers that seem to represent places set aside for distinctive ritual activities. The carefully demarcated use of space suggests different cults or denominations were being accommodated under one big-tent church.

The Fort Ancient Big House was smaller and simpler in plan than the Hopewell Big House, but it was larger than any other structure in the village. The relatively Puritanical simplicity of the Big House and the inwardly-focused community plan of houses huddled like wagons in a circle around a central plaza all suggest a narrowing of the world-view and a more rigidly authoritarian religious outlook.

The religious leaders still were shamans who used hallucinogenic drugs and other techniques for entering the spirit world to commune with animal guardians. Shamanic paraphernalia such as pipes and animals' jaws and teeth that have been cut and drilled are sometimes found as burial offerings. At SunWatch Village, archaeologists excavated a ritual burial of a young male wolf at the north end of the central plaza and, near the southern end of the plaza, a unique effigy pipe carved with a wolf's head at one end and a human head at the other. This suggests the wolf was an especially potent spirit animal for the people of SunWatch Village.

Archaeologists have excavated sweat lodges at SunWatch Village as well as other Late Prehistoric sites in eastern and northeastern Ohio. These were small pit houses where water was poured over hot stones to create a ritual steam bath. Historically, Native Americans in eastern North America used sweat lodges for purification and healing ceremonies.

Late prehistoric burial practices were quite varied. Some villages buried their dead in simple graves, such as those excavated at SunWatch Village. Others buried their honored dead in small mounds of earth and stone, such as the mound at Blain Village.

The most extravagant expression of Late Prehistoric ritual may have been Ohio's great effigy mounds. Serpent Mound in Adams County is Ohio's most famous prehistoric monument. This gigantic serpent effigy, built from earth and stone, stretches for 1,348 feet along a high bluff that projects into the valley of Ohio Brush Creek. The head of the serpent is pointed across the valley at the point on the horizon where the sun sets on the summer solstice.

Alligator Mound was built on a similar bluff

Serpent Mound State Memorial is veiled in a late winter snow as the sun sets on this enigmatic effigy mound stretching along a ridge above Brush Creek in Adams County. Until recently, archaeologists often associated Serpent Mound with the Adena or Hopewell cultures. However, new radiocarbon dates on charcoal collected from the mound in 1991 indicate that it was built about 850 to 990 years ago—a creation of the Fort Ancient culture, that flourished in southern Ohio during the Late Prehistoric Period. Why ancient American Indians built Serpent Mound remains one of Ohio's greatest archaeological mysteries.

Serpent Mound is aligned to the setting sun (left) on the Summer Solstice. Like SunWatch Village, Serpent Mound also may be architecturally linked to the sun. When an observer stands at the neck of the serpent and looks across the center of the oval earthwork (the eye of the snake according to one interpretation supported by a study of Late Prehistoric serpent representations), the point on the horizon at which he or she is looking is where the sun sets on the Summer Solstice.

In 1991, a team of amateur and professional archaeologists re-opened a trench (above) originally excavated by archaeologist Frederic Ward Putman in the late 1880s. Small chunks of charcoal, recovered during the 20th century excavations, were found to be from fires that burned more than nine centuries ago. These new dates suggest the effigy mound was built by the Fort Ancient people. Serpent symbolism was much more important in the art of the Late Prehistoric period than it was in any earlier period.

that projects into the Raccoon Creek Valley of Licking County. It is an effigy of a four-legged, long-tailed creature with a small, round head. It is two hundred feet long following the distinctly un-alligator-like curve of its tail.

The great era of monumental mound-building was during the Early and Middle Woodland periods. For that reason, many archaeologists have assumed that Ohio's effigy mounds were built by the Adena or Hopewell cultures. Animal effigy mounds in Iowa and Wisconsin, however, are known to have been built by a culture contemporary with Ohio's Late Woodland and early Late Prehistoric periods. In 1991, archaeologists recovered charcoal from the Serpent that returned radiocarbon dates of 850 to 990 years BP. Samples from the Alligator Mound, excavated in 1999, yielded an average age of from 800 to 860 years BP. These dates indicate that Late Prehistoric people built both effigies. This is consistent with the age of the other North American animal effigy mounds. Although there is no evidence for any direct connection

THE GRANVILLE EFFIGY

The Granville "Alligator" Mound in Licking County is Ohio's only other known animal effigy mound. While called "Alligator" Mound since the 1800s, the effigy, with its small round head and curling tail, looks more like a panther or an opossum than any reptile. This 1992 aerial photograph (right) shows the 200-foot-long effigy encircled by a housing development. In 1999, archaeologists recovered charcoal from the base of the mound that has been dated to about 800 years ago. The Granville "Alligator" Mound appears to be associated with the Fort Ancient culture of the Late Prehistoric Period.

The oldest known aerial photograph (above) of the Granville "Alligator" Mound was taken in 1928 by Newark businessman and aviation enthusiast Warren Weiant, Jr.

The earliest rendering of the Granville "Alligator" Mound (left) was published by Ephraim Squier and Edwin Davis. Squier and Davis drew attention to the circular stone platform attached to the right side of the effigy, which they identified as an "altar" and noted the stones composing it had been "much burned."

between these two effigy mound-building cultures, it would not be surprising if travelers from Ohio encountered the effigies of the Upper Midwest and were inspired to build something similar here. After all, Native America must have had its own explorers and adventurers, such as Odysseus and Marco Polo, whose exploits were never chronicled.

Ohio's effigies are not burial mounds. The Serpent and the Alligator are Late Prehistoric ritual expressions that take the form of giant sculptures. They may have been built as shrines to the two most powerful supernatural beings whom historic era Native Americans associated with the underworld. The Horned Serpent and the Underwater

Medicine animal of the Winnebagoes

Drawn by Little Hill, a Chief of that tribe.

In thinking about what sort of creature the so-called "Alligator" mound was intended to represent, anthropologists consider the beings who were important in the religious beliefs of historic tribes. Two principal spirit creatures ruled the Underworld—the Great Horned Serpent and the Underwater Panther. If Serpent Mound represents the supernatural serpent spirit, then the "Alligator" might be the Underwater Panther. This depiction of an Underwater Panther, drawn in the mid-1800s by Winnebago Chief Little Hill, was originally published by Henry Schoolcraft 1852. The artwork is labeled "Medicine Animal of the Winnebagoes." Chief Little Hill is reported to have said the animal was "only seen by medicine men after severe fasting."

Panther are frequent subjects of Late Prehistoric and historic period art across eastern North America. Historically, the native peoples of the Great Lakes Region made offerings of tobacco or copper at shrines to these powerful spirits in order to insure a safe journey or victory in war.

The people of the Late Prehistoric period in Ohio faced many challenges. More and more people were becoming concentrated in larger and more permanent villages. Such groups had a narrowing range of options forced upon them. When resources became scarce, they could not simply move to greener pastures because other groups might already be living there. They had to make the most of what they had.

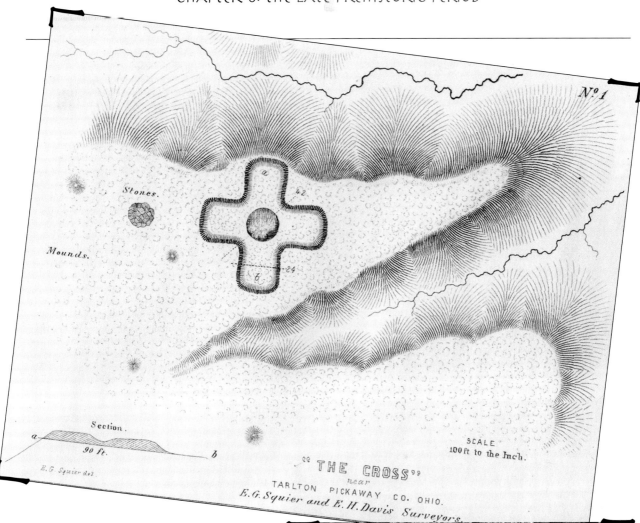

Nº 1

Stones.

Mounds.

Section.

90 ft.

a   b

E.G. Squier del.

SCALE
100 ft to the Inch.

"THE CROSS"
near
TARLTON PICKAWAY CO. OHIO.
E.G. Squier and E.H. Davis Surveyors.

The Tarlton Cross (above) now in Fairfield County measured "ninety feet between the ends, and elevated three feet above the adjacent surface" when surveyed by Ephraim Squier and Edwin Davis for publication in 1848.

Dr. Tod Frolking (right), a geologist from Denison University, and archaeologist Dr. Bradley Lepper examine soil cores taken from the Tarlton Cross mound. Researchers are attempting to determine the structure of the mound and locate charcoal for radiocarbon dating. Unfortunately, no charcoal was found so the age of Tarlton Cross remains one of Ohio's many archaeological mysteries.

221

OHIO'S AMERICAN INDIAN PETROGLYPHS

By W. Kevin Pape, President, Gray & Pape, Inc., Cultural Resources Consultants.

Petroglyphs (carvings) and pictographs (paintings) are two major forms of cultural expression archaeologists call rock art. American Indians made petroglyphs by using a hard rock such as granite to "peck" the outline of an image into softer outcrops such as limestone or sandstone. No pictographs have been identified in Ohio.

James L. Swauger conducted an extensive survey of Ohio petroglyphs in the late 1970s, categorizing 35 petroglyphs of "Native American Origin." His survey, published in *Petroglyphs of Ohio,* Ohio University Press, (1984), indicates that Ohio's petroglyphs are located in two settings likely to yield rock outcrops: hilly uplands and locations adjacent to water. Design motifs tend to reflect animal and human forms and geometric shapes. Intriguingly, Swauger observed that simple designs occur primarily on hillside sites and more complex designs, particularly of human forms, were created on sites near water.

Ohio's petroglyphs pose several challenges for archaeological interpretation. First, petroglyphs do not yield radiocarbon dates. Their exact age is unknown. Yet, relative dating may be possible by estimating the general rate of erosion for softer rock formations. Swauger contends that none of the 35 Ohio petroglyphs of "Native American origin" could have survived from the Paleoindian, Archaic, or Woodland time periods based on erosion rates. Drawing on historical accounts of the gradual fading of once deeply carved images, Swauger contends Ohio's petroglyphs are most likely products of the Late Prehistoric and Protohistoric periods. Swauger also notes there is no evidence of "European contact in their design."

Even in one generation, the impact of erosion is evident on the petroglyphs pecked into Inscription Rock State Memorial on Kelley's Island. This relatively fast erosion rate suggests Ohio's American Indian petroglyphs date no older than the Late Prehistoric period.

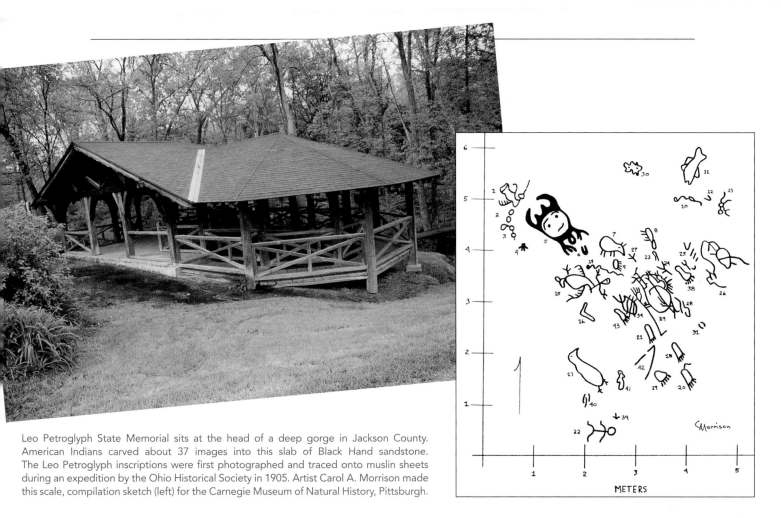

Leo Petroglyph State Memorial sits at the head of a deep gorge in Jackson County. American Indians carved about 37 images into this slab of Black Hand sandstone. The Leo Petroglyph inscriptions were first photographed and traced onto muslin sheets during an expedition by the Ohio Historical Society in 1905. Artist Carol A. Morrison made this scale, compilation sketch (left) for the Carnegie Museum of Natural History, Pittsburgh.

The second challenge is trying to interpret the meaning of hundreds of different designs and images. What do the petroglyphs mean? Some anthropologists have tried to interpret the symbols by comparing them to similar motifs documented in the ethnographic accounts of historic tribes. Some American Indians contend they can still read Ohio's rock art just as easily as a modern highway sign. It may be that meaning was reserved only for the original artists.

Based on similarity of design motifs, researchers generally agree that Ohio's petroglyphs were created by Algonquian people, possibly related to the Ojibwa. In the Ojibwa culture "kinomagewapkong" means "the rocks that teach." "Muzzinabikon" means "rock writing" which most often recorded the visionary experiences of Ojibwa shamans. The conclusion that Ohio's petroglyph sites represent places where people with wisdom came to think and pray does not seem at all unreasonable.

Leo Petroglyph State Memorial

The Ohio Historical Society preserves two American Indian petroglyph sites. Leo Petroglyph State Memorial shelters about 37 images pecked into a large sandstone outcrop in the uplands of Jackson County. The Leo Petroglyph depicts animals, human forms and abstract designs. Archaeologists have identified some animals—an owl, hawk, fish, a bear, and perhaps, a serpent. Many glyphs remain obscure symbols of unknown meaning. This includes a sort of horned "head" with bird feet, which has prompted a stunning assortment of interpretations. The Ohio Historical Society attributes Leo Petroglyph to the surrounding Fort Ancient culture based on design motifs and erosion rates.

Inscription Rock State Memorial

Inscription Rock State Memorial is a 32 by 21 foot limestone slab discovered partially buried in the shoreline of Kelley's Island in 1833. Lieutenant Meigs reported the petroglyph to the Indian Bureau, leading to its documentation by Captain Eastman for Henry Rowe Schoolcraft in 1850. Significant erosion of the designs over the last 150 years, and its proximity to the Kelley Mansion Site (ca. A.D.1450), suggest Inscription Rock probably dates to the Late Prehistoric period. Schoolcraft identified 122 designs and described this petroglyph as "by far the most the most extensive and well preserved inscription of the antiquarian period ever found in America." Ojibwa symbolism suggests that head ornamentation and lines across the chests of human forms indicate persons possessing special powers. Schoolcraft concluded that Inscription Rock was a record of important events. Another petroglyph once rested on the nothern shore of Kelley's Island. But this small, granite bolder with 11 angular images mysteriously vanished sometime in the 1960s.

We may never know the meaning of designs carved into Ohio's petroglyphs but they remain evocative, tangible links to the visions, thoughts, and imagery expressed by native people who lived between the Great Lakes and the Ohio Valley.

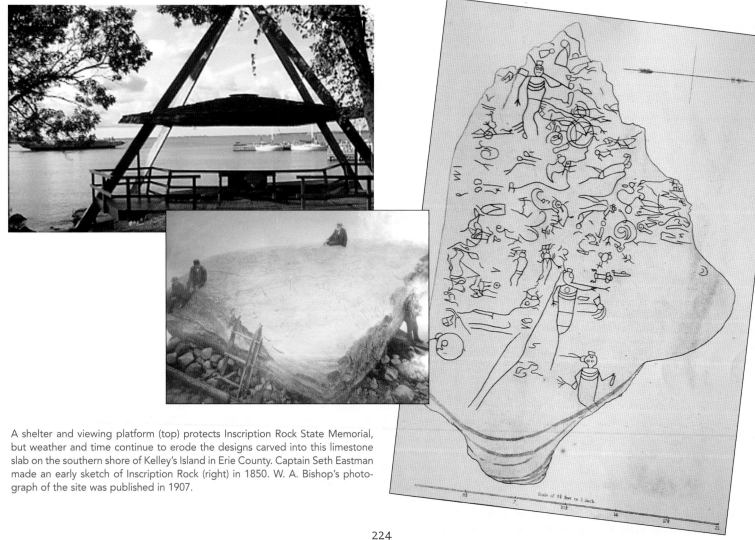

A shelter and viewing platform (top) protects Inscription Rock State Memorial, but weather and time continue to erode the designs carved into this limestone slab on the southern shore of Kelley's Island in Erie County. Captain Seth Eastman made an early sketch of Inscription Rock (right) in 1850. W. A. Bishop's photograph of the site was published in 1907.

This sandstone carving of a pregnant woman is one of the few obvious depictions of females ever recovered by archaeologists in Ohio. The figurine, which may symbolize fertility, comes from a Fort Ancient site in Preble County.

Maize gave them the ability to get more food calories from an acre of ground than they could get from hunting, gathering, or even growing the plants of the Eastern Agricultural Complex. Maize seemed to be a godsend and the rituals surrounding its planting and harvest were invested with appropriately enthusiastic piety. The giant cedar pole at the heart of SunWatch Village and the great effigy mounds reflect the ultimate efforts of Ohio's Late Prehistoric people to secure the goodwill of the spirits who brought the rain and insured an abundance of game animals.

Maize was, however, a mixed blessing. It filled the belly, but it was all carbohydrates and sugar. Cavities, vitamin deficiency diseases, and other ailments plagued the people who relied too heavily on it.

Social problems also bedeviled the people living in the villages of the Late Prehistoric period. Leaders emerged with the authority to control the production and distribution of a food surplus, mediate disputes, negotiate alliances, lead war parties, and organize the village's defenses. The rise of such leaders led to increasing social inequality. The fact that this authority was, in many cases, divided among different people meant that Late Prehistoric societies often were fractured by rivalries and power struggles. It was the continuing absence of a strong, centralized political authority that hindered Native American efforts to resist effectively the incursions of Europeans in the 18th and early 19th centuries.

In many ways, the people of the Late Prehistoric period were victims of progress rather than its beneficiaries. Most of them worked harder, were less healthy, had less freedom, and died at a younger age than their ancestors. The large villages rapidly depleted their natural resources. Conflicts between villages erupted over access to cropland or hunting territory. The winners were the villages with more warriors or more effective war chiefs. With each victory, villages grew larger and the leaders grew more powerful. The gap between the haves and have-nots grew wider. In other regions of ancient America, this cycle culminated with the rise of city-states and empires. In Ohio, the cycle was broken by the aftershocks of two worlds colliding.

Ohio was rich in natural resources, including beaver pelts and other animal hides prized by early European traders on the eastern seaboard of North America. Control of this fur trade, coupled with old hostilities, led to conflicts between the Iroquois Confederacy and other tribes in the Great Lakes region. The Iroquois or Beaver Wars (ca. 1650–1700 AD) brought death, destruction and displacement to the American Indian groups living in Ohio who were already weakened by European diseases, and often fought without guns.

The Late Prehistoric period ended more abruptly than it had begun. The beginning of the end was marked by the appearance of European trade items at sites across Ohio. No European had yet come into the land that would become known as Ohio, but the exotic and seemingly magical things from an alien world were spreading from village to village across the continent. In their wake, exotic viruses from that alien world spread across America, ravaging peoples who had lost almost all their immunity to diseases their ancestors had left behind in the Old World more than 14,000 years ago. The ensuing holocaust also must have seemed magical, but the shaman's sweat lodge and herbal medicines proved unable to cope with the lethal contagion. Varying estimates suggest somewhere between fifty and eighty percent of Ohio's Indigenous population was swept away in wave after wave of epidemic disease. And then, before the survivors could recover from the unthinkable devastation, the coalition of tribes known as the Iroquois Confederacy, armed with European weapons and a growing hunger for more of what Europe could offer, came to finish them off.

The Historic Period in Ohio begins in 1656 with this passage from the Jesuit Relations:

"Our Iroquois, have discovered beyond the Cat Nation [also known as the Erie Indians who lived along the eastern rim of Lake Erie] other and numerous Nations who speak the Algonquian language. There are more than 30 villages whose inhabitants have never had any knowledge of Europeans, they still use only stone hatchets and knives...
Our Iroquois carry fire and war thither..."

The survivors fled to the north, west, and south, but neither history nor archaeology has yet determined where, or whether, they found a safe haven.

Late Prehistoric Period Timeline
Archaeological Sites and Historical/Natural Events
(ca. 1,100-400 BP)

RC Years Ago (BC/AD)	Ohio	North America	World
300 BP (1,580 AD)		Iroquois "Beaver Wars" (ca. 310-250 BP) Plymouth Colony (ca. 329 BP) Champlain founds Quebec (ca. 342 BP)	
	Indian Hills (✳ ca. 350-307 BP)	Roanoke Colony (ca. 366 BP)	
400 BP (1,530 AD)	South Park (✤ ca. 400-300 BP) Petersen (✳ ca. 400-350 BP)	DeSoto's march (ca. 412-409 BP) Cartier explores St. Lawrence (ca. 416 BP)	
	Bear Fort (✳ ca. 450-350 BP)		
	OEC1 (✳ ca. 480-250 BP)		Columbus lands in Caribbean (ca. 458 BP)
500 BP (1,430 AD)	Madisonville [late] (✳ ca. 500-300 BP) Indian Point Park (✤ ca. 500-450 BP)		
			Aztec Empire, Mesoamerica (ca. 523-429 BP)
		Caborn-Welborn Culture, KY (ca. 550-250 BP)	
600 BP (1,350 AD)			
		Little Ice Age (ca. 650-100 BP)	Ottoman Empire, Turkey (ca. 650-750 BP)
700 BP (1,300 AD)	White Fort (✳ ca. 700-350 BP) Madisonville [early] (✳ ca. 700-500 BP)		Marco Polo reaches China (ca. 675 BP) Yoruban Culture, West Africa (ca. 690 BP)
			Inca Empire, South America (ca. 750-420 BP)
800 BP (1,230 AD)	Baum Village (✳ ca. 800-600 BP)		Crusades begin, Middle East (ca. 832 BP)
	SunWatch Village (✳ ca. 850-750 BP) Granville Effigy (✳ ca. 860-800 BP)	Monongahela Culture, PA (ca. 850-250 BP)	Timbuktu founded, Mali (ca. 850 BP) Great Zimbabwe rises, East Africa (ca. 850 BP)
900 BP (1,130 AD)		Angel Mounds, IN (ca. 900-550 BP) Wickliffe Mound, KY (ca. 900-650 BP)	
	Wegerzyn (✳ ca. 950-550 BP)	Medieval Warm Period (ca. 950-650 BP) Moundsville, AL (ca. 950-500 BP)	Vikings land, Newfoundland (ca. 950 BP) Ghana Empire rises, Africa (ca. 950 BP)
1,000 BP (1,070 AD)	Serpent Mound (✳ ca. 990-850 BP) Blain Village (✳ ca. 1,000-400 BP)	Chaco Canyon Pueblos, N.M. (ca. 1,000 BP)	Gunpowder invented, China (ca. 1,000 BP)
	Corn agriculture widespread (ca.1,050 BP)	Hohokam Culture, Southwest (ca. 1,050 BP)	Hindu temples rise, India (ca. 1,050 BP)
1,100 BP (950 AD)		Cahokia Peak, IL (ca. 1,100 BP)	Toltec Culture, Mesoamerica (ca. 1,100-800 BP)
		Mississippian Culture (ca. 1,250-300 BP)	

Left-margin culture bars:
- Sandusky Culture (ca. 700-400 BP)
- Fort Ancient Culture (ca. 900-400 BP)
- Whittlesey Culture (ca. 950-350 BP)

Criteria and Key
This timeline is based on published radiocarbon dates or artifact typology. The dates are listed as ca. (about) BP = Radiocarbon Years Before Present and BC/AD. The "present" is defined by convention as AD 1950, the year standards were set for reporting radiocarbon dates. The timeline includes the best information available at the time of publication. Ohio sites limited to those referenced in text or on maps.
  ✳ = based on radiocarbon (C14) and other laboratory dates
  ✤ = based on typology of artifacts and site features

PROTO HISTORY IN NORTHWEST OHIO

By Dr. David M. Stothers, University of Toledo and
Andrew M. Schneider, Firelands Archaeological Research Center

At the dawn of historic times in northwest Ohio, prehistoric Native American life was significantly affected by Europeans even though they had never seen Europeans. This important time period is named 'proto-history' because in a strange way, it is neither prehistory nor history.

Trade goods from Europe were highly sought after and were valuable items within the Native American economies. Thus, their way of life was dramatically impacted by Europeans, but it would be more than a hundred years before they actually saw Europeans.

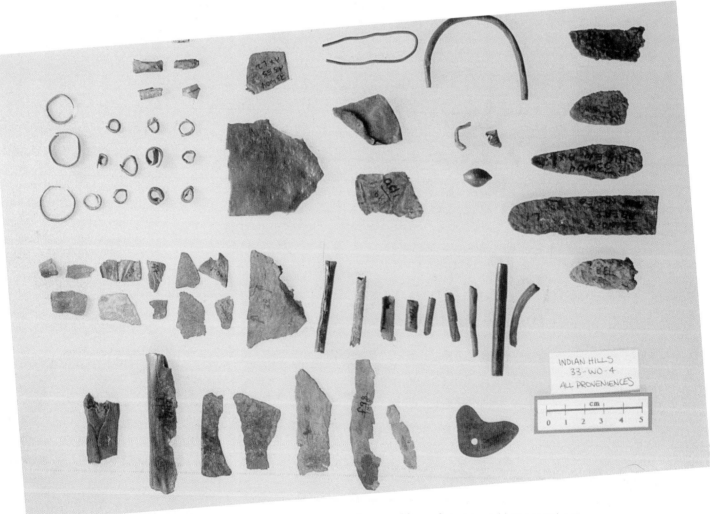

An assemblage of copper and brass metal artifacts from the Indian Hills site in Wood County.

So how did the European trade items get there? We know from diaries and chronicles that Europeans and other explorers were trading with native populations along the St. Lawrence River valley and the eastern seaboard during the 1500s and early 1600s. In addition, the explorers were trying to find a passage west through the Great Lakes. While looking for such a passage in 1603, Samuel de Champlain sailed up the St. Lawrence as far as he could but had to stop near present-day Montreal, Quebec. Through translators, he learned from various Algonquin-speaking tribes about a trade route down through the Great Lakes which took three "moons" (months) by canoe. Their description of the route in specific geographic terms approximates what we know today about Lake Ontario, Niagara Falls, and Lake Erie. They said they had been to the far end of the second lake many times and knew the route well.

Interestingly, modern day archaeological excavations at Late Prehistoric 'Sandusky Tradition' sites in northwest Ohio have produced evidence of European trade items in the form of glass beads, as well as brass and copper scrap and derived items (finger rings, beads, bracelets, and pendants). These sites, such as Indian Hills, Farnsworth, LaSalle, Petersen, Edwards, Muddy Creek and Bear Fort, date from A.D. 1550 to 1643—long before Europeans actually visit northwest Ohio.

Who were the people of the 'Sandusky Tradition'? By the mid-1600s French missionaries were living with Iroquoian groups to the north in Ontario. These Iroquoians told the missionaries about a confederacy of tribal groups to the south referred to as the 'Assistaehronon,' which meant Fire Nation. Archaeologists now think the 'Sandusky Tradition' and the people the Iroquoians named the Fire Nation were actually one and the same.

As was common at the time, the Iroquoian groups sometimes traded with the Fire Nation confederacy, but at other times were at war with them. As European traders became interested in acquiring larger quantities of furs (beaver, muskrat, mink, and otter) to satisfy the great market demands of European clothing fashions, the Black Swamp in northwest Ohio became highly valuable because of its fur-bearing animals. As a result, Iroquoian groups became hostile toward the Fire Nation Confederacy in order to gain control and access to the Black Swamp. In 1643, the missionaries wrote that the Iroquoians defeated the Fire Nation Confederacy after a war that lasted several years. Defeated, the Fire Nation Confederacy fled west to Wisconsin where they met Europeans for the first time. There, they became known by eight new tribal names, such as Mascouten and Kickapoo.

Three European glass beads from the Indian Hills site in Wood County.

Ancient Ohio
Early European Trade Routes
(ca. 400 to 310 BP)
(ca. AD 1,530 to 1,640)

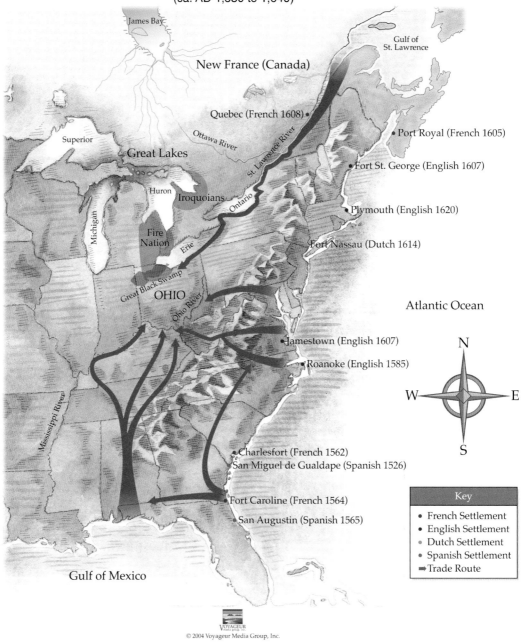

James Bay

Gulf of
St. Lawrence

New France (Canada)

Quebec (French 1608)

Port Royal (French 1605)

Ottawa River

Superior

Great Lakes

St. Lawrence River

Fort St. George (English 1607)

Huron

Iroquoians

Ontario

Plymouth (English 1620)

Michigan

Fire
Nation

Erie

Fort Nassau (Dutch 1614)

Great Black Swamp

OHIO

Ohio River

Atlantic Ocean

Jamestown (English 1607)

Roanoke (English 1585)

Mississippi River

N

W   E

S

Charlesfort (French 1562)
San Miguel de Gualdape (Spanish 1526)

Fort Caroline (French 1564)

San Augustin (Spanish 1565)

Gulf of Mexico

Key
• French Settlement
• English Settlement
• Dutch Settlement
• Spanish Settlement
➡ Trade Route

VOYAGEUR
© 2004 Voyageur Media Group, Inc.

European trade goods made their way into Ohio well before American Indians living here came face to face with European explorers. Items such as copper, brass and glass beads came through established trade routes, primary along the southern shore of the Great Lakes and through trails across the Appalachian Mountains. Indirect European contact marks the end of the Late Prehistoric Period in Ohio and the beginning of the Protohistoric Period (ca. 1560 – 1650 AD), the time just before written accounts emerge about the region.

EARLY EUROPEAN CONTACT IN SOUTHERN OHIO

By Dr. A. Gwynn Henderson, Archaeologist, Kentucky Archaeological Survey.

There can be no doubt that native peoples living in Southern Ohio heard about Europeans long before they ever saw one. By the mid-1500s, the farming peoples in the middle Ohio River valley, including Southern Ohio, were linked indirectly by long-distance native exchange networks to groups in the Northeast, Middle Atlantic and Southeast. News and objects signaling the appearance of Europeans could have come from any one of these places. However, Hernando de Soto's expedition of 1539-1543 was the earliest face-to-face contact with Europeans that occurred closest to Southern Ohio (it reached as far north as Tennessee), so it seems safe to assume that the news of these hairy, light-skinned Spaniards, with their armor, large dogs and many pigs, quickly made its way northward. We will never know when and exactly how the very first report of Europeans reached Southern Ohio, but from this time until 1674, when the first European physically set foot in the middle Ohio River valley, stories of these strange people and their growing settlements and trading posts north, south, east and west of Southern Ohio would have become increasingly common.

As time passed, the objects made from European materials would have become more common, too. Most represented ornaments: indigo, white, red, turquoise, and multicolored glass beads of many shapes and sizes; and strips of copper or brass from European kettles, rolled to form tubular beads, tubes, bracelets, and coils, or flattened sheets cut and folded to form clips and pierced to form pendants. These kinds of items have been found with individuals buried at such sites as Madisonville in Ohio, Hardin Village in Kentucky and Clover, Rolfe Lee and Orchard in West Virginia. They would have come, through down-the-line exchange, from Eastern groups, like the Iroquois or Susquehannocks, who lived in direct or closer contact with Europeans, or from groups living in the interior Southeast.

An assemblage from the Madisonville site shows a mixture of traditional Fort Ancient artifacts surrounding European trade goods, including the Clarksdale Bell, a copper ring, and other copper fragments.

EARLY EUROPEAN CONTACT IN SOUTHERN OHIO

When and exactly how the deadly European diseases, the first probably being smallpox, reached Southern Ohio also is unknown, although there can be no doubt that they surely did appear in the region. The people living in Southern Ohio, like all the native peoples of North America, possessed no natural immunity to the foreign diseases that had developed in European cities.

Researchers generally agree that de Soto's expedition probably was not the source of these diseases, but along the Atlantic and Gulf coasts, native groups experienced the devastating effects of introduced diseases beginning in the 1500s and early 1600s. Disease introduction, though, does not mean disease diffusion. The latter depends on native population densities and communication routes, and the periods during which pathogens are communicable.

Thus groups located farther inland, like those living in Southern Ohio, might not have experienced the effects of these diseases until much later.

Indeed, the Appalachian Mountains served as a natural barrier, and the orientation of the major river drainages and waterways in Ohio directed Europeans, and perhaps their diseases, north along the Great Lakes or west along the Mississippi River until the late 1600s. French documents of the late 1660s mention Honniasontkeronons and Chiouanons living along the Ohio River, upstream from the Falls of the Ohio (what is now Louisville, Kentucky), and maps of the same period, though not based on any direct evidence, also locate indigenous groups like the Chaouanons (Shawnee?) in the middle Ohio Valley. When the captive Gabriel Arthur traversed the New/Kanawha River in 1674, possibly

About 200 years after European trade goods first entered the central Ohio Valley, the lower Shawnee Town near present day Portsmouth was a major English trading post for American Indians and Pennsylvania traders. This winter scene entitled "Early Shawnee Village, 1730" depicts the northern side of the lower Shawnee Town which was located on both sides of the Ohio River.

as far as the Ohio River, his eyewitness account describes a region well-populated by groups that did not own iron tools or guns. Does this mean the diseases had not yet reached the region? The archaeological data are silent on this. Investigators have not documented any mass graves that would indicate when European diseases arrived in the region.

But it was just a matter of time. And the effects of these diseases on Southern Ohio's native populations would have been as devastating for them as they had been to the Eastern groups. Researchers estimate that population loss may have been as high as 90 percent. In the most severe situations, nine out of ten people died. Hardest hit were the oldest, whose memories held their people's history and traditions, and the youngest, who represented the future. The result was that the social fabric of Southern Ohio's native farming societies was irrevocably changed. Responses to the effects of these diseases would have been as diverse as the groups who lived in the region. Some may have completely disappeared. Surviving remnants could have left the region completely, or stayed and worked to rebuild their lives and traditions.

In the decades that followed direct European contact, native communities in Ohio would endure additional threats to their way of life: subsequent disease outbreaks, the construction of trading posts in their midst and the arrival of rum and brandy; the appearance of missionaries who wished to convert them; and settlers who pushed them off their lands. The United States' policy of removal in the early 1800s convinced or forced many groups still living in Ohio to leave for lands set aside for them west of the Mississippi.

Yet the events in Southern Ohio's Indian history hold lessons for us today. They testify to the resiliency of the human spirit, the ability of people to adapt, and their ability to endure. Despite all of these challenges, the descendants of some of Southern Ohio's ancient people are still here.

Historic documents of the mid-1700s describe the lower Shawnee Town as a large, multi-ethnic village that also served as a Shawnee settlement. This artwork by Robert Dafford is one of over 30 murals in the Portsmouth Floodwall Project.

SMITHSONIAN INSTITUTION ARCHAEOLOGIST WILLIAM FITZHUGH HAS DESCRIBED THE arrival of Europeans in America as "a momentous turning point in world history." It marked the closing of a circle of human migration out of Africa that began more than 50,000 years ago. One wave of that migration turned west and colonized Europe. Another turned east and colonized Asia, Australia, the Americas, and Polynesia. Those waves met on the shores of Newfoundland 1,000 years ago. The consequences for Native American peoples were catastrophic, but today, 1,000 years later, the odyssey continues. On reservations in Oklahoma and other western states, in Ohio's cities, towns, and villages, and across eastern North America, descendants of Ohio's ancient people continue to carry on their legacy.

Modern Native Americans have changed many aspects of their traditional ways of life, but change has been a hallmark of human cultures throughout the world. For more than 14,000 years, Ohio's people have been changing in response to changes in the natural environment as well as changing social conditions. Archaeologists have identified and singled out many of those changes to define the various cultural periods considered in this book.

Traces of all of these ancient cultures persist in every part of Ohio. Mounds, broken pots, or flint spearpoints can be found in fields and forests across the state. This is Ohio's unwritten history and it lies all around us. Much of it is being erased by the farmer's plow, the builder's bulldozer, or the looter's shovel. It is the responsibility of those who value our heritage to preserve this irreplaceable legacy of Ohio's ancient people. For their story is not fully known. There are missing chapters and we may have gotten some of it wrong. Future studies will give us new insights and may change many of our current ideas about the past; but future studies will only be possible if we preserve the pages on which the story is written.

A human face pot excavated from the Madisonville site in Hamilton County by archaeologists from Harvard University's Peabody Museum in 1908.

The ancient American Indian earthworks in Ohio were overgrown with large trees when re-discovered by Euro-Americans in the late 1700s. Some remained covered by the forest when formally surveyed by archaeologists in the 1800s. This photograph taken in 1889 shows a team of archaeologists at the "Great Gateway" of Fort Ancient State Memorial in Warren County.

∋ 7 ∈

EARLY ACCOUNTS OF
OHIO'S MOUNDS

By Dr. Terry A. Barnhart, Professor, History Department,
Eastern Illinois University, Charleston, Illinois.

No subject connected with the Ohio Valley in the late eighteenth and nineteenth centuries elicited more popular and scientific interest than the region's extensive prehistoric Indian mounds and earthen enclosures. That is particularly true of what is today the state of Ohio. Indeed, the development of American archaeology in the nineteenth century largely centered on the study of Ohio mounds. Conjectures concerning the origin, antiquity, and purposes of these remains appeared in the journals and diaries of travelers, newspapers and gazetteers, literary periodicals, and the proceedings and transactions of learned societies from the 1780s to the close of the nineteenth century. Archaeology was then an avocational enterprise—the province of often-talented and always-zealous amateurs. Only during the century's closing decades did the nascent discipline begin a gradual process of professionalization and concentration within academic and museum settings. The first archaeologists conducted investigations at their own expense during leisure hours stolen from other pursuits. They expended significant amounts of time, money, and effort in surveying and mapping prehistoric Indian mounds and in gathering valuable collections or "cabinets" of associated artifacts—"Mound Builder relics," to use the parlance of the day. Their labors resulted in significant collections of field notes, survey maps, drawings, artifact collections, correspondence, and publications that collectively denote the pre-professional era of American archaeology.

The earliest known description of a prehistoric earthwork within present-day Ohio occurred in March of 1772, when the Moravian missionary David Zeisberger and a group of Delaware Indians established the Schoenbrunn Mission on the Tuscarawas River. Zeisberger noticed the existence of earthen embankments or enclosures near the site and made the following entry in his journal: "Long ago, perhaps more than a century ago, Indians must have lived here, who fortified themselves against the attack of their enemies. The ramparts are still plainly seen. We found three forts in a distance of a couple of miles. The whole town must have been fortified, but its site is now covered with a thick wood. No one knows to what nation these Indians belonged; it is plain, however, that they were a warlike race." Zeisberger returned to the subject in 1779 and '80 when he wrote his history of the North American Indians. "Here and there traces may be found, particularly along the Muskingum, in which region one may yet see many places, where embankments, still to be seen, were thrown up around a whole town. Here and there, furthermore, near the sites of such town there are mounds, not natural, but made by the hand of man, for in those days the native carried on great wars with one another." Zeisberger speculated that the mounds were used as safe havens during times of siege. "At the top of these mounds there was a hollow place, to which the Indians brought their wives and children when the enemies approached and attacked them, the men ranging themselves round the mound for defensive action." Those who were killed in such attacks were buried in one pit and a mound of earth raised over them, "such as may even now be seen bearing in these days great and mighty trees."

Zeisberger's passing mention of mounds and earthworks is significant in two regards. His description of the earthworks as "fortifications" represents a widespread but often erroneous assumption among early observers. The embankments of prehistoric earthworks (enclosures) at first glance resemble the breastworks of military fortifications, which in the eighteenth and nineteenth centuries gave rise to the popular notion that they were forts. Some of the irregular enclosures do, in fact, mark the sites where stockaded villages once stood, but the more elaborate and geometric works appear to have had a religious purpose, and possibly even an astronomical or calendrical function. Zeisberger also matter-of-factly attributes the mounds to earlier groups of Indians. Many other observers in the late eighteenth and early nineteenth centuries also attributed such remains to unknown Indians. It should be noted, however, that Zeisberger attributed the mounds to an *earlier* group of Indians and not to any of the tribes then living in the region.   The temporal distinction is an important one. Not all of those who denied that the "Indians" had built the mounds necessarily meant *all* Indians, at *all* places, and at *all* times.

The first published drawing and description of a prehistoric earthwork in Ohio appeared in the *Royal American Magazine* of Boston in January of 1775. The anonymous plan and description is of an earthwork designed in the form of a circle and a square located at the present site of Circleville, Ohio, and is dated October 17, 1772. The plan was most likely obtained by a Baptist missionary, The Reverend David Jones, and made by an English trader, John Irwine, who lived among the Ohio Shawnee. The map is not based upon a survey but rather upon approximate calculations made on horseback. The Reverend Jones made no effort to identify the builders of the works, but he did not attribute them to any of the Indian groups living in the Ohio Valley at that time.

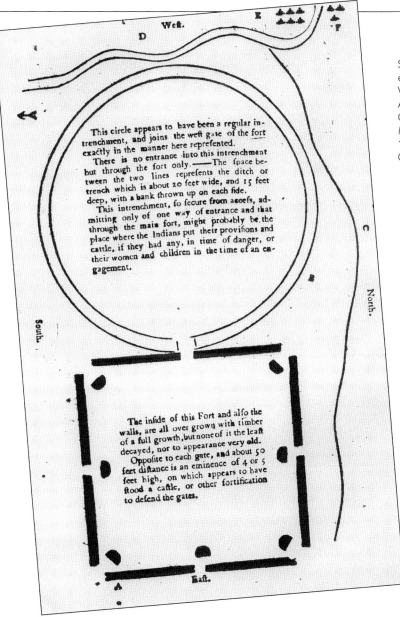

This circle appears to have been a regular intrenchment, and joins the weft gate of the fort exactly in the manner here reprefented.

There is no entrance into this intrenchment but through the fort only.——The fpace between the two lines reprefents the ditch or trench which is about 20 feet wide, and 15 feet deep, with a bank thrown up on each fide.

This intrenchment, fo fecure from accefs, admitting only of one way of entrance and that through the main fort, might probably be the place where the Indians put their provifions and cattle, if they had any, in time of danger, or their women and children in the time of an engagement.

The infide of this Fort and alfo the walls, are all over grown with timber of a full growth, but none of it the leaft decayed, nor to appearance very old.

Oppofite to each gate, and about 50 feet diftance is an eminence of 4 or 5 feet high, on which appears to have ftood a caftle, or other fortification to defend the gates.

Scholars were intrigued by the reported existence of "antiquities" in the Ohio Valley well before the arrival of Euro-American settlers. This map of the Circleville Earthworks, printed in the *Royal American Magazine* of Boston in 1775, is the first published drawing of an Ohio American Indian earthwork.

Who the constructors of it were, the Indians who live in the neighborhood to it, have no tradition upon which we may depend...The present Indian inhabitants were not the builders, and they can give no satisfactory account [of those] who were. By the largeness of the trees growing in the fort, they must be of ancient standing and consequently erected long before the Shawanese and Delawares removed into the country west of the Ohio; for their removal into that country happened since the English took possession of the sea. It seems probable that the former inhabitants were constantly at war, nation against nation, and erected these forts as their "dernier ressorts" in time of danger. They were doubtless better skilled in the arts of fortification and architecture than the present inhabitants.

—*Royal American Magazine*
January, 1775
Author, unknown

The fact that none of the tribes residing in the Ohio Valley in the eighteenth century still constructed mounds, or had reliable traditions about who had done so, did not mean that the ancestors of at least some of those groups had not at one time built them. It is most probable that the prehistoric ancestors of the historic Shawnee, Miami, and other central Algonquian groups at one time built mounds. The situation in the Ohio Valley was further complicated by the fact, as Jones noted, that the groups living there in the eighteenth century had migrated from other parts of the eastern United States. There was no cultural continuity between the prehistoric mound-building cultures and the ethnically distinct Indian groups living in the Ohio Valley at the time of the arrival of Euro-Americans. The possibility that the way of life among the Indian peoples living in the region in the eighteenth century was greatly different from that of their remote ancestors occurred to some early observers, but comparatively few. It

would have been a tall order for eighteenth and early nineteenth century observers to sort all of this out based upon the limited amount of data then available. Indeed, it was not until the early twentieth century that archaeologists began to reconstruct the cultural history of the region and its succession of chronologically and culturally distinct groups of mound-building Indians. The lack of cultural continuity between prehistoric and historic Indian groups in the Ohio Valley was a problem that would continue to befuddle investigators for years to come.

Archaeological inquiry - as a formal discourse about prehistoric remains - began with the expansion of Euro-American settlement into the Ohio Valley during the 1780s. The first published accounts of the mounds and earthworks at Grave Creek on the Upper Ohio and those at Marietta and Cincinnati were made within the context of national expansion as soldiers and settlers arrived on the Ohio frontier. The 1st American Regiment under the

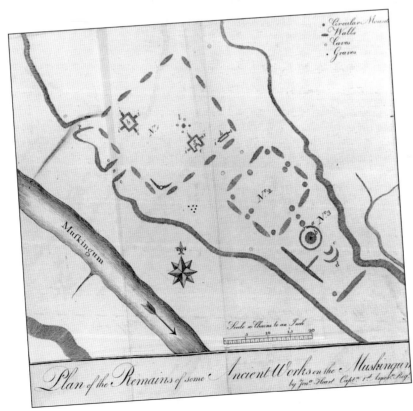

Captain Jonathan Heart's "Plan of the Remains of some Ancient Works on the Muskingum," (The Marietta Earthworks), was published as part of a descriptive article in the *Columbian Magazine* (Volume 1, No. 9, pp. 425-427) of Philadelphia in May, 1787.

command of Lieutenant-Colonel Josiah Harmar arrived at the mouth of the Muskingum and Ohio Rivers in the fall of 1785 where they erected Fort Harmar. The army had been sent there to remove squatters from federal lands, to protect federal surveyors, to establish the authority of the United States government with the Indian tribes living northwest of the Ohio, and ultimately to negotiate a series of Indian land-cession treaties that would open the region to permanent American settlements. Several of the officers at Fort Harmar became interested in the elaborate earthworks situated on the opposite bank of the Muskingum.

Captain Jonathan Heart, who was in command of Fort Harmar during part of 1786, made a plan of the earthworks that appeared in the *Columbian Magazine* of May 1787. Heart also described the exploration of a mound at the Marietta Earthworks, thus recording the first known archaeological excavation in Ohio. Heart was a graduate of Yale College and a close observer of nature. His plan of the Marietta Earthworks is apparently the one referred to by General Samuel Holden Parsons in a letter to President Willard of Harvard written October 2, 1786. Parsons also mentions sending the plan to Ezra Stiles, president of Yale College. Heart's plan and description generated considerable interest among men of letters and science in the east. In a letter written to Stiles in 1788, Noah Webster referred to the plan and supported the theory, first advanced by Benjamin Franklin, that the Muskingum works might have been built by the Spaniards during the ill-fated expedition of Hernando De Soto in 1539. The Webster-Stiles letters appeared in the *American Magazine* in 1787 and 1788.

The Reverend Manasseh Cutler, an accomplished botanist and one of the founders of the Ohio Company of Associates that established the settlement at Marietta in April of 1788, was intensely interested in the Marietta Earthworks. Cutler visited Marietta in August of 1788. An entry in his journal dated September 6th of that year notes that the directors of the Ohio Company made a survey of the works (the survey was made by Rufus Putnam) and that several of the trees that grew upon the works were cut down in order to count their annual growth rings. Cutler examined the concentric growth rings of a tree growing upon an embankment of the earthwork known as the *Sacra Via* with the aid of a magnifying glass, and put the age of the tree between 441 and 445 years. His reasoning on the implications of that evidence is worth recalling. "Attributing the age of the present growth [of trees] to be about 450 years, and that it had been preceded by one of equal size and age, which as probably or otherwise was not the first, the works have been deserted more than 900 years. If they were occupied one hundred years, they were erected more than a thousand years ago." In a letter written to Jeremy Belknap on March 6, 1789, Cutler used the results of his tree-ring dating to refute Noah Webster's conjecture that the earthworks at the Muskingum may have been constructed by De Soto. It was only necessary to establish, as tree-ring dating did, "that these works were of much earlier date than the discovery of America by Columbus" in order to put the De Soto debate to rest. He was of the opinion that construction of the mounds would have required a large population.

The directors of the Ohio Company admired the Marietta Earthworks and to their credit made specific provision between 1788 and 1796 that the remains were to be surveyed, preserved, and ornamented with trees and shrubs. They designated the elevated squares or platform mounds as public squares and dignified them with the Latin names of *Quadranou* and *Capitolium*. The embankments leading from the Muskingum River to *Quadranou* they called the *Sacra Via* (Sacred Way) and the largest mound at the site they called *Conus*. The earthworks were placed under the care of the future mayor of Marietta. As late as 1842, Samuel P. Hildreth reported with pride that members of the community continued to take pains to preserve these venerable structures for posterity. "The public mind is strongly opposed to any violation or disfiguring of the original form of this beautiful structure (the *Conus* mound), as well as of the old works generally." Not even the prudent measures of the Ohio Company and the sensitivity of later generations of Mariettans, however, would save most of the Marietta Earthworks from destruction. The walls of the graded road known as the *Sacra Via* were destroyed in 1882 for the manufacture of bricks along with other portions of the earthworks—a common fate of many mounds throughout Ohio and beyond.

The ancient works located along the Ohio River and its tributaries also received the attention of travelers in the early nineteenth century, which furthered interest in Ohio mounds. Some of these descriptions are casual while others are more substantive. Thaddeus Mason Harris' *Journal of a Tour into the Territory Northwest of the Allegheny Mountains* (1805), includes a detailed description of the Marietta Earthworks and a discussion of the leading questions connected with their origin, antiquity, and purposes: an inquiry, he said, that "All serves to surprise and to embarrass the mind." He attributed the mounds to the Toltecs, who, in the middle of the sixth century, had presumably begun a migration out of their native country southward for one hundred and four years until they arrived in the Valley of Anahuac in Mexico. He believed the Toltecan Mound Builders were descended from the ancient Scythians of Asia, whereas the North American Indians, who had presumably warred on the Toltecs and eventually drove them south into Mexico and Peru, probably had migrated to the New World from northwestern Europe. The earthworks of the western country were places of defense erected by Scythian immigrants from northern Asia. Harris calculated that the Marietta Earthworks were 1,209 years old. He believed that date generally corresponded with Cutler's early estimate of 900 to 1,000, for it allowed 309 years for the forest to regenerate after the site had been abandoned. Harris would not be the last nineteenth century scholar to attribute the Ohio mounds to the Toltecs.

The spread of settlement in Ohio during the first two decades of the nineteenth century resulted in the discovery of new archaeological sites even as it threatened them with destruction. Daniel Drake, a physician and cultural leader at Cincinnati, drew attention to the importance of making careful records of Ohio's ancient works. Drake carefully delineated the form and position of the mounds and earthen embankments located within the upper level of the town plat of Cincinnati in his *Natural and Statistical View, or Picture of Cincinnati and the Miami Country* published in 1815. Drake lamented the superficial and derivative nature of many published accounts of the mounds.

"No objects in the state of Ohio seem to have more forcibly arrested the attention of travellers, nor employed a greater number of pens, than its antiquities. It is to be regretted, however, that so hastily and superficially have they been examined by strangers, and so generally neglected by ourselves, that the materials for a full description have not yet been collected. The former have too often contented themselves by copying from each other; and the latter have commonly substituted wonder for examination."

—Daniel Drake, 1815

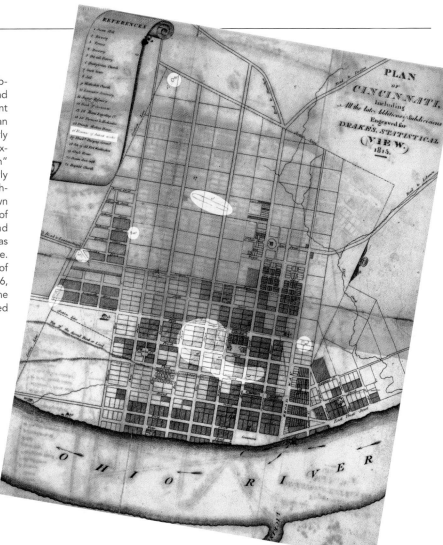

Euro-American settlers often established their towns on the same broad river terraces favored by the ancient architects of Ohio's prehistoric indian mounds and earthworks. By the early 1800s, several large earthwork complexes had been destroyed by "urban" development before being properly surveyed, including extensive earthworks located under modern downtown Cincinnati. The only surviving map of what was likely several Adena and Hopewell mounds and earthworks was made in the 1800s by Dr. Daniel Drake. Drake's map shows the "Remains of Ancient Works" (originally marked as 16, and graphically highlighted). Most of the earthworks had already been covered by homes, businesses and churches.

The study of American antiquities took a significant step forward in 1820 when Caleb Atwater of Circleville, Ohio, published his "Description of the Antiquities Discovered in the State of Ohio and Other Western States" in the first volume of the *Transactions and Collections of the American Antiquarian Society*. It was the "immediate and peculiar design" of the American Antiquarian Society "to discover the antiquities of our own continent," and to make provision for collecting and preserving them. The Reverend William Jenks noted in his address at the first annual meeting of the society in 1813 that its fields of investigation should include the ancient Indian nations of America and the western mounds. What better place to begin than by studying the mounds and earthworks of Ohio? Atwater began his study of those remains soon after his arrival at Circleville, Ohio, in 1815, and communicated his findings to the president of the society in a series of letters. His survey maps and descriptions of the works at Cincinnati, Circleville, Hopewell, Marietta, and Newark represent the first general survey of western antiquities. Atwater recognized that the ornaments, implements, and human remains found in the mounds were frequently of different eras and belonged to different peoples. His descriptions of archaeological materials and sites are still of interest today, but his theory that the mounds of Ohio were built by Hindus who had migrated to the Ohio Valley before moving south to Mexico has not withstood the test of time.

An event of some moment in the history of American archaeology occurred in 1848 with the publication of Ephraim George Squier and Edwin Hamilton Davis's classic *Ancient Monuments of the Mississippi Valley*. The appearance of the work as the first volume of the *Smithsonian*

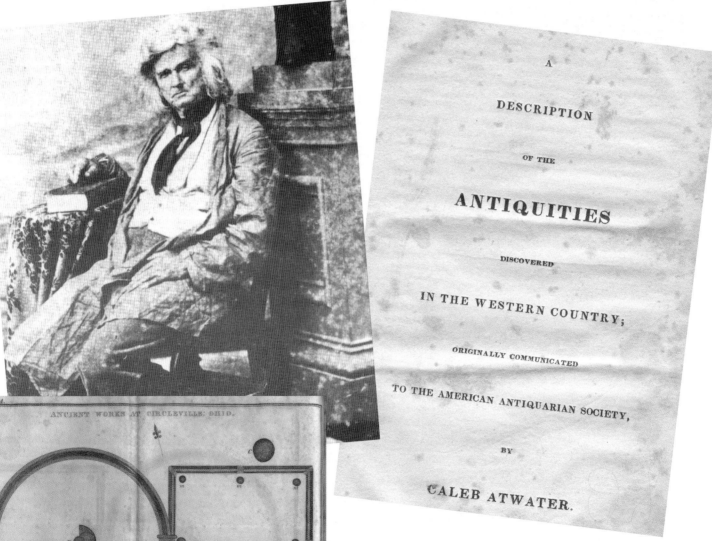

A

DESCRIPTION

OF THE

ANTIQUITIES

DISCOVERED

IN THE WESTERN COUNTRY;

ORIGINALLY COMMUNICATED

TO THE AMERICAN ANTIQUARIAN SOCIETY,

BY

CALEB ATWATER.

Caleb Atwater, seen in his older years in this photograph from the 1860s, was an ambitious postmaster and avid "antiquarian" when we wrote "Description of the Antiquities Discovered in the State of Ohio and Other Western States." The first book-length description on Ohio's ancient earthworks, Atwater's work was published in *Transactions and Collections of the American Antiquarian Society* in 1820. Atwater's book includes several survey maps such as this one (left) of Circleville in Pickaway County. The historic town of Circleville was originally laid out to conform to the circular earthwork built there by American Indians over two thousand years ago.

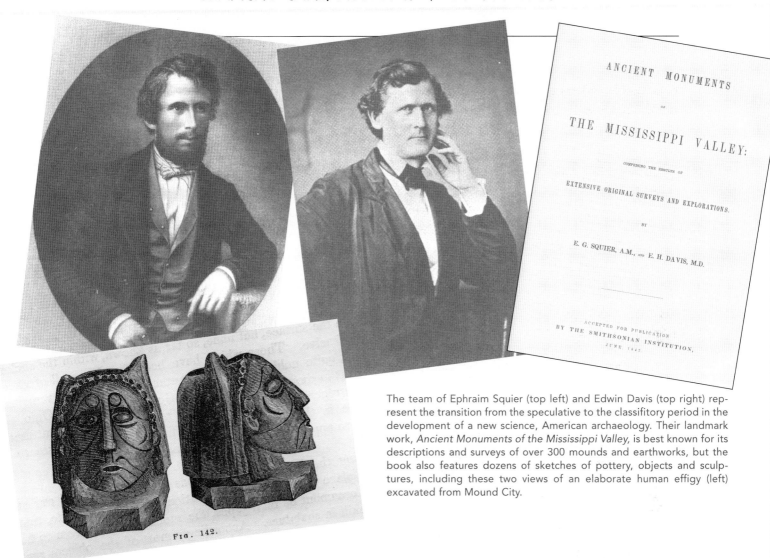

ANCIENT MONUMENTS

OF

THE MISSISSIPPI VALLEY:

COMPRISING THE RESULTS OF

EXTENSIVE ORIGINAL SURVEYS AND EXPLORATIONS.

BY

E. G. SQUIER, A.M., AND E. H. DAVIS, M.D.

ACCEPTED FOR PUBLICATION
BY THE SMITHSONIAN INSTITUTION,
JUNE 1847.

FIG. 142.

The team of Ephraim Squier (top left) and Edwin Davis (top right) represent the transition from the speculative to the classifitory period in the development of a new science, American archaeology. Their landmark work, *Ancient Monuments of the Mississippi Valley,* is best known for its descriptions and surveys of over 300 mounds and earthworks, but the book also features dozens of sketches of pottery, objects and sculptures, including these two views of an elaborate human effigy (left) excavated from Mound City.

Contributions to Knowledge conferred recognition upon its authors, the fledging Smithsonian Institution, and the infant science of American archaeology. Davis, a practicing physician at Chillicothe, had made something of a study of the antiquities of Ohio since his days at Kenyon College. Squier, a native of New York, came to Chillicothe from Hartford, Connecticut, as editor of the Scioto *Gazette*, and possessed an able pen. Squier and Davis excavated approximately two hundred prehistoric Indian mounds, surveyed some one hundred earthen enclosures, and amassed one of the largest archaeological collections in the United States between the spring of 1845 and the summer of 1847. They estimated that some ten thousand mounds and between one thousand to fifteen hundred enclosures were located within the state of Ohio, and that approximately five hundred mounds and one hundred enclosures existed within the Scioto Valley. Squier and Davis also published original surveys by John Locke, James McBride, Charles Whittlesey, Samuel P. Hildreth, and others along with the results of their own investigations. Taken together with the surveys published by Charles Whittlesey in the third volume of the Smithsonian *Contribution to Knowledge*, the work of Squier and Davis provides as complete a view of the subject of Ohio archaeology as it was known in the mid nineteenth century.

Ancient Monuments of the Mississippi Valley endures as an archaeological classic because of its scientific arrangement and descriptive qualities. Squier and Davis classified enclosures and mounds based on their form, position, internal structure, contents, and assumed purposes. They divided enclosures into three classes and the mounds into four. Each division, however, still formed part of a "single system" and were the work of "the same people." Enclosures - sites bounded by embankments of earth or stone - were classified as "Works of Defense," "Sacred Enclosures," and those of a miscellaneous character. The mounds similarly were identified as "Altar" or "Sacrificial Mounds," "Mounds of Sepulture," "Temple Mounds," and "Anomalous Mounds." Altar Mounds were found in or near Sacred Enclosures, possessed stratified soil features, and were erected over symmetrical basins or "altars" of burned clay or stone. Squier and Davis associated the basins or altars with human sacrifices or thought them to have been somehow connected with the religious beliefs and customs of their builders. They found the largest deposits of aboriginal art within this type of mound. Temple Mounds were thought to have been platforms for religious structures. They received close attention from Squier and Davis due to perceived structural similarities between them and the more elaborate teocalli of Mexico and Central America. As for the origin and identity of the Mound Builders, the evidence of their investigations indicated

"...a connection more or less intimate between the race of the mounds and the semi-civilized nations which formerly had their seats among the sierras of the Mexico, upon the plains of Central America and Peru, and who erected the imposing structures which from their number, vastness, and mysterious significance, invest the central portions of the continent with an interest not less absorbing that that which attaches to the valley of the Nile."

Thus, Squier and Davis attempted to link "the race of the mounds" to the aboriginal peoples of Mesoamerica and Peru. They were neither the first nor the last nineteenth century observers to do so.

The Ohio State Archaeological and Historical Society was incorporated on March 12th and 13th,

In the early 1900s, William C. Mills (standing in back row, far right) conducted a series of archaeological investigations across the state as Curator of The Ohio Archaeological and Historical Society. This photograph shows Mills and his crew during the excavation of Seip Mound Number 2 in 1906. Mills was a prolific writer, publishing numerous reports on mound explorations. He also named several of the ancient American Indian cultures, used by archaeologists to this day.

1885. The society began to conduct archaeological excavations in the 1890s, first under the direction of Warren King Moorehead and then William C. Mills. By the early twentieth century, the society had acquired one of the most significant collections of prehistoric Indian artifacts in the nation. The collection has educated thousands of Ohioans about the richness and diversity of Ohio's prehistoric past, first at the Ohio State Museum from 1914 to 1970 and since 1970, at the Ohio Historical Center. The Ohio State Archaeological and Historical Society changed its name to the Ohio Historical Society in 1954. The society also preserves several state archaeological sites and administers museums at Fort Ancient, Fort Hill, the Newark Earthworks and Serpent Mound. Public archaeology and the stewardship of archaeological sites and collections at the Ohio Historical Society continues to fulfill the desire of several generations of Ohioans who articulated the need to promote the study and ensure the future preservation of archaeological remains.

An important period in Ohio archaeology began in March of 1878 when Dr. Charles L. Metz began excavations at the Madisonville Village Site and Cemetery in the Little Miami Valley. The Literary and Scientific Society of Madisonville sponsored Metz's subsequent work at the site, with the costs of the excavation being defrayed through the contributions of its members. The Cincinnati Society of Natural History also contributed funds to the enterprise, which became the repository of the skeletal materials recovered from the site. Reports on the excavations at Madisonville soon drew the attention of Frederic Ward Putnam, Curator of the Peabody Museum of Archaeology and Ethnology of Harvard University. The Peabody Museum was already interested in Ohio archaeology, with Ebenezer Andrews carrying on explorations in the southern part of the state. Putnam visited the Madisonville site in 1881 and made arrangements to carry on the work in cooperation with the Literary and Scientific Society of Madisonville. The Peabody Museum agreed to help fund the excavations (and funded them exclusively after 1882) in return for receiving a portion of the materials recovered for its collections. The Peabody Museum continued to conduct fieldwork in Ohio throughout the first decade of the twentieth century, but the greatest period of activity occurred in the 1880s and 1890s. Many sites were explored in the Little Miami Valley (including the Turner Mound Group), in the Scioto Valley, and scattered sites in other parts of the state.

The activities of Harvard's Peabody Museum in Ohio represent a significant chapter in the history of American archaeology. Putnam sought an annual fund of $3,000 to promote archaeological investigations in Ohio "before it was too late." The time had passed, he noted, when haphazard explorations and "chance gatherings" of materials were considered the chief aims of archaeology. This was the great era of explorations and museum building at the Peabody, when prehistoric materials were leaving Ohio literally by the barrel. Putnam was well on the way to making the museum a major repository of American antiquities. The Peabody had the funds to support systematic fieldwork in Ohio and there were many able hands willing to offer their assistance as Putnam's field agents.

Putnam's fieldwork in Ohio marks the beginning of scientific excavations, although Metz's previous work deserves high marks in this regard, too. Putnam's insistence upon intensive excavation at specific sites and the keeping of detailed records made excavating mounds far less of a quixotic adventure. He was equally committed to the preservation of Ohio's prehistoric sites, and well understood the difficulty of maintaining a

Serpent Mound was being plowed into obscurity when archaeologist Frederic Ward Putnam, Curator of Harvard's Peabody Museum, raised almost $6,000 from private donors to purchase the site in 1886. After three years of excavations and restoration, Serpent Mound became a public park as seen in this photograph from 1908.

precarious balance between the need for excavations, a destructive process, and archaeological preservation and restoration. One of his major contributions was the preservation of Serpent Mound. He visited the site in 1883 with some of his Ohio collaborators and realized that it was rapidly being destroyed by cultivation. He took steps to save it in 1885 by securing a pledge from the owner that the site would remain undisturbed for a year. Putnam enlisted the interest of Alice Fletcher of Boston, who assisted Putnam by raising about $6,000, which enabled Harvard University to purchase the site in 1886. Putnam then explored Serpent Mound and the adjoining mounds, restored them, and opened the site to the public as Serpent Mound

Park. Putnam's efforts to save Serpent Mound prompted the Ohio General Assembly to pass a law in 1888 exempting prehistoric parks from taxation and making other provisions for their preservation. Harvard deeded Serpent Mound Park to the state of Ohio in 1900, when it was placed in the custody of the Ohio State Archaeological and Historical Society.

The Mound Division of the Smithsonian's Bureau of American Ethnology also conducted significant archeological fieldwork in Ohio and other mound building areas of the eastern United States between 1882 and 1889. Cyrus Thomas directed the Bureau's mound survey and his field agents examined 2,000 mounds and collected more than 40,000 artifacts. Thomas' assistants Gerard Fowke and James D. Middleton conducted the Bureau's fieldwork in Ohio. The results of those investigations were published in 1894 by Thomas in his "Report on the Mound Explorations of the Bureau of Ethnology"—a monograph of over 700 pages. Thomas classified mounds by their external form, and not how they were presumably used, in an effort to avoid the functional assumptions of the earlier classifications of Squier and Davis. His chief concern was answering the question of whether the "the Indians" had built the mounds. "If it can be shown that some of the mounds and some of the other antiquities of all the different types and classes were made by Indians, or even by people having the same habits, beliefs, and culture status as the Indians, the inference is justifiable that all are the work of the same race or one closely allied in culture."

Thomas concluded from the evidence recovered that the builders of the mounds and earthworks were ancestral to the historic Indians, that some groups continued to build mounds in the early historic era, and that the Mound Builders were not a racially distinct group of people as had been maintained previously by many writers. The weight of Thomas' evidence and force of argument conclusively linked prehistoric and historic Indians racially, but he was so intent upon establishing that link that he sometimes ignored or minimized cultural differences among prehistoric mound building groups and later Indian peoples. It would be left to later archaeologists to begin the painstaking process of differentiating between the chronologically and culturally distinct mound building groups, but Thomas' debunking of the idea that the mounds had been built by non-Indian peoples significantly connected American archaeology and ethnology in the investigation of a common set of problems relating to the Ohio mounds.

Archaeological method and theory has greatly changed since the end of the Mound Builder debate of the nineteenth century. Archaeologists have examined more sites, recognized more prehistoric cultures, and have developed new methods of analyzing archaeological sites and artifacts. Our understanding of time-depth, cultural change, the emergence of regional cultural traditions, the diffusion patterns of cultural traits, and the importance of analyzing artifacts as a means of interpreting site formation and function has placed great distance between archaeologists and their antiquarian predecessors. Archaeology has become a model of empirical inquiry, even though much about Ohio's prehistoric past remains unknown. Archaeologists have solved many of the problems that perplexed their intellectual ancestors—the antiquarians of the eighteenth and nineteenth centuries. Yet the more empirical of the early investigators made enduring contributions to Ohio archaeology by surveying, describing, and classifying the mounds and their contents. They articulated the need to bring the subject of American antiquities under more critical and systematic study, made a clear distinction between the conjectures of armchair antiquarians and those whose opinions were based upon actual fieldwork, and called upon public-minded citizens to promote the study and preservation of Ohio's endangered and diminishing number of archaeological remains. The opinions of some of those early writers have been again resurrected in the preceding pages, but in an intentionally different spirit. One should give the avocational archaeologists of the past their due, without being uncritical of the prejudices and the dead ends that informed a good portion of early archaeological thought.

American Indians in traditional regalia gather for an intertribal powwow at Fort Ancient State Memorial. The powwow is one of several cultural activities during the annual "Celebration" weekend held in June at this ancient American Indian earthwork in Warren County. The cultural festival was started to educate people regarding the technologies of the past and the importance of American Indian traditions, according to Jack Blosser, Site Manager, Fort Ancient State Memorial. "Celebration has provided the opportunity for people to renew something at Fort Ancient that started nearly 2,000 years ago; to celebrate unity and life, honoring those who once walked this ground and thanking the Creator for the opportunity to do so," says Blosser.

∋ 8 ∈

E P I L O G U E
"LEGACIES"

By Thomas M. Law, Project Director, *Ohio Archaeology;*
and Trustee, Voyageur Media Group, Inc.

The science of archaeology has revealed much about the 12,000 years of American Indian cultural achievement in the lands we now call Ohio. Yet these discoveries have not come without exacting a price. From the early 1800s to the early 1900s, Ohio was a cradle for the development of the science of American archaeology. The "antiquarians" and archaeol-ogists during this era sometimes leveled American Indian mounds and earthworks. Their investigations often focused on the excavation of graves and the recovery of artifacts placed with burials. The concerns of American Indians regarding these activities were rarely, if ever, considered. This, too, is a legacy of Ohio archaeology.

In the early 1800s to the mid 1900s, archaeological excavations such as this one at the Hopewell Mound Group (ca. 1891) destroyed ancient American Indian burial sites in the quest for scientific evidence and artifacts. The archaeology of this era advanced our knowledge of ancient cultures, but did not take into account the cultural concerns of American Indians. The goals and methods of archaeology have changed significantly since the time of this photograph, but scientists, museum curators, American Indians and government officials are still wrestling with this past.

Today, archaeologists, American Indians, museum curators and government officials across the nation are engaged in a profound debate about the role of modern archaeology. Over the past decade, I have been privileged to interview dozens of tribal leaders, archaeologists, museum curators and scholars in Ohio and Oklahoma about the complex cultural, social and political issues surrounding archaeology's past, present and future. This epilogue is intended to introduce readers to a range of opinions on three major issues—the repatriation of human remains and funerary objects, tribal recognition, and site preservation. The essay presents fundamental questions, realizing that each issue is intertwined, that there is no such thing as a pan-Indian or pan-archaeological point of view, and that answers to the questions remain elusive.

Science and Faith

Above all else, it is important to respect the fundamental difference between how some archaeologists and American Indians view the past. It revolves around the divergence between science and faith—what we attempt to prove and what we choose to believe.

American archaeology is based on the western scientific method of inquiry. This system of learning thrives on observation, the development and testing of hypotheses and the search for proof. Archaeology demands precise evidence, mountains of documentation and continual testing. Moreover, the western scientific method has more to do with showing that something is wrong rather than right. Archaeologists are trained to pick apart concepts until they end up with the most plausible explanation. Students are encouraged to challenge even the most widely accepted theories. No idea is sacred. No sage theoretician is beyond criticism. Archaeologists continually share and debate their research at professional conferences, through publications and in the media. Conflict is a constant, healthy part of the archaeological ethos. As one archaeologist quipped, "The definition of a miracle is finding any two archaeologists who completely agree on any one thing."

On the other hand, traditional American Indian culture is based on the oral traditions that contain information about the customs and history of an individual tribe or nation. Oral traditions are passed down from generation to generation in a direct, highly personal manner. This system of learning demands time, acceptance and faith. And faith does not demand proof. Elders are revered for their wisdom. Students rarely challenge widely accepted cultural beliefs. Many

ideas are sacred. Patience is prized. Conflict is subtle. Consensus is often the goal.

These are broad observations to be sure. Archaeologists collaborate more often than they compete in their investigations. More than one American Indian elder is chuckling over my description of those dutiful, attentive young students. Some archaeologists are more conservative with their theories than others. Some American Indians are more traditional than others. However, we need to recognize that there is a tangible cultural gap between the science of archaeology and the traditional culture of American Indians. The First Amendment of the U.S. Constitution prohibits the establishment of a state religion. American governments work hard to separate our spiritual and secular lives—the proverbial church and state. In most traditional American Indian cultures, the political, social, historical and religious aspects of life are deeply intertwined.

An archaeologist screens soil during the excavation of an embankment at the Hopeton Earthworks site in Ross County.

An ancient creation story, based on oral traditions, is depicted in "Our Life on His Back," a contemporary watercolor by artist Julie Lankford Olds of the Miami Tribe of Oklahoma.

The late Charles Dawes, Principal Chief, Ottawa Tribe of Oklahoma, an accomplished engineer, esteemed elder and a respected religious leader, clarified this point during an interview in 1997. "I think the major difference and the consuming difference and the continuing difference is where do we start," said Dawes. "They [archaeologists] start with something that they can prove. We [American Indians] don't necessarily start that way. We didn't demand proof. We were living proof. And so they're [archaeologists] not going to accept it unless they can touch it, or feel it, or consume it, or in some way prove that it exists. And in some cases, proving that it exists includes destroying it. But we don't have that. We don't have that basic philosophy. We accept it without proof. And probably that faith is the biggest difference."

How did American Indians come to occupy North America? The most common ideas presented by archaeologists center on the Bering Strait migration theory. American Indians first crossed into North America from Asia over 23,000 years ago. American Indian tribes have origin stories about traditional beliefs relating to the Creator, Great Spirit, earth divers or the heavens. In many American Indian origin stories, the People have lived in their homelands since the beginning of time.

This is not to say that archaeology rejects oral traditions, or that traditional American Indian culture has no use for the science of archaeology. Archaeologists often cite early written accounts of oral traditions in their research. As shown in this book, American Indians have embraced science for millennia in the fields of physics, botany, mathematics, medicine and astronomy. My first instinct was to compare this cultural difference to the longstanding debate between creationism and evolution, which is grounded in Judeo-Christian interpretations of the written word—the Bible. Daryl Baldwin, Director, The Myaamia Project, The Miami Tribe of Oklahoma, points out a key difference when considering oral traditions. "Our belief stories are always evolving because they are not based in written scriptures," says Baldwin, adding, "Science and religion are complementary in traditional American Indian cultures."

The Native American Graves Protection and Repatriation Act of 1990

How do we balance the scientific goals of archaeology and the traditional beliefs of American Indians in modern American society? In 1990, the U.S. Congress passed the Native American Graves Protection and Repatriation Act. Commonly known by its acronym, NAGPRA, this federal legislation codified some of the long-standing cultural concerns of Native Americans, Native Hawaiians and Native Alaskans regarding the treatment of burial sites, funerary objects and sacred objects. NAGPRA builds on the American Indian Religious Freedom Act of 1978, which protects the traditional religious rights of American Indians, including access to sacred or religious sites on federal lands, the use and possession of sacred objects, and the freedom to worship through ceremonies and traditional rites.

In short, NAGPRA gave American Indians a legal voice in American archaeology. NAGPRA applies to federal agencies (except the Smithsonian Institution) and federal lands, as well as all private and public institutions that receive federal funding. There is little federal land in Ohio, but NAGPRA impacts most of the state's agencies, archaeological institutions, museums and universities.

By 1995, all of the institutions affected by NAGPRA were required to make an inventory of the American Indian human remains and cultural materials in their collections. The institutions were also required to notify federally recognized American Indian tribes about the inventory lists, and to consult with tribes prior to the disturbance of Indian burials on federal lands.

Ohio Hopewell copper cutouts in the form of two open hands on exhibit at Hopewell Culture National Historical Park.

Cultural Repatriation

NAGPRA also outlined a formal process for American Indians to claim human remains and funerary objects held in affected American institutions. This multifaceted process, known as cultural repatriation, is of great concern to archaeologists and American Indians. If known, the NAGPRA inventories must describe how the human remains and cultural materials were acquired. The inventory must further delineate if an item is "clearly identifiable" to a particular Indian tribe or "determined by reasonable belief" to be culturally affiliated with an Indian tribe.

Direct descendants or tribes, with proof of cultural affiliation, may claim human remains or funerary objects for repatriation, which is either the transfer of legal custody of an item, or the actual return of an item. In some cases, American Indian tribes have or plan to rebury cultural materials reclaimed under NAGPRA. Some archaeologists protest the loss to science when human remains and cultural items are reburied. Some American Indians protest the cultural loss when these items were originally excavated from gravesites.

Here lies the rub. Who owns this past? Under NAGPRA, the cultural affiliation of human remains and cultural items may be established by "a preponderance of evidence based upon geographical, kinship, biological, archaeological, anthropological, linguistic, folkloric, oral traditions, historical and other relevant information or expert opinion." The preponderance of evidence may be clear when it comes to human remains and cultural items from the proto-historic or historic periods. The establishment of cultural affiliation is much more difficult when considering materials from the prehistoric period. In Ohio, this generally means sites and items more than 300 years old.

Recognition

Repatriation is connected to another fundamental question, recognition. Who are the descendants of the ancient peoples of Ohio? NAGPRA claims are inexorably linked to American Indian ancestry or lineal descent. The legislation does not specifically cover the disposition of "culturally unaffiliated" materials—items where the ancestry is unknown or in question. NAGPRA officials, American Indian tribes and archaeological institutions are studying the issue, which is currently handled on a case-by-case basis.

In Ohio, most archaeologists contend there are not enough scientific or other forms of evidence to connect a specific prehistoric American Indian culture to a recognizable historic tribe. The evidence has been lost to time, was destroyed during European contact, or has yet to be discovered. But there is also no archaeological evidence that American Indian groups ever migrated from Ohio, or were completely driven out of these lands during the prehistoric period. Most of the professional archaeologists I have interviewed concur that the ancient American Indians of Ohio were an eastern woodland people. Some suggest they were most likely Algonquin speakers—one of several major American Indian language stocks identified by linguists in North America. Some scholars advise us not to discount ancient Iroquoian or Siouan connections to the region. For now, the archaeological jury is out when it comes to establishing direct cultural continuity. Yet most archaeologists would like nothing more than to scientifically establish these cultural connections. That's part of their job.

Oral Traditions

The views of American Indians on the nature and weight of archaeological evidence was cordially expressed at the opening session of "Algonquin

American Indian tribes with historic ties to Ohio are revitalizing their traditions in Oklahoma and Canada. This cultural pride is evident in the vibrant regalia of dancers at the annual intertribal powwow of the Delaware Tribe of Indians in Bartlesville, Oklahoma. Music, dancing, feasting and good old-fashioned "visiting" extend well into the early morning hours at dozens of public, intertribal pow-wows held throughout the summer in northeast Oklahoma. Many tribes sponsor language camps, oral history projects and other cultural programs designed to help members navigate the present by reconnecting to their past. "We learn to walk in two worlds," is a common refrain heard in "Indian Country" from tribal members who work to balance their traditional values and professional lives.

People of the Ohio Valley," an academic symposium held at Miami University in 1996. After providing their name, title and tribal affiliation, the speakers who represented six American Indian tribes began their presentation with this statement, "We know who we are!"

There are about ten federally recognized American Indian tribes or nations with strong cultural ties to Ohio, including tribes historically known as the Chippewa (Ojibwa), Delaware (Lenape), Miami (Myaamia), Ottawa, Pottawatomie, Shawnee, and Wyandot (Wyandotte). Most of these tribes are now based in Oklahoma or Canada. Each tribe is an independent nation with distinct languages, customs and traditions.

European contact had a devastating impact on the oral traditions of American Indian tribes living in present-day Ohio. A tremendous amount of spoken "history" was lost during fifteen generations of epidemics, warfare, and the introduction of new cultures, religions and foreign laws. European diseases were especially hard on elderly, the keepers of oral traditions, and the young, those best able to keep the traditions alive. "Stories were lost, and lots of history was lost through losing those stories," said Linda Poolaw, Grand Chief, Delaware Tribe of Western Oklahoma, during an interview in 1996. This cultural loss culminated in the removal of most American Indian tribes from the eastern United States. By the 1840s, all of the tribes historically based in Ohio had either left or been forcibly removed from the state.

Removal tore apart the cultural fabric of American Indians tribes, a traditional cloth woven from over 12,000 years of experience in the forests, meadows, rivers and lakes of Ohio. Some ancient oral traditions survived intact as tribes re-settled on the western plains of Oklahoma or in small reservations in Canada. Other traditions were modified for new environments and challenges. Early Euro-American writers also documented some tribal histories and customs. But what accounts of these oral traditions are accurate? What cultural history has been revised? Today, elders and scholars within American Indian tribes are trying to sort this out, but repairing such extensive damage to this intricate cultural fabric will take time. Some threads may never be fully restored.

Oral traditions are one form of evidence that may be used to help decide NAGPRA repatriation claims. Who are the descendants of the Ohio Hopewell people? Science and the courts require a strong chain of evidence to establish specific cultural connections. American Indian traditions require neither each link in the chain, nor the chain itself. Why? "We are all connected in some way," states Chief Floyd Leonard, The Miami Tribe of Oklahoma.

American Indian Objections

Opinions about the role of archaeology vary among and within tribes. Most federally recognized American Indian tribes have a cultural committee that deals with archaeological issues. Some tribal leaders state that archaeology provides little direct benefit to their culture and history. Others find some benefit to the information gained through archaeology. A few tribal members are professional anthropologists and archaeologists. During an interview in 2002, Dr. Lathel Duffield, a former associate professor of anthropology at the University of Kentucky, and an enrolled member of the Cherokee Nation of Oklahoma, summarized this range of opinions. "Just as there is great cultural diversity among American Indian groups, there is a great deal of political differences as well," said Dr. Duffield. "Some groups would feel very confident that this is the way we can learn because archaeologists can tell us about our past. Others would see this as a way of desecrating sacred grounds, burial grounds and recovery of artifacts that should be left with the dead. So there's no consensus in all of this."

Beyond general questions, it is important to underscore specific objections of American Indians regarding human remains and funerary objects. Ohio's archaeological museums and academic institutions archive thousands of human remains and associated cultural materials. Several national and international archaeological institutions also hold cultural materials excavated from sites in Ohio. What should be done with these archaeological collections? This is actually a two-part question. The first deals with the academic study of human remains and funerary objects. The second concerns the public exhibit of these cultural materials.

Archaeologist Dawn Walter Gagliano cleans a pottery sherd in the laboratory of the cultural resources management facility of Hopewell Culture National Historical Park

Human Skeletal Remains

Should scientists be prohibited from the study of American Indian human remains and associated cultural materials? Archaeologists, more specifically physical anthropologists, can learn much about the health, diet, population and cultural relationships of ancient peoples by studying human skeletal remains. This information feeds into bigger anthropological questions on world migration, societal interaction and human adaptation. In some cases, the data gathered from the study of human remains have direct practical applications to modern problems such as diabetes, obesity, ecology and environmental restoration. But does the scientific value of physical anthropology outweigh the cultural concerns of American Indians? And who decides?

This issue made national headlines in the case of Kennewick Man, a nearly complete Paleoindian skeleton discovered in a riverbank on federal land in the state of Washington. Several American Indian tribes filed a joint NAGPRA claim for the human remains, which, based on initial radiocarbon tests, are over 9,300 years old. A group of anthropologists filed a federal injunction to secure this rare skeleton for further scientific study, arguing valuable scientific data would be lost if the skeleton was reclaimed and reburied. In August 2002, the District Court found that there was no evidence to show the skeleton is culturally affiliated to the contesting tribes, or that it has any relationship whatsoever to any present-day American Indian tribe. In February of 2004, the Ninth Circuit Court of Appeals affirmed the lower court's decision, but the tribes are exploring other avenues to resolve their objections over further study of the "Ancient One's" remains.

Most, but not all, of the American Indian officials I have interviewed object to the study of human skeletal remains. Some recommend that scientists quickly document remains, and then re-inter them as quickly as possible and as close as possible to the place they were uncovered. Archaeologists raise concerns about future scientific research. Just as radiocarbon dating and DNA testing transformed our understanding of the past, new techniques and technologies will be applied to physical anthropology. Once human remains are reburied, future knowledge is often lost. Paradoxically, one of the most promising avenues for scientifically connecting past cultures to present tribes comes from DNA testing on ancient human skeletal remains.

A clear majority of the American Indian leaders I have interviewed object to the public display of human remains in exhibits, books and other media. In accordance, most archaeological institutions in America have removed displays of American Indian skeletons. However, you can occasionally see an artifact made of human bone in museums and books.

Funerary Objects

Some American Indians also object to the study and display of artifacts associated with gravesites—funerary objects. The disposition of funerary objects is equally problematic. Archaeologists can learn much about ancient crafts, customs and dress from the study of funerary objects. Some contain rare expressions about how ancient American Indians viewed their environment, their cosmology, and themselves. Funerary objects put a human face on a story most often told with stone points and pottery shards.

There is less of a consensus within American Indian communities on this issue. Some American Indian leaders object to the study and display of funerary objects just as strongly as they do with human remains. The objects are "sacred" and

THE RINGLER DUGOUT

The story of the Ringler dugout is a good illustration of the importance of preserving archaeological objects. In 1976, crane operator Harold Slessman discovered this 22-foot-long dugout while dredging Savannah Lake in Ashland County. The rare American Indian watercraft was recovered in remarkable condition thanks to a series of fortuitous events: the natural preservative power of the acidic peat bog; the crane operator's immediate recognition of the object, a week of freezing temperatures, and a call by the landowner (the Ringlers) to archaeologists at the Cleveland Museum of Natural History. A team of archaeologists managed to safely move the dugout back to the museum. Frozen and waterlogged, this fragile artifact weighed nearly one ton.

Preparations were made to try to prevent the craft from disintegrating as it thawed. This conversion process would be lengthy and success was not assured. Therefore, the staff made a cast of the dugout (top of next page) to have a physical record of the boat for study and exhibit (bottom of next page). When the cast was complete, museum staff and volunteers applied daily sprays of a Polyethylene Glycol solution over a period of eight months. The glycol solution kept the cellular structure of the waterlogged dugout from collapsing, according to Katharine Ruhl, Research Associate, The Cleveland Museum of Natural History. Once the solution stabilized the wood, the dugout was allowed to dry out under carefully controlled environmental conditions for an additional two years before being stored in a special archival case for future study and research.

The age of the Ringler dugout is uncertain. Radiocarbon dating and pollen studies from 1976 suggest the dugout is about 3,500 years old, an artifact from the Archaic Period. In 2004, the museum staff moved the dugout into a new archival case designed for better visual observation. They conducted radiocarbon tests on wood fragments found in the old case that appear to have come from the dugout. The new radiocarbon dates suggest the dugout may be only 250 years old, an artifact from the historic period. It is not clear whether the chemicals that preserved the dugout interfered with the latest radiocarbon testing. Archaeologists are considering other dating methods, and also looking to future methods that may provide more definitive dating.

Despite the uncertainty of its age, the Ringler dugout remains a remarkable find. "The Ringler dugout was so well preserved we were able to gather detailed information about how the watercraft was made and used," says Katharine Ruhl. The cut marks and burn marks suggest American Indians used a combination of controlled fire and stone tools to carve the dugout from a large oak log. From its dimensions, archaeologists determined the watercraft could hold up to four crew members with an additional 300 pounds of cargo. The crew probably paddled in a kneeling position based on the pattern of smooth, wear marks on the bottom of the dugout.

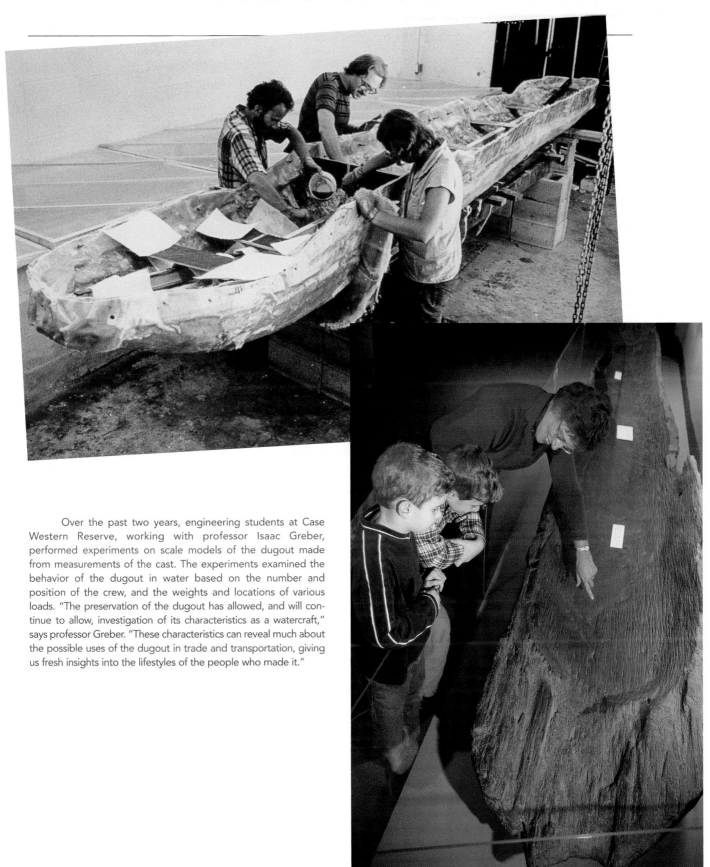

Over the past two years, engineering students at Case Western Reserve, working with professor Isaac Greber, performed experiments on scale models of the dugout made from measurements of the cast. The experiments examined the behavior of the dugout in water based on the number and position of the crew, and the weights and locations of various loads. "The preservation of the dugout has allowed, and will continue to allow, investigation of its characteristics as a watercraft," says professor Greber. "These characteristics can reveal much about the possible uses of the dugout in trade and transportation, giving us fresh insights into the lifestyles of the people who made it."

were "placed in burials for a reason." Others have said that the "cultural damage is already done." While they would prefer that funerary objects were never taken from burials, they concede that the study and display of funerary objects help non-native peoples appreciate the accomplishments of ancient American Indian cultures. Some American Indians do not object to the study and display of funerary objects.

I asked Richard West, Director of the National Museum of the American Indian about this issue after his lecture at the Cincinnati Art Museum in 2002. Over the past several years, West said that he and his staff had been traveling throughout North, Central and South America to discuss a variety of cultural issues with the leaders and elders of indigenous tribes and groups. In general, West reported that a majority of indigenous people he spoke to in North America object to the display of funerary objects, but that most of the indigenous people in South and Central America do not. Mr. West said the National Museum of the American Indian would not show funerary objects when it opens this fall on the Mall in Washington, D.C.

Funerary objects are widely displayed in Ohio museums, archaeological institutions, academic papers, textbooks, websites and other publications, including this book. Some Ohio archaeological institutions and some federally recognized tribes with ties to Ohio are reviewing their policies regarding the study and display of funerary objects. Most of the officials I have spoken to report they are not ready to make formal decisions, citing the complexity of the issue and the enormous repercussions for science, culture and public education. The use of replicas and casts may be a compromise. But quality replicas are expensive, and as one Ohio curator stated, "People still like to see the real thing."

Our production team struggled with this issue when considering whether to develop the Ohio Archaeology project, and publish this book. We decided not to show human skeletal remains, but we did choose to show associated funerary objects. It would be difficult, and visually incomplete, to present the story of Ohio archaeology without showing some of the extraordinary funerary objects that are the focus of scientific research. In doing so, do we honor the achievements of ancient American Indian people, or merely add to the exploitation of American Indian culture? We leave that judgment to the reader.

NAGPRA Outcomes

NAGPRA has forever changed the face of American archaeology. The legislation has given American Indians a rightful role in the study and presentation of their past. It has prompted a growing dialogue between Ohio archaeologists and the leaders of federally recognized American Indian tribes. Yet, as with most legislation, there have been unanticipated outcomes.

Some archaeological institutions have a fraction of the funding needed to deal with the enormity of this federal law. The task of creating and maintaining NAGPRA inventories has been, and continues to be, a monumental task for some institutions. American Indian tribes also lack the funding and staff needed to read, assess and respond to the flood of NAGPRA documents. Several tribes have formed joint NAGPRA committees to deal with the document deluge, but each week more paperwork pours in from dozens of archaeological institutions in states throughout eastern America.

About 27,800 individual human remains and 576,380 associated funerary objects have been repatriated under NAGPRA as of April 2004, according to figures provided by The National Center for

Cultural Resources of the U.S. Department of the Interior. But the process for NAGPRA assessments, notifications, claims and reviews is ponderously slow. "There seems to be a never-ending series of NAGPRA conferences and consultations with little tangible results," stated one tribal administrator. Another common concern is the lack of oral traditions to guide tribal officials in the honorable disposition of repatriated human remains. "We don't have a re-burial ceremony," says Floyd Leonard, Chief, Miami Tribe of Oklahoma, adding, "American Indians never would have considered digging up the dead in the first place."

In addition, NAGPRA does not address the concerns of American Indians who are not enrolled members of a federally recognized tribe. Over 24,000 Ohio citizens claimed American Indian or Alaska Native heritage in the 2000 U.S. Census. There are several American Indian scholars or groups based in Ohio that consult with archaeologists, serve on institutional boards, or participate in cultural festivals, ceremonies and demonstrations. Other individuals and groups actively protest archaeological research and lobby government officials for reforms. The status, authenticity and rights of "unrecognized" American Indians is another complex and emotional issue that often stems from the removal of American Indians from their territories.

In Ohio, there has been relatively little public education regarding NAGPRA and other archaeological/cultural issues. Beyond the professional community, few Ohioans are even aware that NAGPRA exists. Fewer still have ever read the federal law or its regulations. However, there is some positive progress at the professional level. Archaeologists are consulting with American Indians on some excavations. A few Ohio institutions have quietly returned human remains and cultural materials to American Indian tribes. Rebecca Hawkins, my colleague and an Ohio archaeologist who now works for an American Indian tribe in Oklahoma says, "We must realize that some cultural differences between archaeologists and traditional American Indians may never be adequately resolved." Learning how to respect our differences is a common theme at archaeological conferences and American Indian symposia.

Site Preservation

Among all of the contemporary archaeological issues, site preservation offers the greatest common ground. An estimated 10,000 ancient American Indian mounds and earthworks once dotted the central Ohio Valley. Squier and Davis recorded over 500 mounds and earthworks in Ross County alone. About 1,000 ancient mounds and earthworks are preserved in Ohio under the protection of private landowners, nonprofit organizations and local, state and federal agencies. Some survived because of their remote location. Dozens were incorporated into the landscape of early Euro-American cemeteries. Others escaped destruction through adaptive re-use, serving—for better or worse—as fairgrounds, horserace tracks, military camps and golf courses. The Ohio Historical Society preserves 13 prehistoric American Indian sites. Hopewell Culture National Historical Park preserves five sites in Ross County. The Archaeological Conservancy, a national nonprofit organization, preserves 15 archaeological sites in Ohio. Many American Indian mounds and earthworks are preserved under the stewardship of private landowners, especially farmers.

These ancient monuments represent only the tip of the archaeological iceberg. According to the Ohio Historic Preservation Office, about 38,000 historic and prehistoric sites are formally registered

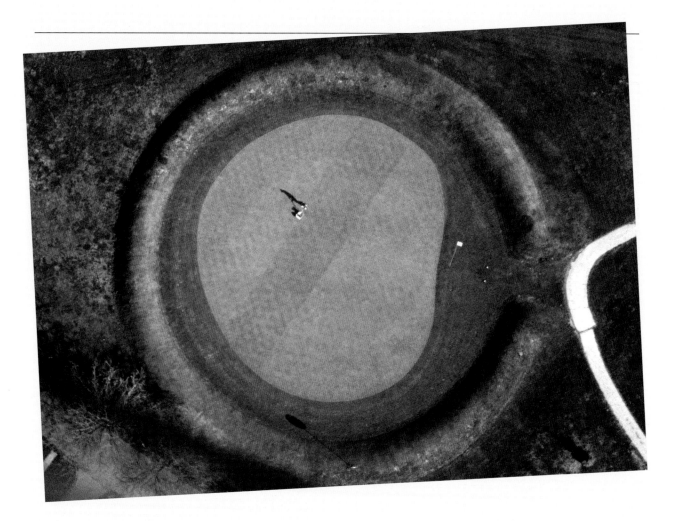

A groundskeeper mows the putting surface of a green built inside a small, circular earthwork on the golf course that now covers the renowned Octagon Earthworks in Newark. In a unique relationship, the Ohio Historical Society leases this Ohio Hopewell site to a private organization, Moundbuilders Country Club. Some contend this preservation arrangement is an economical form of adaptive re-use. Others protest limitations on public access to what they consider to be a sacred American Indian site.

on the Ohio Archaeological Inventory as of July 2004. About 90% of the registered sites have a prehistoric American Indian component. About 61% are on private lands. Many times this number have never been professionally identified, registered or discovered. "Urban sprawl, looting for the antiquities trade and modern agriculture are the principal causes of site destruction in Ohio," according to Paul Gardner, Midwest Regional Director, The Archaeological Conservancy. "Ohio does a relatively poor job preserving archaeological sites compared to other states, "says Gardner, "mainly because of inadequate state laws protecting Native American burials on private lands."

Ohio State Laws

In general, NAGPRA does not apply to private lands or institutions and individuals that do not receive federal funding. About 95% of the land in Ohio is private property. Al Tonetti, Chair of the Ohio Archaeological Council's Government Affairs Committee, says, "One of the foremost problems

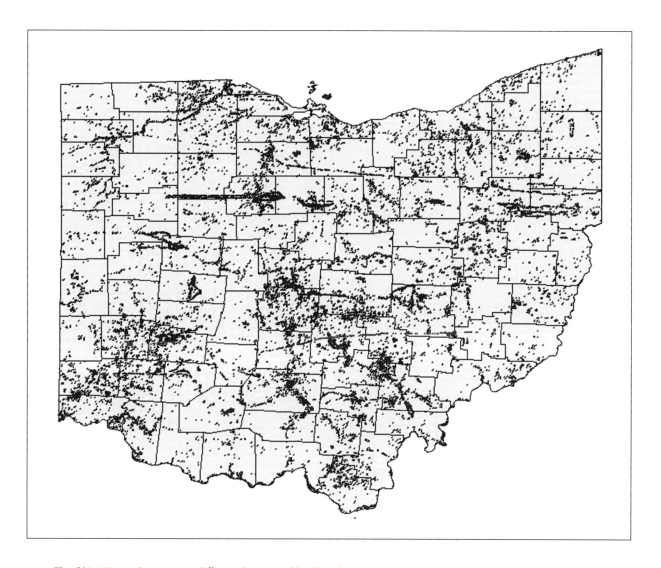

The Ohio Historic Preservation Office, administered by The Ohio Historical Society, identifies and monitors Ohio's historic places and archaeological sites. Since the 1970s, the preservation office has compiled and maintained the Ohio Archaeological Inventory (OAI), a master database of documented historic and prehistoric archaeological sites. This map represents the 34,972 prehistoric sites currently recorded in the Ohio Archaeological Inventory as of July 2004. Brent Eberhard, Acting Archaeology Inventory Manager, explains that archaeological sites in the OAI system may be graphically displayed in relationship to topographic and other digitized environmental context maps. "Comparisons of archaeological sites and environments over time allow for a more complete understanding of patterns in prehistoric cultural distribution and transition," says Eberhard.

The OAI database comes from archaeology surveys and excavations. Until budget cuts in the 1980s, federal grants supported systematic archaeological surveys in Ohio. Today, most OAI data come from inventory forms required from federally funded projects such as road construction, bridges, wetlands, and power and gas lines. As a result, this OAI map shows "natural" archaeological patterns such as clusters of sites along meandering river valleys, and artificial patterns such as straight lines along federally funded road projects such as Route 30 in northwest Ohio. The Ohio Archaeological Inventory is the comprehensive record of Ohio's past, according to Eberhard. "During an era of rapid rural land development, the OAI provides Ohio citizens with the opportunity to jointly record, share, and increase our understanding of the state's prehistory. It serves as both a planning tool for predicting the location of archaeological sites, and frequently, as the only remaining record of those sites that will not be preserved."

facing archaeologists is the lack of adequate and effective state laws protecting archaeological sites and human burial places on private property." The Ohio Revised Code (ORC) has two sections—2909.05 (vandalism) and 2927.11 (desecration)—that prohibit the "unprivileged" disturbance of Native American burials on private lands. Additionally, section 1517.24 prohibits the disturbance of human remains found in caves or rock shelters without the written permission of the property owner. The penalties for violations range from upper level misdemeanors to lower level felonies.

Privilege (a legally defined right) is obtained if you are the property owner, if you have the permission of the property owner, or if you can demonstrate necessity. This means private landowners can basically do whatever they want to prehistoric American Indian burial sites located on their own land. They can excavate archaeological sites without consulting either professional archaeologists or American Indian groups.

NAGPRA does make it a federal offense to sell or purchase illegally obtained funerary objects. It is also a federal offense to knowingly sell, purchase, use for profit, or transport for profit Native American human remains unless the family of the deceased has given permission to do so. Al Tonetti believes that illegal looting and legal, unprofessional excavations on private lands in Ohio is not nearly as significant a problem as unregulated development. "Based on empirical evidence, I think agriculture, sand and gravel mining and other forms of unregulated development are destroying far more Native American archaeological sites than looters ever will," says Tonetti.

Private developers are not legally obligated to do anything when they uncover an ancient gravesite containing human remains. However, the archaeological community recommends that they contact local law enforcement officials, preferably the county coroner or medical examiner. The coroner or medical examiner may determine that the human remains are not within their jurisdiction, meaning the remains are prehistoric and the cause of death does not need to be determined, or that the discovery is not relevant to a criminal investigation. If so, the developer may legally destroy the site without further consideration of the burials.

When such instances occur, the scientific and cultural loss is enormous. "What Ohio needs is a state law that establishes a process that determines the jurisdiction and disposition of buried human remains, regardless of the antiquity or ethnicity of the human remains," says Tonetti. Several attempts have been made to amend state laws dealing with this matter, but Ohio is currently one of only a few states in the U.S. that has no laws governing the protocol when human remains are discovered on private lands.

Archaeologists realize it's impractical to conserve all of the important archaeological sites in Ohio. But which ones are worth preserving? And who decides? I have documented several instances where private developers work around archaeological sites when told of their significance. That's not always the case. In 1993, Serpent Mound State Memorial was named one of the eleven most endangered historic places in America by the National Trust for Historic Preservation. Private developers wanted to dam Brush Creek to form a recreational lake next to Serpent Mound in Adams County. Archaeologists feared the lake would eventually undermine the site. The project was stopped due to other environmental issues, but if the renowned icon of Ohio archaeology can be endangered is any ancient American Indian earthwork in the state ever truly safe?

Serpent Mound State Memorial rests in winter solitude under a blanket of heavy snow.

The Future

So, where do we go from here? What will be the role of archaeology in Ohio at the end of the 21st century? Opinions range from those who foresee little change, to those who predict the extinction of the science. Most envision a middle ground. A few forecast a time when the majority of professional archaeologists in America are American Indians. To some degree, this is happening in Egypt, Mexico and portions of the American Southwest where native people are involved in archaeology and the preservation of their past.

The scientific goals of American archaeology will continue to evolve. Today, nearly all of the archaeological research in Ohio is directed at settlements, camps, houses, trash pits and the spaces between burial mounds and earthworks. While somewhat driven by NAGPRA, this shift also reflects the fact that archaeologists know much more about ancient American Indian *death* than *life*. The daily life of the first Ohioans is relatively unknown territory.

Archaeologists are also using new methods and technologies to reduce the destructive nature of the discipline. Hopewell Culture National Historical Park has become a training center for "strategic" archaeology, a concept that begins with geophysical surveys and the use of equipment such as magnetometers that allow archaeologists to see anomalies in the ground before digging. Geophysical surveys won't replace "dirt" archaeology, but these technologies do increase the precision of archaeological excavations. Archaeologists are employing computer graphics and modeling as a tool in their scientific research. Computer animation such as the "EarthWorks" project at the University of Cincinnati helps archaeologists visualize the scope, context and construction phases of a site based on existing data. Archaeologists are also conducting more demonstration projects and "experimental archaeology" to learn about ancient techniques in house construction, cultivation, food processing, textile production and traditional crafts.

American Indian tribes are also re-establishing control over their own culture and history. Many tribes with historic ties to Ohio now have an official website where scholars, teachers and students can find public information about their traditions. Several tribes have produced their own books, videos and compact disks. In 2001, the Miami Tribe of Oklahoma established The Myaamia Project at Miami University in Oxford, Ohio. Led by tribal members, the Myaamia Project is dedicated to the preservation, promotion and research of Miami history, culture and language. The Miami Tribe is now directly supporting tribal and non-tribal scholars who are engaged in academic research ranging from anthropology and history to linguistics and ethnobotony. The Ohio State University is considering the establishment of a center for the study of American Indian earthworks, culture and history at

its Newark campus. Staffed by American Indian scholars, a major focus of the center would be the Newark Earthworks, which noted author Christopher Scarre named one of the 70 wonders of the ancient world. Only three sites in North America that are north of Mexico attained this status.

Ohio certainly ranks among the top ten most archaeologically significant states in the United States. The state played an integral role in the history and development of American archaeology. Scientists from all over the world come here to study ancient American Indian cultures. Archaeologists continue to make new discoveries about the actual achievements of American Indians that eclipse the most fantastic Moundbuilder myths.

Can we study Ohio's ancient cultures and honor American Indian traditions? I'm optimistic. The science of archaeology and traditions of American Indian culture have complementary strengths and common goals. Both seek enlightenment and knowledge. How we obtain and present this knowledge is now part of the pathway in our exploration of Ohio's incredible American Indian heritage.

Archaeologist Jarrod Burks demonstrates a magnetometer at Mound City, Hopewell Culture National Historical Park. The magnetometer sends out an electronic signal that bounces off anomalies in the soil, sending an "echo" back to the surface like the sonar of a submarine. Archaeologists can then use this geophysical data for strategic excavations intended to examine features such as embankments, encampments and trash pits while avoiding burial sites.

A pathway leads to an ancient American Indian burial ground preserved at the Mound City Group at Hopewell Culture National Historical Park in Ross County.

Suggested Reading

This list of recommended reading materials includes publications that are either written at least in part for the general public, widely accessible, archaeological compendiums, or resources used by the Ohio Archaeology production team. More complete listings of related archaeological reports and publications may be found in the bibliographies of these works, or on the websites of several of Ohio's archaeological institutions.

GENERAL RESOURCES

Fossils of Ohio
Rodney M. Feldmann, Editor-in-Chief; Merrianne Hackathorn, Managing Editor, <u>Bulletin 70</u>, Ohio Department of Natural Resources, Division of Geological Survey, Columbus, Ohio (1996)

Atlas of Great Lakes Indian History
Edited by Helen Hornbeck Tanner, Cartography by Miklos Pinther, Published for The Newberry Library by the University of Oklahoma Press, Norman and London, 1986.

The Settling of North America: The Atlas of the Great Migrations into North America from the Ice Age to the Present"
Edited by Helen Hornbeck Tanner, Macmillan, New York, 1995.

Exploring Ancient Native America: An Archaeological Guide
By David Hurst Thomas, Macmillan, New York, 1994.

In Search of Ancient North America
By Heather Pringle, John Wiley & Sons, New York, 1996.

Indian Mounds of the Middle Ohio Valley: A Guide to Mounds and Earthworks of the Adena, Hopewell, Cole, and Fort Ancient People
By Susan L. Woodward and Jerry N. McDonald, The McDonald & Woodward Publishing Company, Blacksburg, Virginia (2002, 2nd Edition). [This is an excellent guide for those who wish to visit Ohio's publicly accessible archaeological sites].

INTRODUCTIONS FOR KIDS

Archaeology: Boy Scouts of America Merit Badge series
Published by Boy Scouts of America, Irving, Texas, 1997.

Our awesome ancient ancestors
By Elizabeth Levy, Scholastic Books, New York, 2001.

The First Americans, Third Edition: Prehistory-1600 (A History of US, Book I)
By Joy Hakim, Oxford University Press, New York, 2001.

The Human Story: Our Evolution from Prehistoric Ancestors to Today
By Christopher Sloan, *National Geographic,* 2004.

The Young Oxford Book of Archaeology
By Norah Moloney, Oxford University Press, Oxford, 2000.

INTRODUCTIONS FOR ADULTS

Archaeology: A Very Short Introduction
    By Paul Bahn, Oxford University Press, Oxford, 1996.

Archaeology and You
    By George E. Stuart and Francis P. McManamon, Society for American Archaeology, Washington, D.C., 1996.

Frauds, Myths and Mysteries: Science and Pseudoscience in Archaeology
    By Kenneth L. Feder, Mayfield, Mountain View, California, 2001 (4th edition).

Linking to the Past: A Brief Introduction to Archaeology
    By Kenneth L. Feder, Oxford University Press, Oxford, 2004.

Chapter One: THE PALEOINDIAN PERIOD

After the Ice Age: The Return of Life to Glaciated North America
    By E. C. Pielou, University of Chicago Press, 1991.

The First Americans: In Pursuit of Archaeology's Greatest Mystery
    By James M. Adovasio with Jake Page, Random House, Inc., New York, New York, 2002

The First Discovery of America: Archaeological Evidence of the Early Inhabitants of the Ohio Area
    William S. Dancey, Editor, The Ohio Archaeological Council, Columbus, 1994.

The Great Journey: The Peopling of Ancient America
    By Brian M. Fagan, Thames and Hudson, New York, 1987.

Ice Age Ohio
    By Kenneth B. Tankersley and Brian G. Redmond, *Archaeology,* November/December issue, pp. 42-46, 2000.

Ice Ages: Solving the Mystery
    By J. Imbrie, and K. P. Imbrie, Harvard University Press, Cambridge, 1986.

In Search of Ice Age Americans
    By Kenneth B. Tankersley, Gibbs Smith, Publisher, Salt Lake City, Utah, 2002

Pleistocene Peoples of Midcontinental North America
    By Bradley T. Lepper, pp. 362-394, in *Ice Age Peoples of North America, "Environments, Origins, and Adaptations of the First Americans,"* edited by R. Bonnichsen and K. L. Turnmire, Oregon State University Press, Corvallis, 1999.

Search for the First Americans
    By David Meltzer, Smithsonian Books, Washington, D.C., 1993.

Chapter Two: THE ARCHAIC PERIOD

Archaic Hunters and Gatherers in the American Midwest
    J. L. Phillips and J. A. Brown, editors, Academic Press, New York, 1983.

Archaic Transitions in Ohio and Kentucky Prehistory
    Olaf H. Prufer, S. E. Pedde, and R. S. Meindle, editors, Kent State University Press, Kent, 2001

Guns, Germs, and Steel: the Fates of Human Societies
by Jared Diamond, W. W. Norton, New York, 1997.

Koster: Americans in Search of Their Prehistoric Past
By S. Struever and F. Antonelli, Holton New American Library, New York, 1979.

The Status of Archaic Period Research in the Midwestern United States
By Richard W. Jefferies, 23:119-144, *Archaeology of Eastern North America,* 1995.

Tellico Archaeology: 12,000 Years of Native American History
By Jefferson Chapman, *Publications in Anthropology No. 41,* Tennessee Valley Authority, Knoxville, (revised edition) 1994.

Chapter Three: THE EARLY WOODLAND PERIOD

The Adena People - No. 2.
By William S. Webb and Raymond S. Baby, Ohio Historical Society, Columbus, 1957.

The Essential Features of Adena Ritual and Their Implications
By Berle R. Clay, *Southeastern Archaeology* 17(1):1-21, 1998.

Hopewell Antecedents in the Adena Heartland
By Martha P. Otto in *Hopewell Archaeology: the Chillicothe Conference,* edited by D. S. Brose and N. Greber, pp. 9-14. Kent State University Press, Kent, 1979.

The Mound Builders
By Robert Silverberg, Ohio University Press, Athens, Ohio, 1968 (abridged version, 1986).

Mounds for the Dead
By Don W. Dragoo, *Annals of the Carnegie Museum,* No. 37, Pittsburgh, 1963.

A Quiet Revolution: Origins of Agriculture in Eastern North America
By Ruth O. Selig, in *Anthropology Explored: the best of Smithsonian Anthro Notes,* edited by R. O. Selig and M. R. London, pp. 178-192, Smithsonian Institution Press, Washington, D.C., 1998.

Chapter Four: THE MIDDLE WOODLAND PERIOD

Ancient Art of the American Woodland Indians
By David S. Brose, James A. Brown, and David W. Penney, Harry N. Abrams, New York, 1985.

Ancient Astronomers of the Ohio Valley
By Bradley T. Lepper, *Timeline,* The Ohio Historical Society, 15(1):2-11, 1998.

Fort Ancient: Citadel, Cemetery, Cathedral, or Calendar?
By Jack Blosser and Robert C. Glotzhober, The Ohio Historical Society, Columbus, 1995.

The Hopewell Mound Group: Its People and Their Legacy
An Interactive Educational Resource Tool by y Bradley T. Lepper, The Ohio Historical Society, Columbus, 1995.

Mysteries of the Hopewell: Astronomers, Geometers, and Magicians of the Eastern Woodlands
By William Romain, University of Akron Press, Akron, 2000.

The Newark Earthworks: A Wonder of the Ancient World
By Bradley T. Lepper, The Ohio Historical Society, Columbus, 2002.

People of the Mounds: Ohio's Hopewell Culture
By Bradley T. Lepper, Eastern National, Fort Washington, Pennsylvania, revised edition, 1999.

Tracking Ohio's Great Hopewell Road
By Bradley T. Lepper, *Archaeology*, 48(6):52-56, 1995

A View from the Core: A Synthesis of Ohio Hopewell Archaeology
Paul J. Pacheco, Editor, The Ohio Archaeological Council, Columbus, 1996.

Chapter Five: THE LATE WOODLAND PERIOD

History, Progress, and the Facts of Ancient Life
By Mark N. Cohen, in *Anthropology Explored: the best of Smithsonian Anthro Notes,* edited by
Ruth. O. Selig and M. R. London, pp. 109-118, Smithsonian Institution Press, Washington, D.C., 1998.

Late Woodland Societies: Tradition and Transformation Across the Midcontinent
T.E. Emerson, D.L. McElrath, and A. C. Fortier, editors, University of Nebraska Press, Lincoln, 2000.

The Late Woodland Period in Southern Ohio: Basic Issues and Prospects
By Mark F. Seeman and William S. Dancey in *Tradition and Transformation Across the
Midcontinent,* T.E. Emerson, D.L. McElrath, and A.C. Fortier, editors, University of Nebraska Press,
Lincoln, 2000.

The Childers Site and Early Late Woodland Cultures of the Upper Ohio Valley
By Michael J. Shott, Richard W. Jeffries, G. Oetelaar, Nancy O'Malley, M.L. Powell, and Dee A. Wymer,
West Virginia Archeologist 45:1-30, 1993

Chapter Six: THE LATE PREHISTORIC PERIOD

Blain Village and the Fort Ancient Tradition in Ohio
By Olaf H. Prufer, and O.C. Shane, III, Kent State University Press, Kent, Ohio, 1970.

Cultures Before Contact: The Late Prehistory of Ohio and Surrounding Regions
Robert A. Genheimer, Editor, The Ohio Archaeological Council, Columbus, 2000.

Examining the Fort Ancient
By R. Daumeyer, *American Archaeology* 6(2):27-32, 2002.

First Farmers of the Middle Ohio Valley: Fort Ancient Societies, A.D. 1000-1670
By C. Wesley Cowan, Cincinnati Museum of Natural History, Cincinnati, 1987.

Great Serpent
By Bradley T. Lepper, *Timeline,* 15(5):30-45, The Ohio Historical Society, Columbus, 1998

*A History of 17 Years of Excavation and Reconstruction: A Chronicle of 12th Century Human Values
and the Built Environment*
2 Volumes, James M. Heilman, M.C. Lileas, and C.A. Turnbow, editors, Dayton Museum of
Natural History, 1988.

Native Americans in Eastern North America: The Southern Great Lakes and Upper Ohio Valley
By Paul W. Sciulli, and J. Oberly in *The Backbone of History: Health and Nutrition in the Western
Hemisphere,* edited by R. H. Steckel and J. C. Rose, pp. 440-480, Cambridge University Press,
Cambridge, 2002.

Ohio's Alligator
By Bradley T. Lepper, *Timeline*, 18(2):18-25, The Ohio Historical Society, Columbus, 2001

Petroglyphs of Ohio
By James L. Swauger, University of Ohio Press, Athens, 1984.

Societies in Eclipse: Archaeology of the Eastern Woodlands Indians, A.D. 1400-1700.
David S. Brose, C. Wesley Cowan, and R.C. Mainfort, Jr., editors, Smithsonian Institution Press, Washington, D.C., 2001.

White Fort and the Middle Sandusky Tradition Occupation of the Black River Valley in Northern Ohio.
By Brian G. Redmond, Archaeology of Eastern North America, 27:109-156, 1999.

Chapter Seven: "EARLY ACCOUNTS OF OHIO'S MOUNDS"

An American Menagerie: The Cabinet of Squier and Davis
By Terry A. Barnhart, *Timeline*, Volume 2., No. 6, December/January issue, 1985-1986, The Ohio Historical Society.

Ancient Monuments of the Mississippi Valley
By Ephraim G. Squier and Edwin H. Davis, *Smithsonian Classics of Anthropology*, Smithsonian Institution Press, Washington and London, original 1848, re-issue 1998.

Descriptions of the Antiquities discovered in the State of Ohio and other western states
By Caleb Atwater, pp 109-251, in *Archaeologia Americana: Transactions and Collections of the American Antiquarian Society*, Vol. 1, Worcester, Massachusetts, 1820.

Ephraim George Squier and the Development of American Anthropology
By Terry A. Barnhart, in the *Critical Studies in the History of Anthropology* series, University of Nebraska Press Press, scheduled for release in spring 2005.

Fantastic Archaeology: The Wild Side of North American Prehistory
By Stephen Williams, University of Pennsylvania Press, Philadelphia, 1991.

Hidden Cities: The Discovery and Loss of Ancient North American Civilizations
By Roger G. Kennedy, The Free Press, A Division of Macmillan, Inc., New York, 1994.

In his own right: Dr. Edwin Hamilton Davis and the Davis collection of American antiquities.
By Terry A. Barnhart, *Journal of the History of Collections*, Volume 16, No. 1, pages 59-87, 2004.

The Mound Builders
By Robert Silverberg, Ohio University Press, Athens, Ohio, 1968 (abridged version, 1986).

Report on the Mound Explorations of the Bureau of Ethnology: Twelfth Annual Report of the Bureau of Ethnology
By Cyrus Thomas, *Classics of Smithsonian Anthropology*, Smithsonian Institution Press, Washington D.C., original 1894, reprinted 1985.

Epilogue: "LEGACIES"

An Archaeology of the Soul: North American Indian Beliefs and Ritual
By Robert L. Hall, University of Illinois Press, Champaign, Illinois, 1997.

Archaeological Ethics
Edited by Karen D. Vitelli, AltaMira Press, Walnut Creek, California, 1996.

Always A People: Oral Histories of Contemporary Woodland Indians
By Rita Kohn, Senior Editor, Indiana University Press, Bloomington and Indianapolis, 1997.

Digging Into Your Heart
By Joseph Bruchac in *Paraboloa,* Volume 19, No. 4, pp. 36-41, 1994.

500 Nations: An Illustrated History of North American Indians
By Alvin M. Josephy, Jr., Alfred A. Knopf, New York, 1994.

In Front of the Mirror: Native Americans and Academic Archaeology
By Dorethy Lippert in *Native Americans and Archaeologists: Stepping Stones to Common Ground,* edited by Nina Swindler, Kurt E. Dongoske, Roger Anyon, and Alan S. Downer, pp. 120-127, AltaMira Press, Walnut Creek, California, 1997.

Indigenous Archaeology
By Joe Watkins, Rowman & Littlefield, 2001.

Preserving the Past for the Future
By Paul Hooge in *Vanishing Heritage,* edited by P. Hooge and B.T. Lepper, pp 74-92, Licking County Archaeology and Landmarks Society, Newark, 1992.

Public Policy, Academic Archaeology, and The First Americans
By Bradley T. Lepper in *New Perspectives on the First Americans,* edited by B. T. Lepper, pp 203-207, Texas A&M Press, College Station, 2004.

Skull Wars: Kennewick Man, Archaeology, and the battle for Native American Identity.
By David Hurst Thomas, Basic Books, New York, 2000.

Why Anthropologists Study Human Remains
By Patricia M. Landau and D. Gentry Steele, pp. 209-228, in *American Indian Quarterly,* Volume 20, Number 2.

Illustration Credits

Archive key:

AAS = American Antiquarian Society
APS = American Philosophical Society
ASCS = USDA, Agricultural Stabilization and Conservation Service
BPL = Boston Public Library
Carnegie = Carnegie Museum of Natural History, Pittsburg
CERHAS/UC = Center for the Electronic Reconstruction of Historical and Archaeological Sites, University of Cincinnati
CFM = Chicago Field Museum
CHCPL = Cincinnati and Hamilton County Public Library
CHS = Cincinnati Historical Society
CMC = Cincinnati Museum Center
CMNH = Cleveland Museum of Natural History
FORCE = First Ohioans Research Consortium Excavation
GP = Gray & Pape, Inc.
HCNHP = Hopewell Culture National Historical Park (Eastern National, National Park Service)
ISM = Illinois State Museum
KPM = Kanagawa Prefectural Museum of Natural History
KSU = Kent State University
Lithic = Lithic Casting Lab
MAC = Midwest Archaeological Center (NPS)
MAP = Museums at Prophetstown
MWP = Maslowski Wildlife Productions
NAA = National Anthropological Archives
ODNR = Ohio Department of Natural Resources
OHS = Ohio Historical Society
OSU = Ohio State University
Pangea = Pangea Productions Ltd.
Peabody = Peabody Museum of Archaeology and Ethnology (Harvard University)
PCHS = Pickaway County Historical Society
PMI = Portsmouth Murals, Inc.
PO = Picturesque Ohio
SIVAP = SunWatch Indian Village and Archaeological Park
Smithsonian = Smithsonian Institution
USDA = U.S. Department of Agriculture (NRCS Plants database, S. National Technical Center)
VMG = Voyageur Media Group, Inc.

Covers

Page	Subject	Photographer/Artist	Archive
Cover	Serpent Mound	Richard A. Cooke III	photographer
Back Cover	Copper effigy	Dave Barker	OHS
Back flap	Brad Lepper	Dave Barker	OHS/Pangea
End Pages	Serpent Mound survey map	E.G. Squier and E.H. Davis	Bill Pickard/Smithsonian
	Liberty Works	E.G. Squier and E.H. Davis	Bill Pickard/Smithsonian
Advance Pages			
p. vi-vii	Ancient Ohio Timeline	Jim Giles	VMG

Chapter Three: THE EARLY WOODLAND PERIOD

Chapter Four: THE MIDDLE WOODLAND PERIOD

p. 140	Hopeton geophysical map	John Weymouth	MAC
p. 141	High Bank survey	E.G. Squier & E.H. Davis	Bill Pickard/Smithsonian
p. 141	High Bank excavation	Tom Law	VMG
p. 141	High Bank aerial graphic	Beth Fowler/Mark Moch	Pangea
p. 142	Hopewell Mound survey	E.G. Squier & E.H. Davis	Bill Pickard/Smithsonian
p. 142	Copper human effigy	Dave Barker	OHS
p. 142	Hopewell excavation	Jules Angel	VMG
p. 143	Seip survey	E.G. Squier & E.H. Davis	Bill Pickard/Smithsonian
p. 143	Seip pearl necklace	OHS	OHS
p. 143	Seip aerial	Brad Lepper	photographer
p. 144	Copper bird effigy	Michael Bitsko	HCNHP
p. 145	Hopewell exotics map	Jim Giles	VMG
p. 146	Marietta survey	C. Whittlesey and E.G. Squier	Bill Pickard/Smithsonian
p. 147	Marietta Conus Mound	Bill Pickard	photographer
p. 147	Marietta Library Mound	Bill Pickard	photographer
p. 147	Marietta Sacra Via	Bill Pickard	photographer
p. 149	Stubbs survey	Charles Whittlesey	CMC
p. 149	Stubbs aerial	Frank Cowan	photographer
p. 150	Stubbs transect	Frank Cowan	photographer
p. 150	Stubbs postmolds	Frank Cowan	photographer
p. 151	Stubbs excavation	unknown	Frank Cowan
p. 151	Stubbs graphic	EarthWorks	CERHAS/UC
p. 151	Stubbs plot map	Frank Cowan	Frank Cowan
p. 152	Newark Octagon	Richard Pirko	photographer
p. 153	Newark Earthworks survey	James and Charles Salisbury	AAS
p. 154	Ft. Ancient survey	John Locke	Bill Pickard/Smithsonian
p. 154	Ft. Ancient earthworks	Jack Blosser	photographer
p. 155	Ft. Ancient stone mound	Jack Blosser	photographer
p. 155	Ft. Ancient atlatlists	Tom Law	VMG
p. 155	Ft. Ancient museum	Tom Law	VMG
p. 156	Pollock Works survey	S.T. Owens and L.K. Dille	Bill Pickard/Smithsonian
p. 156	Pollock excavation	Tom Law	VMG
p. 157	Williamson Mound	Tom Law	VMG
p. 157	Pollock Works graphic	EarthWorks	CERHAS/UC
p. 158	Great Circle aerial	Brad Lepper	photographer
p. 158	Great Circle excavation	Brad Lepper	photographer
p. 158	Great Circle graphics	EarthWorks	CERHAS/UC
p. 159	Ft. Hill survey	E.G. Squier	Bill Pickard/Smithsonian
p. 159	Ft. Hill aerial photograph	Dache Reeves	Bob Riordon/NAA
p. 160	Hively and Horn	Beth Fowler	VMG
p. 160	Octagon embankment	Tom Law	VMG
p. 161	Newark lunar graphic	EarthWorks	CERHAS/UC
p. 161	High Bank lunar graphic	Jim Giles	VMG
p. 162	Turner graphics	EarthWorks	CERHAS/UC
p. 162	EarthWorks lab	EarthWorks	CERHAS/UC
p. 163	Hopewell Mound graphic	EarthWorks	CERHAS/UC
p. 164	Observatory mound aerial	Brad Lepper	photographer
p. 165	Copper pan pipe	OHS	OHS
p. 166	Copper effigy	OHS	OHS

Chapter Seven: "EARLY ACCOUNTS OF OHIO'S MOUNDS"

Epilogue: "LEGACIES"

Index

Compiled by Laura Russell

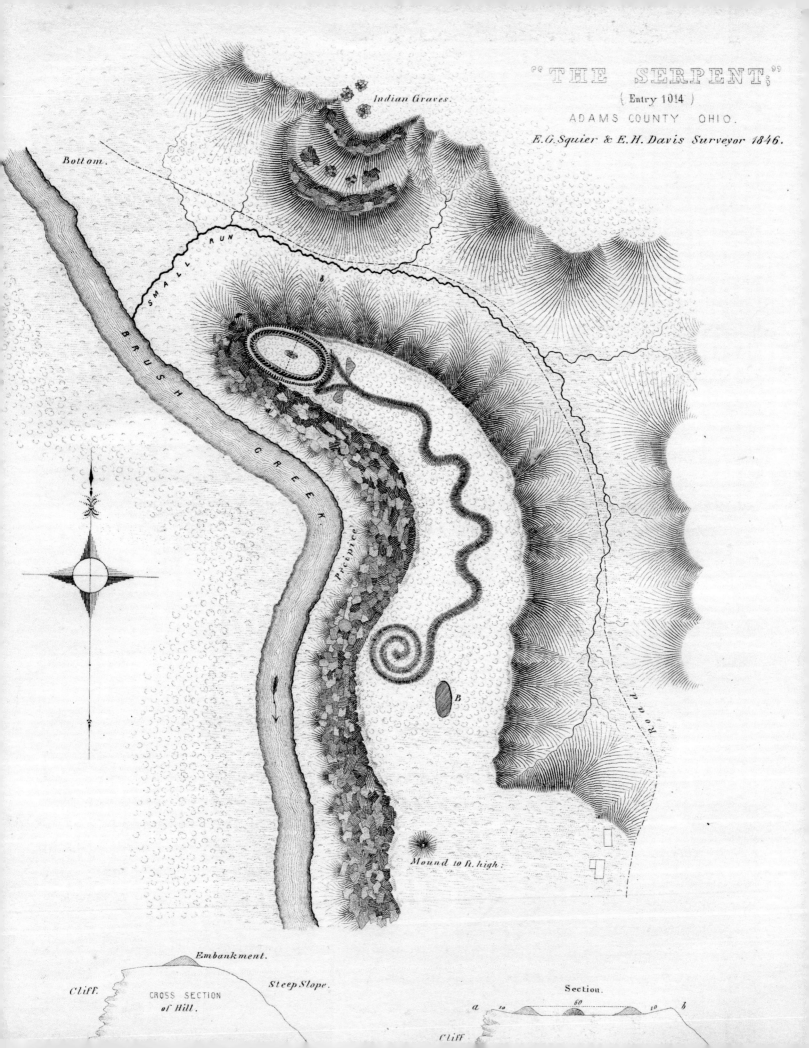

"THE SERPENT."
(Entry 1014)
ADAMS COUNTY OHIO.
E. G. Squier & E. H. Davis Surveyor 1846.

Indian Graves.

Bottom.

SMALL RUN.

BRUSH CREEK

Precipice

B

Mound 10 ft. high.

Road.

Embankment.

Cliff.

CROSS SECTION
of Hill.

Steep Slope.

Section.

a   10   60   10   b

Cliff.